There is a grand evolution taking place right now. You see war, aggression, devastation and Earth changes all around you and doubt that humanity is evolving at all. We see a miracle unfolding greater than it is possible for you to comprehend. The fear based actions in the news and the adjustments to the Earth are simply reactions to the changes underway.

If we could pull the veil aside for just a moment and let you see the wonderment that is directly ahead, you would never give the negativity another thought. As creators your reality is determined by the point of perception from which you view it. This is much more than positive thinking. It is the art of conscious creation.

If we did pull the veil aside for even a moment, you would all simply go Home and stop playing the Game of Spirits pretending to be Human. So instead we offer you a view through our eyes, as gentle Re-minders from Home.

Our greatest desire was to be there to greet you with smiling faces as you opened your eyes, awakening from the dream. Look through our eyes now and expect a miracle. We will help you create it.

Espavo

the Group

# Greetings from Home

A Celebration of a Decade of
"Beacons of Light"

# Greetings from Home

## A Celebration of a Decade of "Beacons of Light"

by Steve Rother and the Group and Barbara Rother

Copyright © 2006 – Steve Rother

### Published by: Lightworker Publications
### a subsidary of Lightworker

www.Lightworker.com

ISBN: 1928806-11-2

The authors and publishers of this book do not dispense medical advice or prescribe any technique as a form of treatment for physical or emotional problems and therefore assume no responsibility for your actions. The intent of this material is to provide general information to help your quest for emotional and spiritual growth. We encourage you to seek professional assistance for all areas of healing.

Lightworker Books CD's and DVD's can be purchased in retail stores, by telephone, or on www.Lightworker.com.

Lightworker 702 871 3317 in Las Vegas, Nevada

Layout and Design: Tony Stubbs (www.tjpublish.com)

Cover Photo: Adam Rowell, (www.rowelldesign.com)

Back Cover Photo: Petra van Vliet (www.petravanvliet.nl)

Lightworker is a registered trademark of the Lightworker corp.

Lightworker is a non-profit corporation dedicated to spreading Light through human empowerment.

# Table of Contents

# Dedication

The Lightworker organization is comprised of about 300 volunteers worldwide. In one way or another they all help us to distribute the messages from the Group. The seminars, trainings, web site, books and internet television shows are all important ways that we help people see the human condition from a point of empowerment. All of these take great dedication from the people who make this possible. Yet all of the success of Lightworker began and is still based around the monthly messages given from the Group on the internet known as the Beacons of Light ~ Reminders From Home. We proudly dedicate this book to the people directly involved with helping us to distribute the Beacons of Light ~ Re-minders from Home.

## Transcription Team Manager

Becky Hannah

## Transcription Team Members

Laura Ainsworth, Gloria Bagwell-Rowland, Linda Bowman, Linda Carter, Lynett Durgin, Lucy Hohn, Denise Hunter-Weck, Diedre Jones-Caluri, Bettina Kotterink, Keri Lynch, Kathleen McCarty-Kawa, Destiny McCune, Cathy Renfro, Kathy Rice, Debbie Rutledge, Sherry Stevens, Kimberly Thompson, Denise Troyer, Eileen Achey, Dale Baughman, Cindy Bergeles, Linda Binns, Pat Brideaux, Julie Cefalu, Jackie Clark, Mary Jane Darragh, Liane De Clerck, Gina Eaker, Margaret Fitzgeral, Ayda Gunduz, Peg Gwinner, Susan Horlick, Shelly Jepson, Mari Kennedy, Kim LePiane, Pam Long, Margaret Maione, Marca Malick, Stan Miles, Karen Moye, Pam Myers, Rowan Pita, Barbara Powell, Dona Reynolds, Nancy Rich, Georgia Sanders, Cicindela Saulean, Suzanne Schevene, Melissa Scherzi, Kay Sellers, Karen Skoczlas, Ruth Somma, Carol Thorne, Jean Tinder, Donna Velasco, Mary K Weinhagen, Doreen Weir, Laura Wheeler, Peggy Whitfield, Terese Whitley

## Proof Readers / Editors

Veronique Andrews

Peter Hyman

Kinga Toth

Gene Bishop

Cheryl Hoar

## VirtualLight Broadcast Staff

Jon Carl     Program Director

Charmaine Lee   Staff Director

Mark William     Sound

Russ Lahoud    Staff Engineer / Sound

Janelle Collard   Guest Coordinator/ Interviewer

Ana Manning  Attendance Coordinator

Janee Vere    Camera / Misc

Tony Stubbs  Publishing / Camera

And a special thanks to our friends at the *Sedona Journal of Emergence* for helping us to spread this Light.

# Introduction

## About the Group

The Group's message and our work is about human empowerment. It's not always an easy message for us to understand because they are not sensational nor will they tell us which way to turn or what we 'should' do. They say that humans are accustomed to giving their power away to credentials or labels. Thus, they rarely talk about themselves, who they are or where they come from. They want us to know that this is not about them … it's about us.

The most the Group has ever revealed about their own origins is contained in the Beacons of Light message entitled "The Family of Michael," which is included in this book and available on the Lightworker web site. Their intention has never been to tell us how great they, are but to show us how great we are. Their greatest hope is to re-mind us what we came here to do and to help us to do it.

According to the Group, the events taking place right now have greater implications than we suspect. As startling and unexpected as some of these have been, they merely mark the beginning. The evolution of mankind has begun. The ball is rolling forward and now there is no turning back … are you ready?

The messages that follow are my favorite selections from the first ten years of the monthly Beacons of Light messages from the Group that drastically changed my life beginning in February 1996. The Group offers us a way to see ourselves from the empowered view of Home. Lives in all walks of life and all over our globe have been empowered by these Reminders from Home since they began more than ten years ago. This book is the one place where the reader can see the best overview of who the Group is and the loving message they bring humanity. This is the most definitive work from the Group published thus far. We offer this collection to you here with the greatest hope that you too will remember the love of Home and see yourself from the perspective of the Group.

Big Hugs and gentle nudges
Steve Rother
Spokesman for the Group

# The Time of Merlia

## March 1999

I have tried to write this twice now and both times have been diverted. I believe there were a few minor pieces that needed to be moved into place before this story was to be told. The Group will add to it over time and others will also appear with pieces of this grand puzzle.

I'll start at the beginning and tell you what I know. I awoke in the middle of the night and went back to my office to write. This happens regularly as I am now a member of the infamous 3 a.m. club. They wake me up and want to know: "Can Stevie can come out and play?" I usually do, yet this time when I got back in my office and got my computer booted up, they suddenly got very serious. They had a message for me, an important one. I would not write anything that night at all. I just sat there for what seemed like hours, staring across my desk, downloading the information. I was not consciously aware of anything coming in yet I knew something big was going on. They had just given me an important package to unwrap. It was time to tell the story of the 'Time of Merlia.'

They have told me that we literally stand at the door of a very exciting time on Earth. We feel this and look to the concepts of 'the ascension' or the veil thinning to conceptualize what we feel. The Group is simply putting this in a different context by letting us know how we will see this time, as we look back upon it hundreds of years from now. The Time of Merlia is about to begin. It is called a 'time' because it is very short in comparison to the ages of our history. In our past, large shifts in consciousness have taken hundreds of years to accomplish. This is not the case anymore in this new energy of ours. The time frame they are referring to is only about 30 to 50 years. Merlia is, in fact, the Merlin energies returning at this time and there is more. There is so much more to what I just said that to say it that simply is 'equivalent' to explaining the nature of the universe as a bunch of planets. When I returned to bed, I understood that I had been given an important task. I was somehow different but couldn't put my finger on it. When I crawled back into bed I glanced at the clock … only fifteen minutes had passed.

Wait a minute, I thought, Merlin was a myth! I've asked the Group about these myths before. What I get is the member of the Group called the Keeper of Time. His job is to determine the most advantageous time to release important information. Apparently the timing of information can be critical to its acceptance. This is his job and here he was, in all of his glory, standing proud with his long, white beard blowing gently in the breeze. He was holding his index finger high in the air, telling me with this beloved, finely honed gesture, that there is more here than I am capable of understanding right now and to wait for the answers to unfold. I have received this same response with other stories that I have questioned, most notably those of Christ and other masters. The energy has recently changed and shifted again, opening minds and moving consciousness to a new level where these concepts can now be at least partially understood. The white-bearded wise man has lowered his finger and stepped aside, allowing this information to now be released. The message I get from the Group is that these stories represent very real aspects of energies behind these mythical figures.

According to the Group, mythical figures were often created to bring in important doctrines and ideals that would otherwise be unfathomable because of the judgments we had about ourselves at the time they were introduced. The way most of these mythical figures are introduced is fascinating. Most of the time, the Group says that they exist in another dimensional time line reality just as 'real' as our own. Occasionally these realities intersect each other, leaving permanent imprints on both that surface as myths that live forever.

Many of my friends have gone through a phase of recalling their past lifetimes. There was a time when the focus was on the age of Camelot and the time of King Arthur. Let's see, I think we had three King Arthur's, six Lancelot's, twelve Guinevere's, and at least two Ladies of the Lake. I thought it odd that there seemed to be no one in those times who actually shoveled the horse shit in the stables. While they shared these remembrances, I felt a little left out, as I never felt any connection to this time in history. I guess I must have missed this one … or so I thought. I can hear the Group laughing as I say this, because most of my past life remembrances of those times have been blocked from me. One of the sources of their amusement is that in present day, my setup is that I travel to various cities carrying a real Excalibur sword. I use this to facilitate Sword of Truth ceremonies to help others awaken and re-member their power and their truth. They finally showed me one life where I was a cross between a jeweler and a blacksmith. I was a special craftsman who made ornate ceremonial swords. These were swords used in ceremony of empowerment and not meant for use in battle. These were swords like the ones used to take warriors to higher levels as in the ceremony of knighting, which is similar to what I get to do now. I not only made these swords but was also entrusted with their care. They call me now as they called me then … the Keeper of the Sword.

What they tell me about these Arthurian times is that the age of Camelot was very real indeed. It was a magical time when seeds of a greater consciousness were being carefully planted on the Earth. The concept of Camelot was much more than the ultimate Kingdom, it was a sacred ideal that formed the blueprint for the coming millennium at that time. These seeds were to find a home and seemingly remain dormant for centuries … until the time was right for them to sprout. That time is here now as we open a new millennium once again.

One of the most important aspects of this magical time is the return of the Goddess energy to our planet, hence the feminine name 'Merlia.' At the start of the Game we call life, we entered the Game board with a balance of the feminine and masculine. The mechanics of the Game board produce a side effect called 'polarity.' This attribute clouds our vision and causes us to see things as up or down, right or wrong, love or fear, masculine or feminine. The result of this is that humanity has been caught up in a massive pendulum swing since what we refer to as the beginning of time. This is only illusion; do not let it fool you. What's happening at this time is that the new energy is allowing us to move into clear vision for the first time. With the raise of vibrations, we can now return to the balance we came in with and, for all intents and purposes, the pendulum will stop in the middle, never to swing again. We are doing this ourselves.

We control the rate at which we raise our planetary vibrations. The way we do this is by clearing our blocks on an individual basis to allow us to carry the higher vibration. This is the immediate challenge for humanity – to take responsibility for doing the inner clearing to allow for the blending of the yin and the yang that will bring back the balance that we started with. This is the reason for the return of Merlia at this time.

The Goddess energy is contained within all of us and it is a very large task at hand to make room for this energy to fully find its way home again. It is much like learning about ourselves all over again. There are parts and facets to us that have been hidden for eons. If we choose to step into this evolution we call ascension and claim our full powers, we do this by opening these facets and allowing in the power they hold for us.

There is a lot of misunderstanding about what the Goddess energy is and how we access it. I can tell you this because even though they have not let me in on all the details yet, I can tell you that there is much laughter on the other side about our interpretation of it. Although we have the basic premise of the energy we call Goddess, we do have some strange tenets we have attached to it in order to make it palatable to us. There is no immediate reason to spend time with these, as they are not important yet. It is important to keep an open mind as more is revealed to us. The Group is nudging me to tell all that what is important is that we look at the Goddess energy as a way of thinking. This is a thought process that allows for more of the heart connection to enter our lives, for this is how spirit channels the higher vibration to each of us individually. A way to easily put this into words would be the blending of thoughts and emotions.

If we look at the current paradigm for the male and females here today, we can see that the genders process thought differently. Females handle emotion in an entirely different way than do males. It is this superior approach to emotion that will eventually facilitate these heart connections. The melding of balanced thought with emotion will allow us to become masters of our thoughts. This is how we can make it safe for Merlia to return now in this time and quickly facilitate our own evolution. Through opening the door to our own hearts, and learning to share all of our innermost thoughts with others, we will be creating the space for the Goddess to bless us with her presence once again and to allow for the true return of Merlia. The goal is to see ourselves as we truly are – spirits of great magnitude, fumbling around in the dark with veils over our eyes, awkwardly bumping into things and each other as we try desperately to find our way home.

On the plane as I sat to write this message, I expected the Group to tell a mystical story about a magical person in colorful flowing robes with a pointed hat decorated with stars and half moons, a dynamic person incarnating on Earth at this time to lead us all into the new age. What I understand now is that there is much more that will be disclosed as we become ready to accept it. There will be much more in the coming writings about the time of Merlia, as well as pieces of the same story from others. Watch for them, for the time of Merlia is upon us now. Merlia is returning as you read this. Make space in your being for her, and her gifts of empowerment are yours without asking. She is here, once again, selflessly trying to point the way home again. Thank you, Merlia, we are honored to have you here.

There is a wonderful silence in the air in this moment. Listen and you will hear the heart beat of the Earth herself. The anticipation is great. Throughout the kingdom there is awareness that the magical energy is about to re-visit the Earth. This energy has visited the Earth before in other forms to aid at crucial junctures. We know this truth by many names. There is one rule that must be observed prior to any visitation on the Earth. We, the players on the Game board, must consciously ask for it.

There have been many times in our past here on the Game board when we did ask for this energy to visit. In most instances, we were not ready to accept the information it offered. Most often, we refused to accept its truth. Still it always came when we asked. The energy came willingly to plant seeds of truth th at oftentimes would not be reaped until generations later. With each return, it offered an abundance of unconditional love and compassion. This energy most often manifested as a teacher, for this was our way of understanding in the lower vibrations of planet Earth. Now for the first time, this energy prepares to return to Earth as an equal. As humans begin to carry more of their own power, we can now see that walking side by side with this energy will quickly lead us to the creation of home on this side of the veil.

The Group falls silent in reverence as she steps into the room. Here in all of her magnificence, she stands before us ready to walk alongside each one. Due to the work we have done and the clearing we have accomplished, we have called her in. It is now time. It is now the Time of Merlia.

Greetings from Home.

We have greeted this gathering of masters many times with a heartfelt honoring. We have attempted to show you in each one of our visits just how special you are to us and to all that is. We have had only limited successes in conveying to you how much you are loved for the experiences you endure on the Game board. You look at your daily life and see only as far as the end of your nose. You do not see that each obstacle you overcome opens the door for many others. We do see this clearly and we thank you for your work. You have successfully increased the vibratory rate of the collective. You have taken control at a critical time on the Game board. You have accepted your power when it was handed to you, even though you did not fully understand it. The colors you will carry from this time forward will mark you among the elite of the Universe. You are the special ones, for you are the players of free choice. The work you have done has made the planet safe for many to follow. This day, we speak to you of the return to the Game board of the Merlia energy. This is only possible because of the Lightwork you have done for so long. The clearing of yourselves for the purpose of carrying Light and the clearing of the planet has made room for this to take place. We are honored to play a role in the introduction of this material, for it will forever change the manner in which you play the game.

Many in your higher vibrations have felt the undeniable pull of the tales you call Camelot. You may know that these are myths that have been written for your amusement. No matter the image held in your head, you also know in your heart that they hold great truth. We will offer a simple explanation, for this is so often how spirit speaks to each one of you. We have explained how your own advancement on the DNA level has opened your perceptions of other dimensions of time. We tell you that these carriers of truth begin at the intersection where these dimensions cross one another. As a path of reality travels forward following the duality of linear time, it often crosses the path of another reality occupying the same time and space. These realities intersect only for a brief moment yet, as they move on, they leave an indelible impression. The energy of each reality leaves its stamp on the other, leaving behind permanent memories lasting for eons. It is no wonder to us that these incidents are often recorded. Because the realities differ so much, they are most often written about as myths or fictional stories. We ask you to follow the truth of the information here and not to judge its origin.

The stories of these times have been placed in your reality for a reason. Look at the many important seeds planted by this one intersection of alternate realities. The idea of the boy who would be King with no royal lineage behind him, speaks of the right to claim the power that each one of you holds. The nature of the game you are playing is to re-member your powers and to use those powers to re-create home on your side of the veil. Was it not King Arthur who created his idea of Heaven on Earth under the name of Camelot? It was striving for the attainment of this goal that set the stage for so many others to create their own ideas of Heaven on Earth. This led to a space in the new government where room was created for the empowered human. The idea behind the Round Table was that no one person was to be in charge. This speaks loudly of the principles we have been offering you for living in the higher vibrations of the new planet Earth. Allowing space for all to take their own power is the way of emulating Universal energy. The idea was proven that to expect greatness from one another would set the stage for that greatness to surface. The paradigm shifted from follow the leader to follow your own truth, as space is made for the empowered human.

Now we will speak again of your true power. We tell you time and again that you have no idea how powerful you really are. You are a finite expression of the infinite creator and, as such, you have the same powers as the creator. You have only to re-member that they are there and how to use them. Where you allow your thoughts to reside creates your own reality in each moment. This is confusing for you because of the time lag that has served you well as a buffer. In the higher dimensions to which you are aspiring, you will see this much more clearly, for the time lag is lessening even in your world at this moment. The power you hold is magical indeed and more powerful than even you could imagine.

We equate this to the time of Camelot when the figure of power was referred to as Merlin. Merlin was a craftsman of power and its uses. Human as he was, he had studied and learned the ways of the magician. We tell you this is much like the powers you are now uncovering within yourselves. Like Merlin, it is necessary for each one to exercise these muscles for full development. When these powers are fully understood, the deeds of Merlin will pale by comparison. Let us also re-mind you that Merlin was the one who lived backward in time. This idea of intentional time control illustrates similar concepts we have helped you re-member. Merlin was the representation of natural power because his power was equal to his alignment with the Universal principles. His strength came from his union with all that is. Such is true for all power. No one can be powerful unto themselves, for it is the union with all things that generates the power.

Many seeds were successfully planted in the collective consciousness of the planet with this single illustration. The hope that was presented in the symbol of Excalibur stands to this day. This is the same sword you see with your interpretation of the one you call Michael. This is the Sword of Truth and always stands to re-mind you that your power is in standing firm with what you know in your own heart. Stand firm in your truth and you will be in your power. In  the days of Camelot, it was only the boy of pure heart that was able to remove the sword from the stone. The integrity of the boy Arthur was an illustration of the truth as known from within. Finding that truth within and having the courage to follow that truth is what makes the connection stronger. Exercising this connection is the process of learning to walk with full connection to your higher self. Find your sword and hold it dear.

Until recently, the illustrations represented in these stories were usually seen through the eyes of the male energy. This has to do with polarity on the Game board. Polarity has provided you with the means of existence on the Game board, yet it taints your vision drastically. You see things as separate when they are not. This leads to a belief in lack when there is none. As you believe, then so you create. This is the simple nature of the game as played on the Game board of free choice. Movement into Plan B means moving from a field of polarity to a field of wholeness. This is a concept that may be difficult for some to assimilate. Some of your belief systems have been built on judgment rather than discernment. It is these judgments that create energy strings that always tie you to that which you have judged. We re-mind you that we have often said, "There is no judgment on our side of the veil, other than that which you bring with you." Judgment is only possible within a field of polarity. As you move out of this field of polarity, it will be necessary to re-evaluate these core belief systems. Opening to the potential of wholeness brings new strength and wisdom. This is now in progress on your planet. You are now in movement from a field of polarity to a field of completeness. With that movement comes a new complete vision.

It is this movement that has cleared the way for the full expression of female energy to return to planet Earth. This is not a time of dominance or competition, for those are strictly illusions of polarity. As seen through the eyes of whole beings, this is a return to full and complete natural power. Because of the clearing work you have done on this planet, this is now possible. The full feminine energy can once again return to the planet and make it whole. This is the full complement of the Yin and the Yang supporting each other in their wholeness. This is a return to the whole reflection of God within each one of you.

It is with great pride that we tell you that the time of Merlia is now upon you. It is you who have made this possible through your choices on the Game board. Because of the work you have chosen to do, you have made it possible for the full feminine energy to return and unite with the whole. You can clearly see that this reunion has begun on your planet. The numbers on your planet have never been so large and yet your crime rates have continued to decline. You are making a difference and changing your world with each thought that enters your heart. It is this balance between the head and the heart that so clearly shows the re-membering of Merlia. Making space for this part of each one of you will enable the re-membering process to continue. Balance the third-dimensional thinking with the feelings from your own heart ... and watch the magic return.

Merlia is the Merlin energy returning to Earth in feminine form to offer the balance needed for the step out of polarity into wholeness. This return has been prophesied in many of your writings. We ask you to make space for Merlia as she returns to offer her balance. She does not come to sit in judgment or to be a leader of humanity. This was indicative of the old energy. The Second Wave has opened a new energy of walking within self-empowerment. She offers to walk alongside each one of you and balance the energy of the planet naturally. She represents an opportunity to utilize your full power by incorporating all aspects of yourself. Until recently, it was not safe for this energy to return but, through your choices, you have made it so. You now see evidence of this progression in your collective thinking. Women are making advances in many areas on the Game board at this time. This will continue as this energy gently assimilates and naturally finds a balance. This energy has been mistrusted and suppressed for some time. Now it will find its way back to seek a natural balance. Balancing the heart and the head will open doors never thought possible.

Once the energy equilibrium is reestablished on the planet, the doors will open for the next phase of evolution of humanity. This will be the introduction of those of crystal vibration onto the planet. These are gentle beings who will be the next incarnation of humanity on planet Earth. They will bring you to understand the full implications of walking hand-in-hand with your own higher self. This will mark a time of peace on the planet that has never before been known.

It is your own daily struggle with life in the third dimension that has cleared the way for this to unfold. It was only possible to build the Game board in this fashion. Many of you look at your daily life and feel stuck because there is so much you want to do. So often you say, "If only I had this or that, then I would be able to do what I came here to do." We tell you that with the veils firmly in place, it is not possible for you to see the effect you have already had. We tell you that you have already changed the outcome many times over. This was only possible in this manner. You have chosen to redefine the Game. These seeds of our own evolution and the new Game have already been planted. You have done very well preparing the soil. We are deeply honored to be a small part of this process. Through your actions and choices, you have called the original families back together once again. This reunion is a grand one indeed, and is not limited to your side of the veil. We, too, have been reunited with a part of our family that we thought was all but lost. We are joyful to see you return. Welcome home.

It is with the greatest of love that we ask you to treat each other with respect, nurture one another and play well together.

the Group

# The Family of Michael

## Circles of Light

## February 1999

From the very beginning of this information, the Group has been silent about their origin. When I first started channeling, people warned me to be sure that I knew who was sending the information. I was told that if the source would not identify itself, then that would indicate that it was from the dark side. I therefore promptly asked three questions: "Who are you? What are your names? And where are you from?"

They came back with an immediate response that went like this: "You have asked three questions and we will give you three answers: It is none of your business, it is none of your business and it is none of your business." Then I heard the gentle loving laughter that I have since learned to love so much. At the time, I was dumbfounded and re-membering the words of advice, I informed these entities that I could not channel them if they wouldn't identify themselves. In response to that, they told me something I will never forget. They said, "We honor your choices" and with that statement, they were gone. After two days of having a hole where my heart used to be, I went back to them and asked to resume the communication. The moment I asked, they were there waiting, and I felt whole again. I was still hesitant but asked them why they wouldn't tell me who they were. The answer was: "We wish you to discern the message for the love content of the message itself and not because of some label placed upon it. This is discernment and is the first tool of the new energy." Then they gave me a guide for using the tool. They said: "If it pulls at your heart strings then take it as your own. If there is anything less, then release it without judgment, for it was simply placed there for another." They went on to explain that if I believed they were 'Bad Guys,' what made me think they wouldn't say they were 'Good Guys.' I laughed and the relationship between us began to really grow.

Needless to say, I was very hesitant to ask a lot of questions about their origins, but I did manage to slip in a few things now and then. They did tell me that they had never incarnated on the Earth, but silence was the general response when asked for more information. It was actually several months into the messages that I included a casual reference to 'the Group of entities just over my shoulder.' That was the first time I called them 'the Group.' To my surprise, they seemed to like it because it didn't imply a lot of mysticism. Still, every time I asked, there was no answer as to their origins.

About a year later, they surprised me. During one of the messages I was writing, the Group spoke almost out of context to say: "We will now tell you something that you already know. We are from the family of what you would call Michael." I was not sure what that meant but I can tell you, the moment they said it, I knew it was true.

They gave me further explanation of their origins during a live channel in Charleston, West Virginia. Here, they said outright, that they were from what we know as the Angelic realm. There was little more on this subject until we found ourselves doing a live channel at the United Nations in Vienna, Austria. During this channel, they mentioned several times references about the family of Michael. I can tell you, from inside my head, those words resonated very deeply within me. Several days later in another live channel in Vienna, they spoke about the family of Michael having a portal in the Earth at that physical location. Although they didn't say much more, they mentioned it a lot during that channel. Later that year, I was doing a live channel in Cancun, Mexico. During this channel, they mentioned that this was a physical location where the family of Michael had a portal in the ocean.

I get a lot of e-mail from people, as the Group speaks to many people on different levels with the same words. Some of them get very excited because they feel they know who the Group is. I have heard from people that they are Sirians, Pleiadians, Arcturians, the Greys and a few I can't even pronounce. The interesting part is, I don't even ask that question of the Group anymore. They speak to me from the very depth of my own heart and that is enough identification for me. Now it seems they are ready to fill in some of the gaps.

Greetings from Home

Our time with this special gathering of souls grows more precious to us with every moment that passes. Your choices on the Game board of Free Choice are the final expression of the Creator energy in finite form. The choices you have made in the playing of your Game have allowed the direction to shift toward Unity once again. Your willingness to play the Game in this fashion behind veils that keep you from seeing your true nature is honored beyond your understanding. We love you so for your willingness to reach for higher truths, even in the times when you doubt yourself.

Know that there are many eyes in the Universe that are watching your every choice. Even the times when you feel so very alone and in despair, there are many around you that eagerly share your pain. In that manner, it allows them to be a part of the Game that is shifting the reality of All That Is. Those around you number far beyond your understanding. If you could only see the preparations that are needed to accommodate such a large number of entities, you would easily understand how important you really are. This is why we so often encourage you to treat each other with respect for all of you on the Game board are important beyond what you can possibly see.

The Grand Wizard of Timing has just lowered his finger, illustrating that it is now time to reveal more information about your true nature. We wish to speak to you at this gathering of the family you call Michael. We are what you know to be representatives of this great family. Even when you speak the word, it resonates deep within your being. This is the family vibration of which you are very much connected.

There is much confusion as we see you attempting to apply human traits to spiritual matters, so we will offer you further explanations to help you re-member that which you already know. What you call Michael is not just a singular entity, but also a collection of energies that form a singular vibration. This is why we describe it to you as a family. Although the number fluctuates constantly, the family you call Michael is actually the collective vibration of 144,000 souls on this side of the veil. The singular vibration was formed to achieve a singular purpose, and all things that are attracted to that vibration are related to that purpose.

## Who Is Michael?

He "who is as God" is the singular Archangel you have know as Michael. The greatest of warriors fought constantly for the right to end all war. The final battle is now at hand as humanity is making decisions to use their swords for a higher purpose. The original battle was one where the Angels began to believe that they were superior to the humans they were overseeing. This was a misdirection of energy and it was Michael who stood firmly in the understanding that to be truly strong, it was necessary to become open and vulnerable. Michael was the one who drew his sword to stand firmly in his own truth and therefore declared allegiance to the Light. This began a family vibration as many followed this lead. This inner strength is prevalent even today, as more are beginning to carry their own power and stand firmly in their own truth. This is the true strength of the "Warrior of the Light" you know to be the Archangel Michael. Today, the family of Michael is at the forefront of your vibrational changes as you step into the next stage of evolution as spirits.

## Pebbles in the Pond

Take a small pebble and toss it in a pond. You will see circles of vibration that travel from the center outward. What you have done with this action is to introduce the vibration of the pebble in motion, to the vibration of the water. The circles of vibration that travel outward are the energy of the pebble in motion being assimilated by the pond. This emulates the Universal flow of energy of seeking balance through blending.

Understand that the original vibration of the pebble still remains as it now sits at the bottom of the pond. The truth is, the introduction of this one pebble forever changed the entire overall vibration of the pond.

Now see the effect on the water as you throw several pebbles for it to incorporate at one time. Now you see many circles on the water begin rapidly expanding and crossing over each other as they intertwine in their search to be part of the whole of the pond. Each one travels an individual path as it seeks to blend, but now you see it cross the path of other energies in the same quest. This design of intertwining circles is where we will begin to describe the family you know to be Michael.

## Heritage of the Family of Michael

This family is one of choice. You may be born into this family or it may be chosen during the Game, yet to remain and hold the energy of this family is always a choice. Members of this great family will never retreat from a conflict of light and dark. They have chosen to be at the cutting edge of the change in all areas. Once a step has been made to take one's place as a Lightworker, one connects with their inner power. Rarely is it possible to reverse the direction after connecting with this power. Everything on the Game board is ruled by free choice and, as such, it is possible to push yourself in another direction. Yet this is not done without a cost. Turning your back on your higher purpose is a misdirection of energy and quickly drains your energy. Denying the pulling within your heart that you have chosen as your highest purpose will have a negative effect on your biology and your higher self. It is only possible to leave the family and therefore the purpose of the family, if you choose another family and take up that cause in its place.

This is possible since most belong to several families at one time, yet it is very rarely done. Stepping into your own work and creating Plan B contracts is the work of this family that most of you will aspire to.

## Messengers from Home

We tell you once again, there are beings in special service directly to the Archangels. These intermediaries interact on the Game board with instructions directly from Home. These are the "Angels" you see visiting the Game, lending guidance and assistance. They appear to you only in forms that your belief systems will accept. That is the reason many do not see them at all. These are special beings who work from the midpoint of the divinity ladder. You have known them by many labels. They are grand beings and, if you make space for them, they will be there when you need them most.

## The Hierarchy of Home

Imagine there is a large circle that sits at the center of Heaven. Now see the slightly smaller circles that overlap the original and support the whole. These are what you know to be other Archangels. There are many more of them than you presently have represented in your writings. Now see many smaller circles that support and offer slightly different purposes than the sponsoring larger circle. This is a simple way to understanding the Hierarchy of Home. This is where many families support one another in a united purpose. The largest of these circles is the family of Michael. This is the family that holds the energy for all of the larger purpose of Heaven. That overall purpose we have shared with you many times, yet the properties of the veil do not allow you to fully comprehend the meaning. The purpose of the entire angelic realm is to honor and support that part of us which is you. This was at the base of the Lucifer experiment, for here the pendulum of advancement was pulled very far to one side, allowing us to determine our direction and intent very clearly.

Like the pond in motion with the circles of energy blending into the whole, we ask you to imagine many circles overlapping one another. Angelic families are similar to what you call extended families on the Game board. One is never restricted to a single family. It is very common for a soul to be a part of several families simultaneously. In the overlapping areas of the circles, one is a member of all of those families represented. In these instances, you will find a natural pull to all of the family purposes. This has been confusing, as you on the Game board like to relate to one purpose at a time. We tell you that you will easily adapt to the new ways.

## Angelic Purpose - the Family Business

Many times we have been asked to describe the nature of the Angelic families. Humanity has now reached a level of vibration high enough to accept some of these basic truths. There are many families within the Angelic Realm. What you know to be angels are the messengers that hold the highest vibration discernible to man. They have presented themselves to you in terms that you would easily understand. They interact in your Game by your invitation only, carrying instructions from Home. They work very closely with your guides in assisting you to connect with your own higher selves. What you know to be Archangels are actually family designations. Each Archangel, or family, has an overall vibration, which stands for a singular purpose. It is no accident that we call our human partner by the title of the Keeper of the Sword. He has held this role for eons of your time, and now is once again playing the part. We tell you it is also no accident that the Archangel Michael has always been portrayed with a sword. For on your Game board, the sword has symbolized truth and empowerment.

The energy known as Michael played an important part at the beginning of the Game, as he earned the status of Archangel and leader of the angels who remained faithful to the Light during the Lucifer experiment. The entire family of Michael has carried the title of 'Warrior of the Light' in some form as a result of the first days of the Game. Now the scripted end times and the last days of the Game are upon us, and once again, there are choices to be made. This is what has called the family of Michael so forcefully into action. These are the times on the Game board when speaking your truth and holding your sword high will lead humanity into evolution instead of extinction. These are the attributes and the highest purpose of the family of Michael.

Empowerment is the attribute that was needed to awaken the Game board of Free Choice to the higher truth. It is for this reason that the family of Michael has been at the cutting edge of the awakening process. You will find many within this family who are Master Healers. The awakening of humanity began by first awakening the Healers needed to re-unite the whole. The next level of awakening will be facilitated by the many healers who will now move to their next level of work in teaching. There are also Master Healers who are not within this family, but the majority resonates with the Michael vibration. In your Game, it would appear that this would be the 'family business,' so to speak. Learning first to heal yourself, to hold the higher vibrations, is moving into empowerment and holding your true power while in biology. This is in progress with the Second Wave of empowerment now on the planet. This is a challenging task for humans, for you have played without it for so long. Holding your power will return you to the truth of your powers of creation. It is the reunion with this power that will affect the creation of Heaven on Earth.

## Connecting Circles of Light

Michael is a crystal pure vibration of such magnitude that many are attracted to it. The family known as Michael is the energy that binds the many circles of Light together. This, as with all, stands in Heaven as it does on Earth. We have told you from the beginning of these messages, of the importance of the re-union of spiritual families in your awakening process. This is the one action that most rapidly advances your own vibration as you move into the higher levels. This is also in progress on this side of the veil. The many circles of Light are in a search for connection once again. This is the movement toward unity consciousness which humanity is now experiencing. For the circles to connect in Heaven, it is necessary for the circles to connect on the Game board. This is facilitated when members of this great family on the Game board come together with intent to move forward.

## Light Centers - - - A Shared Dream

A call has gone out from Home for this connection of these circles of Light to begin on many levels. Being of this family, there are many of you who have heard this call and placed your human interpretations upon it. You have the dream of the Light Centers that you also call the Healing Centers. The dream, as it is being interpreted, is to create locations where all can come together and share the learning, healing and Light. We tell you that this dream is an interpretation of the higher call from Home to connect the Circles of Light. Many have attempted to create the Light Centers only to find them unsupported. Some of you have fallen into disillusionment upon attempting to create what you know to be true in your heart. There is one thing that is missing in some of your human interpretations of this idea. This is the calling back together of the Circles of Light. Please re-member that this original call was to connect the Circles of Light and call them back into overlapping connection with each other. No matter the purity of intent, as you began building these healing centers, if the implementation did not include connecting to others with the same dream, it was not supported. So often, we see you attaching this dream to a physical location. A physical location limits the expansion of the circle and often serves to cut the dream short. Understand first that the dream is to connect the Circles of Light we know to be families of angelic purpose. Incorporating this higher aspect of the original call will create the support needed. Understand that, although it may have a physical location, that location is not the true center. Those of you who hold this dream have this Circle of Light revolving around you. Make space for many of the same dream to share resources, ideas and information. Make space for the many original spiritual families to re-unite and find each other. Make your first intent to create a Circle of Light to aid in the unity process on the Game board, not only to connect others to the Light but also to connect the many Circles to each other. This will facilitate the original call and find full support in the implementation. This will also complete the cycle on our side of the veil. As Below, So Above.

## It Is Time

We have all waited patiently as the Grand Wizard of Time held his finger in the air. Now, the finger has fallen, signifying that it is time to be about your higher work. We ask you to not reach too far in searching for your higher purpose, as most of the time it lies directly at your feet. Do not concern yourself if you are not sure where your path is. Watch for the crystals on your path that lead to your highest expression of spirit in human form. These are the crystals you have placed here yourselves in your planning sessions. These crystals carry the vibration of Home and serve to re-mind you of the true joy of Home. Know that you have placed them well and they will appear to you as you take the first step toward your own joy. Dare to dream the highest of dreams and step into that dream. Now is the time.

## The Gift of Michael ... Your Michael Crystal

The energy, courage and strength of this family are with you always. There is a step into higher vibration you will soon be taking. More will come of this special step in our sessions ahead. For now, simply know it to be a step into 'OverLight.' This will begin when all of the portals of this family are open and connected. To prepare for this, we ask you to carry the vibrations of this family with you consciously at all times. The Gift of Michael is a small crystal that you carry with you that holds this sacred vibration. This crystal will come to you soon if it has not been with you already. It will be a gift from a loved one or perhaps from a teacher. You may find that you have always had a special crystal in your possession but did not know its meaning. It may jump off the shelf in the store as you pass by. Open and allow it to find you. When you connect with it, please take a moment and intentionally store the vibration of the family of Michael in this crystal with ceremony. This is the blending of spirit, in the vibrations of Michael, with the crystal of Earth. This is beginning the process of physically bringing Heaven to Earth. Carry this crystal proudly as your 'Michael crystal,' as it helps you balance your energy and stand firmly in your own truth. If you experience doubt, have lost your way, or just need direction, pull out your Michael crystal and receive the answer from within your own heart. Carry it with you always and use it with intention as you then bring Home to your side of the veil. This is the physical representation of the completion of the crystalline grid and a signal for the Children of Crystal Vibration to begin their ascent onto the Game board.

## The Other Half of the Assignment

Accepting and carrying your crystal is only half of your assignment. Once you have received your crystal, we ask you to give at least three others their Michael crystals. Take your own Michael crystal and place it in ocean water along with the crystals you will be giving to the others. Do this overnight and remove them from the salt water with ceremony, as you once again imprint the crystals with the family of Michael vibration. Give these gifts to the special family members within your own spiritual family. Explain the intent and use of these gifts of Heaven and Earth. Also charge them with the same assignment of spreading the vibrations of Home by the gift of Michael crystals to others. Soon a critical mass will be reached, as the number of Family crystals carried on Earth reaches the number of Family crystals carried here in Heaven. As Above, so Below. This begins the next level of the creation of Home on your side of the veil as the blending of Heaven on Earth.

## This Group of Nine

We have refrained from the beginning of these messages to explain in full detail the origins of this Group of nine. The human interpretation of very high ideals is often twisted. There is an imagined spiritual competition on the Game board that does not exist. This human trait detracts greatly from the value you can receive from the information itself. We now wish to tell you more of who we are. We are those who place the instructions into the hands of the intermediate angels who walk among you. This Group is a series of nine connected circles at the very center of the largest circle known as Michael. We tell you this not because we want to be placed on some imaginary ladder of importance, but rather, because we wish you to truly hear our next words clearly. It is our greatest honor to be of service in helping you to re-member your magnificence. You are winning the Game and we are honored to be your family. It is with our utmost respect and love that we ask you to treat each other, and yourself, with respect and honor, nurture one another and play well together.

I have a tradition that I always travel with my hat. That silly hat is often seen in the pictures on the web site and I often use it to cover my eyes if I sleep on an airplane. On top of my favorite hat is a small medicine bag. That bag has small garnets in it. Garnets are my birthstone. From the beginnings of my travels with this work, I have worn that hat. In each new place I travel, I take a garnet and exchange it for a small stone, which I then carry in the bag on my hat. It has been a wonderful tradition that the Group suggested several years ago. It illustrates the blending of vibrations that the Group says is the Universal energy flow. Recently, while showing this bag to a very special person in Holland, the Group told me to give him a special crystal I was carrying in my bag. This crystal was very clear and called a Herkimer Diamond.

The day after proofreading this message, Barbara gave me a gift. She said it was to replace the crystal I gave away in Holland. Her gift was a beautiful Herkimer Diamond. The moment she gave it to me, I recalled the words of the Group from the message I had just written. "The Gift of Michael is a small crystal that you carry with you that holds this sacred vibration. This crystal will come to you soon if it has not been with you already." In that moment, I knew we both had been given our 'Michael crystals.'

And so it is …

From the heart of the family of Michael, we wish you all a very joyous beginning in this new century. May your path be well lit and full of passion. Expect a miracle. May all your dreams come true as we all bring this grand family together once again.

Steve & Barbara

# Wings

## January 2000

Taken from a live presentation in Attleboro, MA.

Numerous times during private sessions, the Group often shows me people who have recently had the Phantom Death experience. They say this is the time they originally scripted to leave. Now that we have changed the paradigm, we have the opportunity to stay and script new contracts for ourselves. Still, when our originally scripted time to leave comes, we generally experience some opportunity to leave and return Home. It is an opportunity to make a choice. It may be an unexplained illness or a close call in traffic. Often it is a dream where our greeters come for us and we have the choice to stay if we wish. The Group has showed me many times when this has happened to people, and we often tell them about this. Often, they never really put it together that this is what they experienced until we mention it. After telling this to hundreds of people in sessions, I have never had anything like this ever happen to me. This is not unusual. I find that often, when people are experiencing things on a global scale and the Group speaks about it, I am somehow removed from the experience. I never really gave it much thought until I was in session the other day and the person asked me if I ever had the Phantom Death experience myself. I started to say no, but then the Group showed me that I had this experience during the recent channel in the Scepter of Self-Love in Attleboro, Massachusetts.

At the lunch break on the second day of the seminar, the Group wanted to talk. I sat off by myself in a comfortable chair, thinking they were going to give me some information about the channel that was right after lunch. They used to tell me right before the channel what we were going to talk about so that I could start gathering the words. This wasn't what they had in mind, and I found myself in a very comfortable state between sleep and wakefulness. I thought nothing more about it. We then gathered all the chairs around in a comfortable setting. I really like the channels to be very informal and comfortable. I sat down to begin the introduction and the Group stopped me. There was a Master Healer named Raymond sitting to the left and just behind me. The Group wanted me to move him forward so that he was not sitting behind me. I didn't understand why, but Raymond was gracious and moved forward at my request.

We then began the channel. This is a very timely channel and I have taken the transcript and offered it here. The Questions and Answers, and more importantly the discussion that followed about what people experienced during this channel, are given at the end as it happened. When the dust settled and we were complete, I stopped the recorder, pulled out the tape, and labeled it 'Wings.' I am very proud to offer you the experience of 'Wings.'

Greetings from Home.

We love saying those words, for we love sharing the vibrations from home with you who have made your temporary home here on Earth. You have done well in your choices and now the Game goes to the next level. We thank you for playing the parts that you play so well. When you scripted these parts, you had no idea that they would entail the ending that you are seeing as played out in front of you. For there was a time limit on the Game board and now that time limit has passed and you are still here. You have made it so through your choices, through opening your hearts, and through holding the energy of this family within your own hearts. You have done well and we tell you that it is us that are honored to sit at your feet.

We wish to tell you this day a little more of the Angelic realm of which you are so curious. One point in particular we wish to speak of and that is our wings. You have many wonderful tales that speak of earning your wings, we particularly love the one about the bell because it is closer than you may imagine, and we are referring to the tale that whenever a bell rings, an Angel has earned his/her wings. There are many such representations in your Game that link your world directly to ours. We tell you, they are there for a reason and, even if you look at the bell, you can easily see that it is a representation of vibrational healing. Once the vibrational level is attained, the wings are added. One thing we wish to clarify to you is that we do not need the wings to fly. As you know, we fly quite well without them. But they are, in fact,, wings, and they are a representation of part of your world that represents the freedom to fly. But more than anything else, these wings have a specific purpose, a purpose that actually has reason and uses within your field of your three dimensions. Our highest purpose is to reflect your magnificence. Our wings are used for the singular purpose of reflecting the energy of humans. The veils you have agreed to wear are thick and very effective. Therefore, it takes a concentrated reflection to see even a small part of your own magnificent energy through the veil. If you were to closely observe our wings, you would see that they are a concave shape. This allows us to focus your energy as we reflect it back to you, and enables us to let you feel and see who you really are. Before we can reflect your energy, you must be open to receiving that energy. Up to this point in the Game, very few opportunities have been given us to spread our wings for you. Now, through your choices, you have purposely raised your own vibration and the collective vibration of all of humanity. We are so very proud of the work you have done. For that reason, we are so terribly honored to be able to spread our wings in front of you. You have called us here to reflect your magnificence and we are so honored to do so. As you get comfortable with this energy, we tell you this is the energy of Home.

You may be here on the Game board playing your game but you are carrying the vibration of home in your own hands. The crystals you hold, in which you give so much power, tell you they are a representation for there is no magic within the crystal, much as there is no magic within our wings. Yet, both of them reflect your energy and your magnificence and help you to remember who you are. This is the true source of the magic you seek. For such is your own great heritage and the magic is held within each of you. We tell you that you are not pieces of God; in fact you are God. We love you so and we thank you for having the courage to play the game.

We take a moment while we adjust the energy in the room. We tell you that it is very, very crowded in here. (Laughter.) There are so many who wish to see what is happening in this room. It is not us they have come to see, for they see us all the time. It is you. It is the Grand Masters who have the courage to play the Game behind the veils. By placing the veil of forgetfulness on your own face, you are playing out the greatest scenarios on the Game board, for you are remembering your true power. And in bringing the power of this side of the veil to your home, you are extending Heaven. You are winning the game. Welcome Home.

This day, we ask you to take the crystals from this room. Not only the crystals that you carry within your hands, but also the crystals that you carry within your hearts. For you have earned them so much through your toils and your struggles. You have earned more than you can possibly imagine. You have set your tone. You have taken away the veil for just a moment and said, "This is who I am to be." And in doing so, you align energy on many different levels that cannot help but bring you the reality you are choosing. And we thank you for those choices, for you are the representation of us. It is our greatest honor to reflect the love that we hold for you. That love is so far beyond your understanding that it can only be expressed as a feeling.

At the beginning of this year, you received a very special gift. You have had it all along and yet it was just activated. You are powerful beyond your imagination and that power was greatly amplified as you stepped into the next level of the next turning of the clock. You stepped into the year of crystal intent. And that year is a year for you to crystallize and focus and infuse your own intent into your lives. To purposely take the Quill and script your own life, to purposely set things into motion and create your own reality is the most honored task now before you. We tell you that your actions, your love, and your words, during this next year will set the energy and intent for the following twelve years. The next twelve years on the planet will determine the energy that will pervade the next millennium. You hold that future in your hands at this moment. Many of you have the Earth-ticket, as the Keeper calls it, for you have stood in line to be here at exactly this moment. Many of you rushed in, not getting ample rest between incarnations only so that you could be here at this very second of time. For that reason, we honor you. You have chosen to be at the very cutting edge of the new paradigms. You have chosen to be at the cutting edge of the new energy. Of course, you at the cutting edge also receive most of the heat for the books about how to do it have not been written yet. Many of you look at the higher vibrations through the eyes of the lower and think you are not moving. Many of you feel stuck. We ask you to be patient and kind to yourselves. Had we asked you to take a seat a little bit further back in the class, you would have said, "No, I must be in the front row!" Now some of you sit and wait for the rest to catch up. Be patient and follow your hearts, for you will be the ones to help the others that follow. We honor you for you have done well. You are leaders, you are energy leaders.

There are many spaces within this part of the country that are boiling at this moment. This is humorous to the Keeper for there is snow on the ground, yet we tell you that this is the boiling. As the energy opens within the heart, you feel the warmth of the soul. And that has created many pockets of warmth that we see as pockets of boiling energy. We charge you in this area to go out and find those pockets and connect the Circles of Light that are forming. Those are the Centers of Light you have searched for so long. They are now opening right here in your own back yard. They are opening in many, many parts of the globe, yet your own work begins here in your own area. From there you take it to other areas, for everywhere you travel you carry this energy. Everywhere you look, every time that you pick up the telephone, you spread this to others. Use the Universal Energy and the fusion of the Michael energy, and purposely set your tone to be heard by all. Carry it well, for we entrust you, for you are the Guardians and Ambassadors of the Light. We honor you so for taking these roles. As Ambassadors of the Light, each and every one of you will have an opportunity to carry this wonderful vibration of home. We thank you for that.

We tell you that there will be another infusion much like the one you experienced on the first of the year. This infusion of energy will be very powerful. It is no coincidence that the Keeper will be returning to this area upon the infusion. We tell you that there will be an alignment on May fifth of this year that will bring another level of energy to this planet and to your Game board. Do not allow yourselves to be wrapped into fear. This is a gift you have earned. This is your right to accept this new level of power. This is a gift that will take you to the next level. And much like the infusion that you experienced last year in August, this will be the completion of a nine-month cycle of the birth of the New Light. The power that this energy carries can be intentionally directed for the highest good of the planet and the highest good of the players on the Game board. It is truly another step toward creating Heaven on Earth. Imagine yourself with wings similar to ours for that is truer than you may know. We ask you to spread your wings and focus this energy to create the highest potential for yourselves. That is your ascension. That is what you chose to do as the highest possible outcome of the Game and now it lies before you.

You have chosen to re-script your contracts for many of you were to leave. Five of you in this room were to leave in the last three months. You have stayed. You have re-scripted your contracts. You have done so for a reason. Plant the seeds. Connect the Circles of Light. Let people see your heart. Let people see who you are. We have carried the sword for so long and now we pass it to you. Now you have an opportunity to use the sword to find your own truth so that it never will be used as a weapon again.

Several in the room have asked for healing. We wish to tell you that you were healed the moment you asked for it. You have the power to do this for yourselves. We are honored that you would ask us, and we tell you that you have already have received it. It is yours for the asking. You have had the courage to ask. Now we ask you to have the courage to accept that which you have asked for. Now we ask you to have the courage to walk away from that familiar pain. Now we ask you to have the courage to step forth into your empowerment.

We are here to offer you the strength for all of you to walk forward into the next level of your existence. We are here to reflect your energy and help you re-member who you really are. We are here to help you re-member the feelings of Home. We take a moment to do something we have never done before. Through the Keeper, we will now spread our wings to reflect your magnificence ...

[In that moment, I felt myself spreading my arms out to both sides, as if I were spreading my wings. The energy that began to run through me was indescribable. I felt the tears as they fell in a steady flow from my face to my chest. I became aware that everyone in the room was also feeling the effects of this energy from the sounds I heard. The energy was building and becoming more intense as the people in the room accepted it. This beautiful energy that I can only describe as the energy of Home was beginning to allow me to feel as if I was Home. The veil was getting very thin and I could feel the energy building very quickly. Barbara was sitting to my left and I became aware that she was concerned about me. It felt as though she was holding my feet to the ground. I also felt the wonderful energy of Raymond who was now sitting just to my right. I knew that the two of them were holding the energy for me to do this. The energy was still increasing and then, in that instant, the Group took me. I did not know where I was, but I was no longer in the room. Even though I could hear tears from the others as they felt this energy from Home, I was removed and insulated from what I would be feeling if I were still in my body. Then, I felt my arms pulling back in as I re-entered my body. Once again, I was feeling the tears streaming down my face and my shirt being wet from them, and I once again felt the intense energy running through me. I knew that if they had not pulled me in that moment, I would have simply crossed the line and stepped into Heaven. I was that close, and the pull was very strong indeed. As the flow of information resumed, I continued the channel. All of this happened in the space of about 30 seconds. That was perhaps the longest and most wonderful 30 seconds of my life thus far. In that moment, I was Home and I will carry that feeling with me always.]

The Group resumes:

That explains why we have never done this before. (Laughter) You have received a charge. Carry the crystals that you came with today, for they are now charged with your own energy. Carry them in your heart always. Show them to others freely and if they are admired, then give them away. Share the energy of your love for, in giving it away, you too spread your wings. Nurture each other and the planet in the way that only you can do with each other. We can sit here and tell you of your magnificence and it is nothing compared to when you tell each other. You share the same dimension, you share the same experience, and you share the veil. Remind each other often of who you really are. When you feel lost and alone, and cannot remember who you are, allow yourself to be hugged, for we are there hugging you often. You have set the new energy into motion. You have breathed life into the new Game. You have made it so, and you are honored beyond your imagination.

It is with our greatest honor that we sit here and ask you to please treat each other with respect. Nurture one another to your greatest avail and please play well together.

the Group

After I opened my eyes again I realized why the Group wanted me to ask Raymond to move closer. They wanted him to help hold the energy while they took me on this journey. Raymond and Barbara on either side of me were holding the energy for what I experienced. In fact, had they not been on either side of me, I most likely would have returned Home.

# The Story of the Circle and the Light

## Enter the Human Angels

November 2001

The room was filled as I entered. There was not an empty seat and some were even sitting on the floor on the sides of the isle. As I walked into the room, I saw the people all watching the stage in anticipation. It was obvious that a miracle was about to happen. I knew I was to be a part of this miracle but I was also very much aware that it was their wonderful anticipation that was actually creating the miracle that was about to unfold. I felt the most wonderful unconditional love as I walked up the side isle to where Barbara was already waiting for me on the stage. As I put on my microphone, I looked into the audience and was amazed at how many faces I recognized. In that moment, I knew we had crossed the boundaries of the veil. We were Home.

The second Light Circles Congress held in Veldhoven, Holland with 800 Family members on October 16th 2001. We are very proud to present the live channel from that special day of love and light.

Greetings from Home

Can you feel the energy? Can you feel the essence of who you are as you look into each other's eyes? Can you feel that you are here for a reason? Yes, of course you can. These, dear ones, are the memories of Home. You understand from your own heart that you have been placed here at exactly at this moment and time to do what you came here to do. You have looked to us and you have asked, "What is this about? What is the meaning of life? What am I here to do?" If only it were possible for us to answer you. If only it were possible for us to tell you that if you would simply turn right instead of turning left, you would find your passion. That is not for us to do, as it would take your power from you. It is the search for this passion that allows each and every one of you to experience being the creators that you truly are.

You wonder why you cannot see where you are going. You ask, "Why does it have to be so confusing?" Ah, we love the fact that you ask but we tell you, you are the ones who have decided for it to be so confusing. You are the ones who have scripted the Game and you have done that well for you truly do not even re-member who you are. You are the ones who choose to come down here to this wonderful little Game board, where you would wake up in your bubbles of biology and you would be confused. It was even your intent to be completely confused. Oh, we tell you, you have done better than you expected, have you not? But you are starting to see through the veil now. Time is getting quicker. The lag of time in which you create is becoming shorter all the time. Choose your thoughts well, dear ones, for they hold the reality of your future and now you will experience it faster than before. You have no choice over what comes into your head, for you are part of the Universal Subconscious Mind and there is a steady stream of thoughts going through your head at all times. Ah, but you do have complete choice over what stays in your head. Choose those thoughts well and choose only those vibrations that blend with your heart, and there will be no more war on planet Earth. There are some new times ahead. There are so many challenges that you now face.

We tell you that you have greater opportunities for each and every one of you than you are aware of. Yet to try and tell you exactly where that will be and exactly how that will look would be to take your power from you. So instead, we will tell you a story.

## The Story of the Circle and the Light

In the beginning, there was the word. The word was 'om,' and this vibration was the origin of All That Is. As the sacred sound of the word vibrated against the fabric of Universal Energy, it created a Circle and that Circle was energy in motion. Since the Circle was a creation of the fabric of the Universal Energy, it was a Circle of creation. The formation of this Circle was the beginning of everything. Ah, this was a marvelous creator Circle.

Soon the Circle got up from its fabric of the Universal Energy and started moving around. It bounded, bounced and rolled as it moved everywhere. Soon it began creating and it created the most wonderful wonders that you can imagine. The Circle loved to  create and did so all of the time. The Universal Energy had a way of blending everything together so it was as if it were a great canvas upon which to create anything and everything. The Circle experienced the wonders of creation for it was able to create and do anything. As the Circle rolled around creating, it saw the most majestic sights and became aware of the creations it was creating. The Circle loved to play. There were times the Circle turned on its side and started spinning much like a helicopter and flew all over the place. The Circle learned to bounce, and it began to roll. It learned to spin like a coin spinning on edge. The Circle found that there were really no boundaries it could not cross. The Circle was free and easy and the Circle was happy.

At one point, the Circle got comfortable with creating and began creating very large creations that showed the vastness of the Universal Energy. It took it upon itself to attempt to create something that would exceed the boundaries of the Universal Energy. Try as it did, the Circle was never able to define the boundaries it was seeking. The more it created, the more it realized it could never find the beginning or the end of the Universal Energy. Much like the Universal Energy, the Circle became aware that it (the Circle) could see everything but itself. The only thing that the Circle could not create was an under-standing of itself. It could roll anywhere it wanted to roll. It could fly anywhere it wanted to fly. It could bounce all over the place, shrink and expand yet still it could see only small parts of itself at one time. The Circle began to question its perfect existence because it understood that it could never understand its own existence. The Circle was unable to say, "I AM."

The Circle was the first dimension for it was the first Circle. It was here that the Circle decided to venture into another form. The Circle thought that if it took another form it might be able to see itself and say, "I AM." Here the Circle stepped into the second dimension. At that moment, the Circle decided to create something it had never created before and it created another Circle. "Ah, this will be easy. Now I will simply be able to look at the other Circle and I will be able to see who I am," said the Circle. Once again the Circle was disappointed for, as it looked, it could not see the entire Circle it had created. It could only see small pieces of it. Like its own Circle, the second Circle was constantly moving in energy, with no beginning and no end. Therefore it could not be contained to actualize or realize itself. The words, "I AM" eluded the Circle once again.

"Ah, so what happened next?" you ask. Here, the second Circle entered into the second dimension inside the first Circle, where it twisted upon itself and formed the figure eight. The figure eight took a place inside the first circle in a horizontal position. As  the energy in the second Circle continued to move around the Circle, it crossed itself in the center of the eight. So now the second Circle was rotating in a figure eight inside of the first Circle. Now, with the first Circle, there were three circles, since the second Circle was twisted into two. In this fashion, the expression of the Universal Energy found itself in the third dimension.

The energy moving through the second Circle crossed the magical spot in the center in the third dimension. Here the energy crossed itself and sparks flew off. The first Circle spoke with the voice of creation: "Let there be Light" and there was Light. The sparks that flew off were made of the same Universal Energy as the first Circle. Therefore it had the same abilities of creation as the first Circle, but they could not re-member their abilities for they saw themselves as separate in the third dimension. So now the Circle within the Circle was still moving and these little sparks started to fly all over the place and create Light. Oh such wondrous times they started to have. They could not see themselves and they thought their existence in the third dimension was all there was. The original Circle could now look at the Light and see it as separate, for it passed through the polarity of the second dimension. Now the Light began to feel totally separate as it spoke the magic words, "I AM." The Circle laughed joyfully as the Light spoke these words. The Light could only speak the words because it thought it was separate from the Circle … and the Circle was happy.

Over time the Light began to create as the Circle watched with joy. Such fun to watch as the Light created everything yet could not even see that it was creating its own reality. Such fun it was for the Circle to see itself in this fashion.

The Light created even more as it continued to become aware. It was not long before the Light began to become aware of the large Circle surrounding it. Even as the Light felt the Circle in their hearts, they could not see it. The Light began to accept the reality of the Circle even though it could not be seen or touched, and it began to speak to the Circle. "Dear Circle, tell us why we are here. Tell us the meaning of life."

The Circle was amused yet remained silent for the Circle knew it could never tell the Light the meaning of life for the Light had yet to create that meaning and that life. Only if the Light fully accepted its own powers of creation could it truly be the finite expression of the Circle. The Circle remained silent as the Game continued … and the Circle was happy.

On it went, and as the little sparks of Light started taking responsibility for their own Light, they started creating for themselves. They, too, were housed in the fabric of the Universal Energy, which made them the same creators as the first Circle. The Light began to play and found ways of rolling and spinning and flying, much the way the first Circle did in the beginning. The Circle looked upon them with joy and the Circle was happy. As the little sparks of Light started shining and using their Light, they started having fun. They started blinking and playing with their Light. They started getting very imaginative and created colors with their Light. They found that they could either be the Light or reflect the Light, and they got good at doing both. Soon they were even signaling each other with their own Light, as they began to see that the Light was their own. They started having all sorts of fun as they created everything with their Light … and the Circle was happy.

There came a time when the Lights found they could not reach any further into the Universal Energy and they started their own circles for, as creators, they started creating their greatest desires. They did not even know they were doing it because the veil of forgetfulness they wear was so thick that they could not see they were a part of the larger Circle. But there they were in the third dimension, and they created a wonderful galaxy of planets in the fabric of the Universal Energy in which to play their games. The Lights created this wonderful Game board over here and this Game over there and they started creating all sorts of wonderful games to blink their lights at each other and to use their Lights. The Circle stood back and watched in amazement … and the Circle was happy.

Even after several games were in place for the Light to see itself, the Lights began to think they were all that is and the memories of the Circle faded. Seeing this, the Circle understood that the real test of the Light would be if it were able to see itself and re-member that it was actually a part of the Circle. Then the Light would have all of its abilities of creation restored and the Circle would fully see itself as the Light. It was this re-union that caused the united creation of one special Game. Here the Lights' higher aspects combined with the Circle to create a very special Game. The Circle, in all its grand wisdom, knew that the only way that the Light could take its full power was for it to take full responsibility for creation. Therefore a grand Game was created with only one guideline: In all matters there would be free choice.

So the Lights started playing on the Game board of free choice. They started as before, blinking and enjoying each other. Only this time they made the Game very difficult with the use of a veil of forgetfulness. Not only did the Lights not know they were part of the Circle but they also chose to wake up and be very confused. At first, the Circle thought that the Game would not work as hoped, for the free choice idea led the Lights to make some very poor choices. Still the Circle looked on as the Game unfolded and it was there with Love to rekindle the Lights with Love whenever the Light faded. The Light drew energy from the Circle every time used its own powers of creation. The hardest part for the Light was to know that the power of creation it held was its own, for the veil kept that secret well. It was not long before the Light found a great hidden secret. It found that when the Light became dim and faded, it can be quickly rejuvenate by connecting to the Circle through any expression of Love. The Light got very excited by this discovery. The Circle also got very excited at this development for it meant that the Light was beginning to re-member.

The Lights got so into the Game that they fell into a comfortable place as their power slipped away from them. After long periods of time, the Lights began to create a fascination for darkness and shadows. For it was only possible to really see Light with a contrast of darkness, they reasoned. There were times where they really forgot about the Circle and got fully wrapped in the darkness. The Circle watched in amazement as the Lights played their Game. The Lights fell into believing that the reality of what they had created was all there was. They believed that if they could not see it, feel it or touch it, then it did not exist. They even printed in their newspapers that the "Circle was Dead." The Circle looked on with joy that the Lights' creation of their veils was so very complete. Here the Circle was in joy, for it allowed the Circle to see a part of itself that it never dreamed of … and the Circle was happy.

Every so often, two or more of the Lights would look into each other's eyes and they would somehow re-member that they are part of a great Circle. They asked the Circle to protect them from the darkness and they reached into the darkness of fear and shined the most exquisite Light. The Circle beamed with pride as it looked on and saw the Lights take responsibility. The Circle offered to help the Light to understand that the darkness was just an illusion of polarity and a lack of Light.

The darkness is only there as part of the Game so they can see their own Light and provide them with a space to use it. It was so difficult, for with the veils of forgetfulness firmly in place, the sparks of Light could see their Light only as a reflection.

It was very difficult for the Lights to see outside and grasp the larger picture. Their hope was to wake up totally confused … and they were very successful at that creation. They were so confused that many of them gave their power to the darkness thinking the answer must be there. Since their powers of creation held no limits, the darkness appeared to have power. The Circle laughed wildly at this creation, for their powers were so great and the veil was so thick that here they created something from nothing. Since they created with Light but could not see that it was they who were creating, they gave their power to the darkness, which of course is only a lack of Light. The Circle thought how wonderful this was that the Game was so very complete. "These Lights are so amusing!" thought the Circle.

So it went, for they started creating everywhere they looked. They even began creating games within games that have absolutely no meaning. The Circle thought to itself, "Aren't they imaginative? Isn't it wonderful to see how they create everything that they touch, everything that they think of, and everything that they feel?" The Circle began to see itself in the beauty of the Light … and the Circle was happy.

The Light continued to play the Game in a field of polarity for it has passed through the two inner circles twisted upon itself. The two inner circles represented the duality of the second dimension. For as it passed through the second dimension, it was necessary to split off from itself or at least give that illusion. Everything that the light saw in this field of polarity while it visited the third dimension was an illusion, for it saw itself as separate from the Circle and it was not. It saw itself as light and dark, and it was not. It saw itself as up and down, as love and fear, as good and bad, as right or wrong. It was not. It was only an illusion needed for the expression of Light. Every so often, the wondrous lights got a glimpse of their own light as reflected from another. When they did, they were rejuvenated for it touched their own hearts. It touched the essence of who they were. In that moment it sent back a ripple of energy to the Circle and the Circle was happy.

The Circle of the Universal Energy has no beginning and no end but within the second inner Circle, the energy must have a beginning and an end otherwise, it could not be seen by the first Circle. All the Games created by the Light have a time limit. Such was also the case for the Game of Free Choice. Now even the greatest of hopes of the Circle may fade, for the planet of Free Choice is coming to an end of its time. The Light even saw it coming, for it was foretold. The Lights looked at each other and said, "What do we do? Where are we? Who is going to save us? They prayed to the Circle and the Circle smiled back lovingly. They asked the Circle to step in and to save them and direct them. "Just show us the way," the Light asked. The Circle smiled and did everything it could to hold the mirror in front of the Light for it to see itself. Yet the veil was so thick that the Light could not see that the Light was its own. The Circle saw that its greatest hope of seeing itself was about to end. Even so, the Circle was happy.

Then at the very last moments on the Game board, the Circle saw that the Light was getting brighter. It was getting so bright and was about to pierce the veil. "Do you re-member who you are?" asked the Circle. There was no answer from the Light. "Do you know that you are in fact the Circle?" the Circle again spoke but there was still no answer. The Light was getting very bright but was still unable to comprehend that it was the Circle. The Circle was getting very excited now for the Light was getting so bright that it began to take Responsibility for holding its own Light. The Light began to awaken, very slowly at first … one awakened and then another. A higher truth began to appear on the Game board as Light got brighter. Fear of the darkness lessened and they began to understand that much like the first Circle, in order for them to have Light, it was necessary to have darkness. In fact, the darkness gave them the ability to express their Light. It was all part of the larger Circle. The Circle now became overwhelmed at the possibility that the Light would truly see itself … and the Circle was happy.

Lights everywhere came to the realization that they held their own destiny. Even other Games looked on and saw what was happening. They began to plant seeds of Light and nurture them with Responsibility and Love. As these seeds began to sprout, the final end of the Game drew near. At the very last moments of the Game board, the Light got so bright that the smallest ray of Light pierced the veil. The Circle was elated as the Light began to hold its own power of creation.

The Light extended the Game by its own choice. It also learned to enhance its powers of creation through the use of Responsibility and Love. It claimed the Responsibility to use its own powers of creation and it learned to Love itself. That day, a new Light shone on the Game board of Free Choice as even the fabric of the Universal Energy began to change. Every Light in every Game began to shift due to the awakening of the Light. Each one of the lights began to reach for a higher truth and, in so doing, the Game board of Free Choice reached a higher vibration.

It went through the color range of its own vibratory levels and began to create new ones. As it did, it scripted new contracts for itself. Yes, there were setbacks. Yes, as the higher energy and higher truth started filtering in, there was resistance. There were five steps forward and two back. Then five more steps forward and then only one back. The Circle was happy.

At this point, the Circle itself stepped in and sent an idea to the Light and said, "Light, you are the creator. You do not understand. You have always been asking for information and we tell you, you hold that within your powers for you are the Light of Home. You, in fact, are Light that you seek. Do not reach for it outside of yourself. Go inside and you will find the answers on all the creation that you need to create your highest reality."

At first, the Light did not know what to think as it heard the words of the Circle. For so long it had asked to hear the words clearly and now that the words came, they were heard within. "Ah, so this is the secret of the Circle!" said the Light. "It has talked to us all along yet we could not hear it as long as we looked outside of ourselves." It was then that the Light first grasped an important higher truth. It realized that, for the Circle to talk within, it must be a part of themselves. And so the Light understood that they were actually a part of the Circle itself. In their excitement, the Lights began to blink and flash their colors wildly.

There was great excitement that shot throughout the entire fabric of the Universal Energy, changing everything in its path. From that day forward, the Lights began to plant seeds openly and freely. The Lights no longer feared the dark. They no longer feared the shadow, as they understood that the shadows really are a place for the Light to shine. It was then that the Light even blessed the darkness as an integral part of itself … and the Circle was happy.

On their own accord, the Lights created a third Circle. They emulated the second Circle and they twisted it upon itself so it, too, made the same figure eight. This figure eight was also positioned within the first Circle, but in a vertical direction. In this act, the second Planet of Free Choice was born. Now you have the two figure eights within the larger Circle and if you count all the circles you will see that there are now five, which represent the fifth dimension where the next expression of Light will reside. The Circle spoke to the Light: "You have won the Game, dear ones. You have dared to say 'I AM' and to hold your power. Now the next step is before you. You now take the role of overseers of the Light as a new Game begins. First you will help the other Lights make the transition ahead of them and then you will become the overseers of the Light for the New Game. You are taking your own Game to the next level. Fear it not and re-member that darkness is really an opportunity for the Light to shine."

With that the Circle smiled … and the Circle was happy.


Do you understand the nature of this story, dear ones? Do you understand that you are stepping off the bridge of the forth dimension and into the fifth right now? Do you understand that you are the Light you have been seeking outside of yourselves? Do you understand that you are the Circle and the Light? If you understand this, then you understand that you will script what is to happen next. There is no grand plan on the Game board of Free Choice, as you have not written it yet.

This is what you have come here to do. We tell you, you are just to the point where you are beginning to reach into the fifth-dimensional reality. You are the forerunners, for you have gotten here first. You will be helping the others over. The step off the bridge of the fourth dimension to the fifth dimension takes trust. It takes courage. It takes a knowingness that all will be in order. You can help each other. Do not ask the Circle to help you, for you are the Circle. You are the Light. Take responsibility for your own Light and for your own passion. Find a small piece of that passion and carry it proud always. Enhance your Light with Responsibility and Love. Reach out, for when two or more come together and create their own

Circles of Light, the magic begins. We tell you that you are the Circle. You are the Light.

Each and every one of you are the sparks of Light. All we ask you to do is to see the light for what it is and take Responsibility for your own creations and your own Light. Find your passion, and your Light will shine bright. Do not try to heal the world. Do not try to change everything that is. Allow those steps to go five forward and two back if they must. Hold your Light firm and high. Blink it and shine the colors you hold within. Express it and dare to be the Light in its entire splendor. For that is where your true power is, dear ones. You are becoming the Human Angels. Your next role is to help the others cross over and take responsibility for their own empowerment and creations. Soon after, you will become the Angels to the second planet of Free Choice, for that is already in motion. The symbol we have shown you is not new. It has been on your Game board all along waiting for you to take your power. This is the sign of the Human Angel, and it represents the Light in the fifth dimension.

The story of the Circle and the Light does not end here, for you are just writing the next chapters. We tell you that we were with you in this place one year ago and we spoke the words to you that you are no longer the only planet of Free Choice. Now there is another one. There are many of you that ask us, "What does that mean? What does that look like? Is it out in the stars? Are they in the embryo phase? Are they humans? Are they aliens?" We love your questions for you are so imaginative. Re-member that the Light you shine is the Light of Home. Share it with each other and all who ask to receive it. Share it with yourselves. Hold it high and proud and there will be no more shadows on planet Earth.

You have opened the door to the infiltration of the new Light and the blended energy of the male / female Crystal energy. This has been done by your choosing. You are the ones who have created this. Does it surprise you that there will be some who resist that? Does it surprise you that there are some who are so far grounded in their reality that they cannot see this coming? Does it surprise you that they take drastic steps because they are in fear? Hold your Light, dear ones, each and every one of you. You do not need to fix that which is not broken. Re-member that darkness is an opportunity to shine Light. Hold the hands of the person next to you and share your Light. Create your own Circles of Light. Re-member that all the Light is within the first Circle and therefore is in Unity with all that is. Honor the Unity in each other and you will honor all of the Light.

You are the creators, dear ones. Hold the sign of the Human Angel within your own heart. Do not give your power to it but rather use it as a re-minder of who you are. We tell you this is only a warm up for what you have come to do. You will be the angels of the second Planet of Free Choice. Now the triggers will begin for now you know some of the base truth. Now you know how this works. You talk to the angels and you ask Archangel Michael to watch over you and for the angelic realm and all the divine family of Light to come and help you. We tell you we are always there for you. The same as you will always be there for those who you will watch over. Your greatest task as Angels will be to reflect the Light within, without taking the power from those you reflect upon. As you learn to do that, you will begin to reflect the Light of the magnificence of the second Planet of Free Choice.

Watch for the signal of eight zero eight. It is the signal of the Human Angel that will now start activating your own DNA. Take that signal if you so choose.

It is hard for you to understand that even in the darkness, the Circle is happy. Emulate that happiness, dear ones. Do not let the events of your planet on your Game of Free Choice dim your Light. Be the creators that you are. Know that you are loved beyond your wildest expectations, as you are the Circle and the Light.

It is with the greatest honor that we, the angels in Heaven, sit before the Lights of the Game board of Free Choice. We ask you to nurture one another and treat each other with respect and play well together in the Light.

And so it is …

Espavo.

the Group

## The Beacons of Light Meditation

### By Barbara Rother

### Dedicated to the Circles of Light Groups

Together we allow the light to grow brighter. Breathe deep. With each breath that you take, celebrate the light of the new day. Each exhale releases the dark that is only the absence of the light. Create this light at this very moment. Envision the light. Feel the warm, healing glow of this energy. As the light moves in circles surrounding all that is, it becomes the circle of light. With each turn of the light it becomes brighter. It has dared to shine. It shares with all within its field the peacefulness of its center.

The circle has been turning ever so slowly through life. It begins first dimly lighting its path through the every day existence of life. It is shining but not fully allowing its abundance of sparks to show. Now another circle comes next to you and says, "You are so complete in your circle. Your glow illuminates with an electrifying aura. When you touch another circle, sparks fly off and there is a connection that inspires them to glow as well. Do you not see your own light and power? Let me be a mirror for you so that I might reflect your own magnificence. You inspire other circles to create with their own thoughts the power to light up their own circles."

Feel now the excitement of when two circles meet, much like the feeling when you meet with others of like mind in your Circles of Light. Feel your passion. Be your passion. Be free to share it with all around you encouraging them to shine their own light. You feel yourself daring to shine your light on a permanent basis. No longer are you afraid of what others might think. You are proud to be the light, lighting the path for others to see. All will see you shine as you roll along life. See yourself bump into another circle, shining but not as bright. By touching each other and sharing the light, both of your lights are brighter. Instead of being two separate circles of light, you become part of the whole. Your circle is but apart of the whole circle of God. You are God. Together with the other circles, you make up the whole complete circle of the higher being. Each circle you continue to touch increases the ever expanding glow of the endless circle of light.

You find yourself anxiously anticipating meeting other circles along your way. Feel the glowing warmth of this light resonate from within to all outside your personal circle. Know that this inward glow expands to connect to all the circles that you touch in your life. Dare to be the Circle of Light. Re-member who you are. Feel your importance of how you are here to connect to others. Release all that has held you back from shining. Keep your mental attitude constructive and live without judgment but with love and understanding. As you continue to roll through life, spread your light to all that you touch. With a kind word, a warming smile, allow all to feel your heartfelt energy. Be confident in your power that you are making a difference in this world. Be your own individual circle shining your light. Connect with the larger circle of the world. We are one. As you continue to roll through life, you may hit rough spots. Be strong. Rise above these times by being in the center of your circle. At times, you may encounter those who seem to threaten your smooth path as you roll along through life. Know that these are just lessons. Welcome these challenges for the growth they are presenting to you.

You know in the past you have experienced your own growing periods before you knew the way to be in your full light. Those who are challenging you are only rolling on their own circle, not yet understanding the full light. Understand the path of others. Know that you are learning from each bump you find along your way. Do not be critical of those who present these lessons to you, for these are only lessons toward your light. Rise above and empower these individuals. Hold your altitude toward helping other circles. You can only offer them a way to connect in the Light. It is up to them if they choose to connect. Bask in your own light.

As your circle continues experiencing each delightful lesson, you build confidence. This confidence makes your circle glow even brighter. Feel the glow from your very center of your circle. It begins there and illuminates from you, touching outward to all who come into your path. Spread your light. Be the light. They will see the glowing circle of light you have created. They will ask how they can create their own circle. Gather together with those of like mind. Reflect in each other's light. The light will become a golden ring. Be the circles of light first individually, then by joining your circles together. The circle is the light. By joining together, we are one.

And so it is …

# Farewell to the Sword

## Love over Terror in the New Game

### September 2001

From a live channel presented at Mt Shasta, CA

From Steve:

A flash of lightning followed by the crack of thunder woke me from the first deep sleep I had all week. It was 6:30 a.m., and all I could think of were the plans we had made to take all the Lightworkers to the meadow half way up Mt Shasta. As I took a deep breath, I realized that this entire week had been an exercise in flexibility for me. The first day of the Espavo conference was 9/11, the day the terrorists hit the World Trade Center towers. From the moment I got the call and was told that we would not be flying anywhere, the entire experience took on a new importance. The Group immediately wanted me to put a message on the site. I did and then we decided to drive the 14 hours to get to Mt Shasta. From the moment we left, it was as if we had taken on an important mission. The week-long event was very powerful and all but 11 people made it. Those 11 people, many stuck in airports for several days, were also a part of the energy. Some even called at regular intervals to tell us they were still attempting to come. Only one made it.

Yes, we did go up to the meadow, and it rained all around us but left us dry and in the perfect energy to create the New Game. This New Game is also reflected in the global events that are unfolding now. The book Re-member begins with a chapter called "The Grand Game of Hide and Seek." That chapter begins: "All of us are gathered in a meadow at the base of a mountain. We are Home and playing together in perfect love." We returned to that meadow this day and began to write the New Game.

As I walked out of my cabin, I grabbed the Sword. The Group calls me the Keeper of the Sword. This is the sword of truth, the Sword of Michael and the sword of empowerment. This is Excalibur. They once told me a beautiful story of who I was in the days of Camelot. They said I was a cross between a jeweler and a blacksmith. I made special ceremonial swords. These swords were never used in battle but only used to take people to their next levels of existence as in knighting. Not only did I make these swords but it seems that I was entrusted with their care between ceremonies and was therefore known as the Keeper of the Sword. Today we had yet another chance to use this sword to take people to their next levels. Today we would use the ceremony of the sword to set into motion the New Game in the meadow up on the mountain.

Driving up the mountain, I was listening for any indication of what the Group would talk about. There was reverent silence. As the caravan pulled into a parking area, I looked up at the mountain and saw what the Group calls the guardian of the mount. This is an outcropping of rocks energetically in charge of the valley below. We stopped, held hands and asked the guardian permission to proceed. Little did we know when we finally found our way to the meadow, that same guardian was directly in front of us, looking down with a hint of a smile.

There were a lot of firsts in this channel, and we think it is appropriate to share this with you now. We proudly present the live channel that the Group gave us that day in the meadow at the base of the mountain as we began the New Game.

Greetings from home, dear ones.

We tell you we are not over there where you look for us, we are here with you. We are a part of your energy. You are a part of us and we honor so much your willingness to sacrifice, to be a part of making the new world. We cannot tell you the honor we have for you, for you are the ones who are changing the paradigms of All That Is. You are the ones who are changing the energy and making it possible to create the New Planet Earth. We tell you that in the New Earth, things are different. We tell you for the first time, we ask the Keeper to open his eyes. [Keeper (Steve) opened his eyes and was overwhelmed by tears. For the first time this entire channel was given with eyes open as he looked from one person to the next.]

Much is going on here and each one of you can see the brilliance in each other as you look in each other's hearts. As you look past each others souls, as you look past the bubbles of biology that you wear while you are here, we tell you things are different. The New Planet Earth is at hand. You have created it through your own love and your choices, and we thank you. We honor you beyond your understanding for what you have created. We tell you, you are the ones that have set it into motion and you are the ones who will take each piece of this new energy and make the beauty that is here even more beautiful. As you leave this place today, you take a piece of this with you. As you leave today, you take a connection to the planet that is beyond your understanding for you are creating this every moment of every day. You connect your hearts. You connect your energies. You take these crystals with you. You incorporate them into your own being. You incorporate them into your own self, and you take it with you for the New Planet Earth is your choice. You have chosen to stay, even after completing the Game. You have chosen to stay and watch as the turmoil and the resistance to the New Energy plays out. We thank you for that for you have asked to be there to open the door to the Light in times of apparent darkness. It is only possible to do this from your own vantage point and, therefore, we are in the greatest awe of you, for we are in the presence of the masters of the Grand Game.

We tell you, you do not see who you are. You cannot see the rest of the energy and yet you will, for the veil is thinning, dear ones. You are redefining everything about yourselves and everything about what you are doing. We tell you, there will come a time when you will no longer need swords on the New Planet Earth. That day is coming very soon. We tell you if you use the sword of empowerment the way it was truly meant to be used, you will no longer have need for it in physical form. It was only meant to knight, to take you to the next level of awareness, and to awaken you to your own empowerment. The days of the use of the sword are gone. Find another use for it, dear ones, and you will be in the creation of Heaven on Earth. The days for the sword to return to the stone are here and you will see it within your lifetimes.

Take your power, dear ones. Take your power and find that energy which is yours. Find that center of your own energy and become the greatest Beacon of Light that you can be. Now is the time to shed the Light of the New Earth. For we tell you, there are two ways to deal with Light. We ask you to do both. One is to reflect the Light. Take the Light of Home within your prisms of who you are, much the ways the crystals do. Allow it to dance within your own being and send it back out with the proud reflection of who you are. The second is to be the Light, for you have the Light within your own souls, each one of you. You have the Light of Home that you carry within yourselves. Let everyone see it proudly at this time. Let everyone feel it, whether you are in the grocery store, in your church, or up here in the mountains. Even as you are passing each other in the street, let your light shine. You are the chosen ones dear ones. [Thunder in the background.] No, it is not us that have chosen you. It is you who have chosen you. [More thunder.] You have chosen to be the forbearers of the Light. You have chosen to take the awesome responsibility in the greatest times of turmoil in your own planet as the old Game leaves and the New Game begins. You have chosen to be the ones to make the transition between the two energies. You have chosen to be the Light and to hold the door open.

You are the greatest presence on this planet that has ever been. You look to those in the past called Jesus and Buddha and Merlin. You look to the ones who many have named as the great masters and we tell you there are none greater than those who sit in front of us right at this moment, for you hold the energy of Home. You have dared to be here at exactly this moment to help hold the energy of the Light at times of darkness. All those who sit here this day and all those who choose to hear these words, whether they are read or whether they are listened to, you are the ones who are choosing to claim the title of crystal vibration. [A strong breeze blows.] This is the Christed energy.

The New Earth is right in front of you, for you have created it even with the words you have spoken just now. You have set it into motion this day through your intent and by gathering together to create the vortex. We tell you, you have no idea what you have set into motion. Every moment you feel the breeze rising up, it is that breeze that is taking your crystalline intent and incorporating into the magic of what you call Mt. Shasta. For the vortex here is real. The vortex here has been created by you the first time you came. That vortex is your own creation to which you are now reconnecting. To have you stand here in the same meadow that you started the Game in is beyond description to us. See the beauty as you look out onto the mountains and the trees. . See the beauty of the vibrant colors of the moss and the flowers that are all in bloom just for you. We tell you, it does not compare to the beauty in this meadow right now as we look at each of you. Your own energy is beautiful beyond description. Dare to be those vibrant colors. Dare to take yourself to the next level. Dare to allow yourself to be the Light. For that is what you have come here to do. [Thunder.] That is why you are back right now.

Many of you know the connection you have had here before. Some of you think it odd that you were drawn here. We tell you, you have placed lifetime after lifetime to be here at exactly this moment. There are many of you out there who will be connecting soon. Please find them. Please help them to understand who they are, for you are now the Human Angels. We will take this opportunity to do something we have only done once before, and that is to spread our wings. [The Keeper spreads his arms out to each side. Everyone in attendance also spreads their arms out at this moment.] For our wings are not for flight, our wings are to reflect the magnificence of humans. For you are our greatest hope, dear ones. We are your hope and we will hold the Light for you when you cannot re-member it. When you find yourselves in the darkness we are there spreading our wings helping to light your way. Now we ask you to spread your wings and help the others, for it is time. What you have come here to do is at hand. It is not only the creation of Heaven on Earth but it is the creation of the angelic realm on the first planet of free choice. (Thunder)

Yes, we tell you there is a second planet of free choice that has already begun as a result of your own actions and choice. It is very closely tied in with your own energies, with your own game. [Thunder.] We tell you the energy must follow its path and let you experience sadness. The other day on the Game board of free choice [thunder], there was a pull into polarity. This will enable those that could not see before, to see Light. Please, we ask you to begin the creation and incorporate the rules you have set into motion for yourself this very day. Find

ways of treating your greatest enemies on the New Planet
Earth with the same respect and love that you set into motion
for yourself as you stood there and held this mighty crystal.
[Thunder.] Then you will create Home right where you are,
right now.

In this action, there will be backlashes, for you are still
within a field of polarity. You still see things as up and down,
black and white, right or wrong, love and fear. We tell you,
please understand that even though your first reaction is to
fall into the field of polarity, it is an illusion that you have created to see the Light while you are in the Game board. That
illusion is thinning. You will find the magic within each one of
you, as you now become the Light. For it is no longer necessary to have the darkness to see the Light. The New Planet
Earth is different and the energy is changing. Find the way
to be the Light, and you no longer will be the darkness. You
will find support, not only with others of like-mind, but even
with those you have called enemies. You found yourselves
seeking to have an experience of spirit in human form. That
has confused you so. You woke up one day, and you did not
know what to do with these bubbles of biology. You were not
able to travel around the same way you did in the ethereal.
You looked for ways to define yourself and you found a tool
that you called judgment and, although it worked well for the
lower vibrations of who you were, we tell you that tool is no
longer valid. Find the use of discernment instead and you will
become higher vibrational beings. That has already begun.
Discern the part that is for you in all things and leave the rest
without judgment.

You will feel support also in direct relationship to the
support that you give Mother Earth. That is the reason you
began this journey on the Game board of Free Choice in
that meadow right over there. That is the reason you are back
here with these wonderful dense bodies of yours to begin the

second game right now. The connection with the Mother is important for you, for you are a part of her and she is a part of you. We talked about her as a 'she' only because it is a way you understand her. There is no polarity of male and female energy within the planet. Earth is a divine essence of all the energy of what you call God in physical form. The Earth is a sentient living being who is self-aware. The Earth herself is now beginning to shift. The Earth herself is now incorporating the male and female aspects that were necessary to distribute and to segregate from one another so that you could see who you were here. We tell you now that is changing. In the days, and months, and years ahead, you will see some of your vortices changing direction. You will see some of the rocks that sit in front of you (crystals), as well as some of the rocks you are actually seated upon, changing density. It will happen first on the very inner core and work its way out. For the mineral kingdom is in the process of shifting to the next level of vibration. You will see this very rapidly. In the beauty of the life forms you know to be crystals, you will see inclusions beginning. You will see things that were there disappearing. You were see crystals that have been fogged over beginning to clear and clear ones beginning to fog over. Fear not these changes; simply celebrate them, for they indicate that you are now beginning to move. You will find also the opportunity to include the beauty of the natural crystals with the man-hanced, for there is magic. You are seeing the blend of what you call nature and the creative abilities of man beginning to blend, for we do not see that as separate; we see that as one.

We tell you, dear ones, in the new Earth do not neglect the humor and if we find you getting too serious, we will tickle your funny bone to remind you it is a Game. For you are not the humans that we see with tears in your eyes; you are spirits greater than you can possibly imagine and the badges of color that you already wear will be with you for an eternity. The badges of color and honor will indicate you as being one of the players of the first Game of Free Choice. You are the third graders who have changed the universe. Your honor will be known for wherever you go in the universe, whatever you decide to do, whatever games you decide to devise and play, you will be known as the chosen ones that shifted the paradigms of All That Is. We tell you, it is not by accident that the Keeper saw the guardian of the gate up there on the mount. It is not by accident that you have chosen the one meadow the guardian overlooks. We tell you, there are more entities on that peak watching what is happening right here right now than you can possibly imagine. We tell you, they will leave their mark. We tell you, you have altered so many inter-dimensional realities with your choices, with your searching, your work, [thunder] and your sacrifice. We tell you, was the reason the rains came this morning. It was to make space for all the entities that are now here with you. You will feel them with you. You will feel them over your shoulder. No, they are not your guides, nor are they your angels. They are visitors watching. They are looking only at how you are changing the reality of your Game. For it is not about them, it is about you. Stay centered, dear ones. We tell you, in fact, it is not ego that prompts us to tell you this; it is simply that you are each the individual center of your own universe. If you will treat yourself accordingly, you will find all things falling into place. Please understand, you are not the only universe, for there are many. If you make space for the many universes that walk around you, if you make space for the many belief systems even on your own planet Earth, if you make space for Light in all of its forms, you will have created Home in that (snap) of a moment.

You have already made a difference on the Game board of free choice. You have already shifted your energy to the next level and we tell you now, you have chosen to stay. You have chosen to take this to the next level and actually stay and make something more. And for that, we and all the entities on this mountain are in your debt of gratitude. As we began this channel, a dear one here decided to ground the Keeper by putting dirt on top of his feet, and we tell you it is our greatest honor to sit at your feet and wash your feet with the crystals of the earth, to help you re-member who you are. [Michele placed dirt on my bare feet to ground me.] Take the challenge dear ones [thunder] for the challenge is not only about you but it is about everyone you touch. It is about taking this life and doing the work within, so that you may clear your own energy tubes, so that you may smile at someone in the grocery store, [thunder] so that you may meet someone on the street, so that you may pass someone getting on a bus and, as you smile, you touch their soul for as you smile, you are the Light.

We deeply honor you, dear ones. You have no idea who you are and yet we tell you, you are here on purpose with the greatest of intent. You are here through the struggles of not being able to re-member who you are and now that veil is beginning to thin. Watch as the Mother helps in this shift. Reach for her. Be a part of that energy. And as those around you get scared of the changes that are happening, we ask you to be the center of Light. You be the one who stands up and says, "I am not your leader, yet I am here to lend a hand. I am here to be here to help you find your balance for the paradigms have changed."

The role of leadership on planet Earth is beginning to sift and that is what is now playing out. That is what has been playing, for you will find in your own direction, you have an opportunity in the months and days ahead to redefine the role of leadership on your own planet. Work from the heart as one, dear ones. Work as a unity consciousness. Take the guidelines you have suggested for your own new Game, for you are the ones who created it the first time. Take your power. Hold your love and know we are here applauding you. We are opening the doors whenever we can at those moments when you cannot re-member who you are. We are here to help you. We are here with the touch of an angel! It is ours to reach over and touch you on the heart chakra for just a brief moment so that you can carry those seeds with you. We ask that you do this for one another. Reach out, dear ones, and touch one another, for you are the greatest of the Human Angels who will be on planet Earth. The new Game has begun. You have made it so.

We tell you, we have a gift this day, for we tell you this day, we will no longer call the Keeper of the Sword by that name. He will become the Keeper of the Flame, for the sword is no longer needed on the New Planet Earth.

It is with the greatest of honor, dear ones, that we ask you to treat each other with respect. Re-member who you are. Nurture one another as you help them re-member. Play well together. And so it is.

the Group


We then held the ceremony of the sword, where each person set into motion their intent for the New Game. Our work began several years ago with the Sword of Truth ceremony which we did around the Kryon seminars. There was a tinge of sadness in the fact that we are to put away the sword and yet I knew in my heart, the moment it was spoken, this was in perfect order. The Group showed me we will use the sword only three more times. The first was that day immediately following this channel. The pictures of this day can be seen on a special page on the Lightworker website. The second of these was a month later in France at the Week to Re-member. The final time was when we returned to Mt Shasta for the Espavo conference the next year. It is time to claim the tools of the higher vibrations and release the old. I can't think of a better time to say goodbye.

Big hugs and gentle nudges
Steve Rother

PS:

We did return to Mt Shasta for the final Sword of Truth cere-mony the following year at the ESPAVO conference. We returned to the same magical place near Panther Meadows on Mt. Shasta and prepared for the final ceremony. We all took turn with the sword that day, standing on a large magical rock in the meadow speaking our truth. Of course, being the Keeper, I was the last. After I spoke, I saw a crack in the rock and firmly placed the sword back in the stone. We all stood there admiring the beauty of the sword and the moment. Yet, we all knew it was time to move on. We turned, wiped a tear and walked from that meadow that day, leaving the sword in the stone.

# The Sacred Room

## Creating Space in the New World

### January 2002

The following was a live channel presented at the Week to Re-member in Ardeche, France, October 23, 2001. This message is a call to action. As we step into the fifth dimension, we invite you to join in the action as we now create the Sacred Room.

After we returned home from France, I decided this message was so important that I wanted to use it as the Beacons of Light monthly message for January 2002. Late at night, I edited it, marked it up onto the Lightworker site and sent it out.

After I finished, I got side tracked and started playing with some web design software. Several hours later, at 5 a.m. the next morning, I put the finishing touches to the 8 Sacred Rooms interactive experience on the Lightworker site. The 8 Sacred Rooms of Creation are still very active today and have helped thousands manifest their reality. I was so driven to do this that at one point, I felt as if I was actually channeling HTML code. Boy, the Group really gets around, huh?

Greetings from Home.

Did you feel the energy change in the room? Do you feel the love that we have for you? We ask you to breathe it in and let it become part of yourselves for we are connecting you with yourselves. It is our highest purpose to be with you during these special times, to reflect your magnificence. For, as we speak through the Keeper on the stage in this wonderful room, we tell you there are many entities here watching with great expectation, for you are not just changing your own world, you are not just changing and shifting your own paradigms, but you are also shifting All That Is. We thank you for doing it. You have built your Game board so well. You have placed in front of you the veil of forgetfulness. Your whole intent to be here on the Game board was to wake up confused, and you have done well. You are constantly asking, "What is the meaning of life? What did I come here to do? Where is my passion?" Oh, dear ones, if you could see it as we do; if you could see yourselves the way we do, you would understand that you are the masters who are hiding behind the veils, unable to re-member your true magnificence, for that is the nature of the Game you have made. That is the essence of what you have done, and now that you are taking even the next step, you find the veil thinning yet not moving away. It is still important to carry the attributes of the veil. Why? Very simply, if you were to raise your veils today, you would look around the room and say, "Ahh, I know you. I re-member you, so that is who you are." And you would have a grand re-union in this very room. And you would hug, and you would have a wonderful time re-membering, and then each and every one of you would go Home. There is still much to do. So we suggest that instead of removing the veil. you follow your hearts and have that re-union anyway. Even though you may not have full re-collection, embrace the people around you as the brothers and sisters and mothers and fathers and lovers that they have been to you. Re-member them from the heart and your head will follow.

## 77 excited onlookers

You are in a special state as the veil thins, for you are beginning to become the Human Angels. Can you hear the reverence in our voice as we speak those words? Can you hear us as we tell you that you are taking the place of what we have been to you? We are so very honored to be in the presence of the masters of the Universe. You have done something in your own worlds that all the might in Heaven could not accomplish. You are awakening from the dream. You have taken the reflection of God within yourselves and hidden it from your own view. Now you are starting to re-member. Can you see our excitement? Can you see all the energies in the room? Can you see what is happening from a global standpoint? It is much larger than your single planet. It is much larger than what you call the Universe. There are no words that describe All That Is,

yet you are the masters that are beginning to make the changes
that will change the paradigm of All That Is. For that very reason, each of you here in this room have no less than seventy-
seven entities behind you, watching over your shoulder, here
to watch your every step. Some of them are from your own
planetary systems, as you know them. Some are not. Some of
them are from your own families, for there are grandfathers
and grandmothers and husbands and wives and others looking
over your shoulder with great joy for you are changing each
and every one of those.

## The Challenge

We ask you, as the family of light, to do something that
is very difficult for you. In this moment, we are going to ask
you to intentionally lower the walls you have built around
you. Many of those walls have been built with purpose. Many
of those walls protect you from leaking out, or so you think.
Many of those walls protect you from energy invading your
space, or so you think. Those walls have helped you define
who are and helped you understand where your energy field
stops and another energy field starts, or so you thought. Now
we ask you in this safe time, in this safe space, in the energy
of pure love of Home, that you release those walls. Take a
deep breath, dear ones, and as you exhale that air, just for a
moment, let the walls down completely. As you dismantle the
wall, stack the stones neatly, blessing each one for a job well
done. Feel the energy of Home as it enters your heart. That is
the only way we can show you who you are.

## Welcome to the fifth dimension

The times are special, dear ones, and there is work to do.
We are so honored to be with you during the times that you
have together. For each time that you look, not only in each
other's eyes, but also in the eyes of others, you will be offering

the seeds of Light in the form of the sign of the angels. And in that offering, there is much to do, for the work is just beginning on the Planet Earth. You are moving well out of the third dimension of vibration. We have told you before to watch for the fifth dimension, as this has been unfolding. That which you call the fourth has been before you for a very long time. You have been on the bridge of the fourth dimension for, as you travel across it, it is not a place to rest, it is only a place to travel through. And much like the second dimension, it was necessary for you to travel through and receive the attributes of the fourth dimension for you to exist in the fifth dimension. Now we tell you, you have arrived. The very first of you are now stepping off the bridge. As you do we greet you with a heartfelt Welcome Home.

You are creating Heaven on Earth in the fifth dimension. Please do not confuse yourselves with questions forming in your minds; "Why does this look the same as before?" Please know that what you see is a direct relationship of what you expect to see. In the fifth dimension, point of perception determines reality. The time lag of creation in the fifth dimension is very short. All that is necessary for you to hold your power is to hold the responsibility of your own power. Understand that, in the fifth dimension, if you do not like what you see in your reality, you have the power and the responsibility to change it. Here, it is your task to create the highest and the best for yourselves and dare to place yourself first in the energy flow. That is your rightful place. And that is the only way that you can take your power as Human Angels.

There is a special time on the planet at this moment, for you have felt the stress. As you are some of the first ones to cross upon the bridge into the fifth dimension, we ask that you take your role as the 'chosen ones,' for there is work to do. You have chosen yourselves to be the first ones across the bridge, and as difficult as that has been sometimes, we tell you that you have done well. Even though you have been very success-ful at waking up confused, you are beginning to re-member.

## The Sacred Room

There is a task that we ask of you. All of you who hear this in voice, or read this message in print, we ask of you a great task. And if you choose, it may be your first task in the fifth dimension. There is need for a sacred space in the fifth dimension. This is a space of healing and a sacred space for those who will cross the bridge confused and feeling lost. This room will be used for acclimation for those who arrive scared and angry that their world has changed. This room will be for the Old Guard to acclimate to the New Energy. You have cho-sen to lower your personal protective walls to be the Human Angels. You now have the option of picking those stones up and taking them back with you re-building those walls. We ask you to consider another possibility. If it feels right for you, if you so choose, combine your stones with the others, not only within this room, but of those of you who are stepping off first into the fifth dimension. The stones that lie at your feet from your own walls being dismantled will now rise again to create the magical space of the sacred room. In that sacred space, those who find themselves coming across the fourth dimension and falling into the fifth dimension, and who are not prepared, may find a safe haven. This is for those who do not know the love that is possible on the New Planet Earth. It is for those that get scared at being overwhelmed at the heart chakra. For to live in this energy, it is necessary for you to stretch your heart chakras so far open that you can let it all in. That has been and will be the source of many tears.

If after today, you leave here and go back to your daily lives and wonder, "Where is my passion? What do I do to find what I came here to do?" just re-member this night, and re-member that you took part in building the Sacred Room in the fifth dimension. For some of you, that may have been your first act as a Human Angel. A Human Angel is a person who makes a commitment to be there at exactly the right time when you are called. It is not for a Human Angel to be evangelical or to reach out and touch someone who has not asked to be touched. It is not for a Human Angel to create or fix something that is not broken. Ahh, but you love to do that, do you not? As a Human Angel, you will reach through your own higher self and touch those who are ready to accept. Those were the rules you set about yourselves, and now it is activating.

## Integration of Higher Self

Many of you here have said, "Where have my guides gone? How come I cannot hear the voices the way I could only last week?" We tell you that you cannot hear the voices the same because in the fifth dimension, that which has been external has now fully integrated into you. They are now a part of your own being. As you step off the bridge into the fifth dimension, you will begin to see only little glimpses of it. But the more you lean against it, the more you trust it, the more you practice with it, the more you will understand your connection to Source. For that is the essence of whom you are. That is the Godself that is within each one of you that was hidden behind the walls you so carefully guarded. With your walls down, you not only can let it in, but you can let it shine, and allow others to see it. And it is not to say, "Look at me, I am a Human Angel." Rather, it is to simply hold the energy in quiet dignity, for it will not be long before someone comes to you and says, "What is the smile on your face all about? As you take a deep breath, you know that you have just heard the call into action of the Human Angels.

So many things are happening on your own planet that you see as setbacks to the energy. We tell you, please do not fear this. Please do not put more power into this than is necessary. For it is simply a re-shuffling of the energy. And if you make this sacred space, this sacred room of healing of the fifth dimension, those who do not feel safe in the fourth dimension will react here rather than overreact on Earth. You are building this room not only with the stones that have served you well, but build it back with the mortar of the pure love of who you are. Oh, dear ones, you have touched more people than you will ever know. You have made a difference already on your planet, and here you sit asking, "How can I help? How can I do more?" Do you understand the love we have for you? Do you understand the gratitude we have? Feel what we are sending you right now in this moment. We ask you to breathe in the energy and claim it as your own. You are the Human Angels of the New Planet Earth.

Hold your power firmly dear ones, for in the fifth dimension, your powers of creativity are substantially increased. And as many step off the bridge from the fourth dimension into the fifth, they will receive these powers of creation. We ask you to re-member the words of the Universe, for all requests are answered with the words: "and so it is." So as they step off the bridge from the fourth dimension into the fifth, they look around and they say, "I do not see anything any different. This looks the same to me." And the Universe answers: "and so it is." Hence, they play the Game in a third-dimensional reality even as they sit in the fifth dimension. That, too, is the purpose of this special room. We ask you to place in this room your love and your education and your knowledge for all those who choose to go into it and to find themselves and to claim their creator selves.

Espavo, dear ones, Espavo.

# The Second Planet of Free Choice

We have news this night. Because of your movement, we tell you there is movement in All That Is. Another milestone has been reached that we wish to divulge to you. For you continually think this is all about you. You have looked at your planet and the many dimensional realities that exist within that time and space, the mineral kingdom, and the plant kingdom, and the biological kingdom, and now technological kingdom. Oh, you humans are so imaginative. We tell you, there are so many more that you have not yet discovered, but they all move together as one. That is the magic that you have created, for you are here re-turned from the days of Atlantis. You are the magicians who decided to come back and try it again to see if you can do it different this time. We call you the chosen ones because you have chosen of your own accord to cash in all of your karma chips to be here at exactly this moment on the wildest hope that you would be sitting in this room, on this evening, and here you are. Oh, dear ones, you have done so well. And now you take the entire Game to next level.

The Second Planet of Free Choice is alive and well. Your movement into the fifth dimension will now facilitate the movement of the Second Planet of Free Choice to take its place in the third dimension, which you will be vacating. You have heard many stories, dear ones, of how some will be left behind and those who are not enlightened will be left behind as you ascend into the fifth dimension. We tell you that is not what will happen. For it is no longer possible for you to leave another part of yourselves behind. All is connected within a unity consciousness. As two enemies battle on the battlefields, they do not see that they are one, for if they did, they would not be in battle. You can help them see that, dear ones. And that is what you came here to do. Those are the attributes of a Human Angel. Since you have learned to deal with the confusion so well, you may now help others with their confusion. Do not take responsibility for changing the world. Rather, take responsibility for your life and your joy, holding the essence of that in your own heart. That is how you will make a difference. The collective consciousness will rise as each one of you takes your power. Hold that power firm, hold it high, and hold it proud. You, dear ones, are the family of Light. You are those at the very tip of the arrowhead that is piercing and changing the paradigms of All That Is. Treat yourselves well. We need you now.

You will be assuming new roles as you move into the fifth dimension. First, you will become the Human Angels who will work with other humans, which will help you assimilate the higher vibrations of the New Planet Earth, for you are building Heaven on Earth and we are so very proud. You will soon know the answers to all the questions you have asked of us. And we tell you something else, as you begin to move further into this, you will receive more of your own answers through your higher source. Although there will be many new sources of information, your discernment will become very acute. That is where the magic is, dear ones. We ask you not to take every word we say and hold it as your own truth for, in doing so, you would be giving your power to us and that is not appropriate in the higher vibrations of the fifth dimension. Take only the pieces that resonate with you. That is your power. Hold it firm and stand with it. Home will be created where you now sit. There is much at hand, dear ones, and soon you will find more. You will be writing the books and lessons that will help the others to transform. You will help others to raise their vibration and, in doing so, the call of the Human Angel will be heard. Build the sacred room, dear ones, with the stones of your own walls mixed with the mortar of the love of Home. We tell you that the sadness you have had deep within is nothing more than the longing for Home. Imagine a day when that longing will be fulfilled right where you are and you will miss it no longer. That day is at hand.

## The Gift

There are magical times ahead on Planet Earth. You look at your storybooks and think of all the fairy tales that have happened, and about the wondrous magic of time. And you look to the tales of Merlin, the only person who has ever been able to walk backwards in time. We tell you that he is actually the only person who has ever walked forward in time, for it is all of you who walk backwards. Ahh, but that will now be changing for, in the fifth dimension of reality, it is possible to see your direction. Play with it dear ones. Take your power. Stretch the limits. Infuse all and watch for the changes right now on the mineral level of your planet. Work with the crystals in all forms. Hold your power and know that we are watching over your shoulder with the greatest of joy. In much the way that you will take great pride as the Second Planet of Free Choice starts evolving, you will understand the great pride and love we have for you. You are more courageous than you know. Take your power. Create. Dare to create your heart's desire. Dare to accept it after you have created it. Each and every one of you is in a situation now where you can make a difference. It is exactly why you are the chosen ones; you simply do not remember that you are the heir to the throne. Take your place. Hold it firm. Hold it with love. Hold it with gratitude. You may then adopt the call of the Human Angels: "There Before the Grace of You Go I." That is our gift to you as you step off the bridge. Carry it well, dear ones, and Welcome Home.

It is the greatest of honor that we sit with you this night. We ask you to treat each other with respect, nurture one another often, and play well together.

And so it is …

the Group

A Note from Steve for the publication of this book:

The Beacons of Light began in February 1996 as an Internet meditation. The Group started channeling through me from the very first one. On the first Beacons, they did a form of introduction to the meditation that we called 'The Message.' After a few months, the messages from the Group were getting longer, and the actual meditations was getting shortened to make room for them. After several years, I wanted to stop the meditation portion all together as it seemed unnecessary. Barbara then stepped forward and decided that she would take over the meditation portion so I could focus on the messages. She did a great job and very few people noticed that I was not writing the meditations anymore. After three years, Barbara also said that it was time to cease the meditations. But people had grown accustomed to hearing from her each month so at the readers request she agreed to do a short column each month on 'Connecting the Heart.'

What follows is the last Beacons of Light meditation ever published. Even though she didn't know this would be the last at the time, it's interesting to note that the title is: 'New Beginnings'.

## The Beacons of Light Meditation

### By Barbara Rother

So often when the new year arrives we say. "This is a new beginning, a fresh start." There is only one answer to that: And so it is. Now is the time to dare to change. Your past ways have been a comfortable path long enough. They have served you well. Thank the past and move forward. Now is the time. Celebrate the new you!

Breathe deep the light of the New Year. Exhale the blockage that has held you in your comfort zone. Welcome in this time of change. Embrace the change.

Many times, we look for assistance on our path, whether it be through astrology, numerology, readings from people who have a gift from Spirit, or simply asking friends what they think. All the outside help is wonderful but they are simply tools to help you find your direction. Listen to your heart. See the synchronicities in your life. Most important is to trust. Trust yourself. You are the master of your own creations.

Embrace this exciting time that unfolds around you. Look at the values in all areas of your life. Imagine the circle of life. See the circle as the world around you, your world. This world is divided into six magical sections.

The first section is your career. Think about it. When you wake up in the morning, are you excited about your day? You cannot wait to get to your work! Adopting an attitude of excitement, even in a mundane job, can make it more interesting. Look forward to how you spend your day. You are never stuck in a job; you always have choice. Dare to change. Be in your passion, even if it's only part of the time. Feel the stirring of your soul with the very thought of enjoying the majority of your time. Enjoy what you do everyday.

Second is Spirituality. When you touch the center of your being, when you feel life flows in such a peaceful way, you are connected with your Spiritual side. Be with Spiritual Family. Look deep inside toward how you feel about life. Be alive with your Spiritual self. Feel your warm glow from inside permeating your entire being.

Health and fitness are next. We are body, mind and soul, and they are all so connected. The physical body is so important to our center. Exercise, eat what your body knows is good for it. You will feel more balanced when you honor this area of your life.

Personal growth and development are fourth on the wheel of life. This ties into all sections of life. Dare to grow. Many of us fear change. Change can feel uncomfortable, upsetting our daily routine. Envision the rewarding results of growing into the person you always knew you could become.

Relationships. The most important relationship you have is with yourself. Honor yourself. Love yourself. Only then can you be ready for others in your life. You are the most important person in your own life. This is not selfish, but 'self first.' There is a big difference.

Family is the completion of your circle. It is important to know and honor ourselves first but then to reach out for family. This can be biological family as well as Spiritual Family and friends. Reach out for others of like mind and you will quickly find family. Feel yourself blossom when you share your Light. Stay out of judgment. Encourage each other to be the best they can be. Support each other in your personal growth. We are all one. We are family.

Take each day and celebrate your circle of life. Connect with yourself and with others. Areas that you focus on will improve.

And so it is …

Barbara

# The Color Clear

## An Exercise in Seeing
## Beyond Duality

## November 2002

Taken from a live presentation in St. Louis, MO.

I may look at a red rose and take in all the beauty it has to offer. I may share the vision of the rose with you and we may agree that the red we are seeing is a beautiful color.

But who is to say each one of us is seeing the same thing? What if the color I see is actually a different color than you are seeing, even though we both call that color 'red'? Now to take that a step further. What if you were looking at the rose with sunglasses on; would you still call the rose red? The answer lies in the incredible beauty of the mind. Anyone who wears glasses knows how much the mind can adapt to changes in vision. You would still see the rose as red even with sunglasses because your mind would make the adjustment for you.

In this message, the Group begins talking about the way we see our world in words that describe vision. They have said many times that our reality is based on the point of perception from which we view it. So, are we seeing our world through sunglasses, and if so, how are they distorting our vision and therefore our reality? Once they have that established in the message, they begin speaking about the color 'clear' as our base motivation, telling us that our base motivation actually colors our world and therefore our reality.

We are pleased to offer it here, in hopes that it will help you to see your color clear.

Greetings from Home

Welcome Home. As you look around the room, you see each other for perhaps for the very first time. Here you see a brother who finds a sister he has not seen in many lifetimes. And over there, you see another, neighbors who have fought and are now best friends. So many times, you have played the Game, attempting to put you right in the heart of your passion. So many times, you have played the game, trying only to re-member what your passion was. You hear our laughter and sometimes, it confuses you. Dear ones, you have no idea how we see things from this side of the veil. We greet you with the memories of Home so that you, too, may re-member the wonderful humor that we share here. Humor is the only energy that passes unhampered between our side of the veil and yours. Yet, sometimes, you feel like the joke is on you and that frustrates you. The Keeper has told us many times, when we sit here and laugh, that next time he will sit up here and laugh, and we will come down and play the Game. We will see, will we not? Do you hear our laughter now? We tell you, the laughter we share with you is direct from the heart of what you call the family of Michael. The smile upon your face at this very moment is opening your being to a flow of energy that brings you Home again. Welcome Home. You are part of us and we are part of you, and when you share the energy one unto another, as we have just shared it with you, you create Home where you are at this very moment. You are the Human Angels.

It is so hard for you sometimes, where you have come here with the express intent of not being able to see yourself. You have come here with the greatest intent of joining the Game on Planet Earth, taking form in biology as confused beings. We tell you, you have certainly done well with that. You look to us for answers as you ask: "Where am I going? What is next? Where am I to be the highest use?" And our favorite: "Where is my passion?" Dear ones, we cannot see the future, for you have yet to write it. We can, however, see the direction you are traveling and what contracts you have placed in your own path. We tell you now, there is no grand plan in place, for you have surpassed even the highest potential. Please understand that every minute of every day, you are the ones in control. That is why your passion is now more important than ever, for it is the road map to your highest purpose, and with that, you are dong much better than you know.

## Evolution of Sight

Dear ones, this day we wish to share with you part of your own evolution in the area of sight. We have spoken before about new colors that will be showing up on the first Planet of Free Choice. We tell you this day. there is color you have never understood. You see it often, and yet you have never understood what you have seen, nor its greater meaning. Now it is time to start understanding what you are seeing. We have spoken of the Universal Energy as the energy that exists in all things. In fact, it is the backdrop against which you play your game of hide and seek. In much the same fashion, there is a color that underlies each and every thing that you see. It taints all of your vision within the field of polarity. Becoming aware of this color and seeing it as the base against which all things are colored will help you in your next stage of evolution as you now move out of duality. It is the color clear. Many times during the Game, you reach for an understanding that mysteriously eludes you. Mostly this is because you did not understand the base color of clear. The background against which you built your understanding was not clear; therefore, all things seen against it are tainted. If you can, imagine what it is like for you to travel around all day with the most wonderful rose-colored sunglasses. We think you humans are so imaginative in how you attempt to shift your base perception. Here you are working with the color clear, for you are changing your base perception with the colored glasses. Humans are so imaginative! With the glasses, the physical biology quickly adapts and considers the rose tint to be normal or 'clear.' The challenge comes when you view a red rose and cannot perceive the true color because the color 'clear' has shifted.

## Rose-Colored Glasses

The color clear is not limited to your sense of sight. In human form, you have many more senses than you are aware of. Your sense of absorption is an area where this information will be most helpful. Absorption is the manner in which you absorb all forms of energy, including emotional energy. It may be helpful for you to understand that, with your senses, you do not perceive actual color, sound, fragrances or energy. In actuality, you only perceive changes in those things. Your biology can easily adjust to shifting the base in all of these areas. Therefore the true color of clear is very important as a base for all that you experience. If you live next to a perfume factory, you will only smell the perfume when you first return home for that is when you perceive the change. Later that night, you no longer smell it. Likewise, if you live in a busy city where there is noise outside your window all times of the day and night, you may find the silence of a week on a farm in the country deafening. Everything that you see through your glasses is slightly tainted and, therefore, altered in some way. It is helpful to know that, even when you put the sunglasses on, the color clear is underlying all that you perceive, including the rose tint of the glasses. Find the color clear, and you will have a base for all you experience as Spirit masquerading in a human costume.

## The Color Clear

Let us show you some areas that you can see the color clear, for it is becoming more important each day, not only in your evolution of sight, but also in the way you live your lives in the higher vibrations of the New Planet. Your lives can be confusing as the change starts taking place. As you make a decision to step into your passion, it may mean that you step out of something else to make room for that passion. As you become higher vibrational humans, you no longer have the tolerance you had in the lower vibrations. It is no longer possible for you to be in a lower vibrational job that does not support your higher vibration. Many of you have intentionally lowered your vibration in order to go to work every day. You no longer have that luxury. Now it is about passion. It is about joy. This is not new, only more important in the new energy as the tolerance has now been removed. The shift toward living your life in search of passion and joy requires substantial energy. To make a shift of this nature, you will need a solid base. To gain that base, you must understand the color clear.

Each person's color clear may be slightly different. The color clear is what causes you to feel attraction or repulsion to another when you first meet them. Two people with the same color clear may meet one day and bond as if they had been friends for lifetimes. In fact, it may have been that having many life experiences together has given them both the same color clear. Most dramas are played because the color clear is slightly different for each other. As humans, you are in the continuous motion of reconciling your color clear with everyone you meet.

Your whole experience on Earth is what we see as the Grand Game. This Game is a grand play being staged with great detail. The Game itself is a form of human drama and is a needed component of the game. Also understand that energy is always drawn to drama. This is as it should be, except when the drama feeds upon itself and forms a loop. Then, it is quite possible to be wrapped up in the endless loop, losing sight of your base and what is truly important. Yet if you understand the color clear, you can play in the dramas of life and never lose sight of the true meaning.

With humanity moving at the speed of love toward the next evolutionary step, there will be many dramas playing out on the stage. As the painter begins a new canvas, his first step is to mix the colors on his pallet. What we are suggesting here is that, before you mix the colors for your next stage of life, you closely examine the base color of the pallet itself, for it will modify every stoke of your brush from this point forward.

## Seeing Your Color Clear

To find the color clear, we ask you fearlessly examine your motivations in all actions of your life. Fear not your motivations, for they are simply motivations. The field of polarity is growing thinner as you move closer to Home. Accordingly, the illusions of polarity are beginning to become more transparent. You are beginning to see that Right and Wrong, Good and Bad, Up and Down, Love and Fear and even Black and White are all illusions. In reality, there is not black, nor white, only shades of gray. They are part of the Game that you are scripting for yourselves in each moment of each day. To find the color clear, we ask that you to release the judgments you have of your own motivations. There are no correct ones, nor are there any bad ones. Throughout all of nature a simple rule applies:

For every action, there is motivation.

Truthfully identify your motivations and take inventory of them without judgment. Then and only then will you begin to see the color clear. The funny part to us is that, as hideous as all of you think your motivations are, your base motivations are all very similar. The veil that you wear makes it very difficult to see yourself, yet, by setting your intent and allowing your vision to clear by releasing judgment, you will see yourself in a new light.

## Step 1 Clear Ceremony

Before you step through the doors that will be opening soon, we suggest that you take time and co create ceremony to locate the color clear. Sit in a quiet time, breath to clear your field and center your own energy. If you choose, ask your guides, angels or higher self to help arrange the pictures that you are about to see. Set yourself in a theatre, as the show is about to begin on the screen in front of you. Before the show begins, consciously suspend your judgment for a time and give yourself permission to just enjoy the show. Then begin as you watch the pictures that follow about random events in you life. As each one passes by, examine it to see if you can identify a single thread of motivation that runs through it. As you begin to see the motivations, you will begin to see the color clear. These motivations are not right or wrong; they just are.

Now, as you become more comfortable with the process, we ask you to boldly label each of these motivations temporarily, even though the labels themselves may repulse you at first. Continue to allow many more of these visions to enter your thoughts, and fearlessly identify and label the motivations in each one. Once you have identified the color clear as seen through base motivation, you can begin to identify those motivations within the dramas that you play on the Game board. Now begin the flow of pictures that show the most life-altering dramas that have played out in your life. Again watch as your base motivations are revealed to you. Here you may also find that by examining your own base motivations, you will more clearly see the motivations of the other participants in these dramas. It is important to totally release judgment for this exercise, as judgment itself is an exercise in polarity. As you identify base motivations, you can understand your real needs as Spirits masquerading in human bodies. All Spirits have wants and desires in the human form. There are no wrong or selfish needs, as all needs are real. The challenge comes when you hide those basic needs from yourself because of a belief system or judgment you carry. Look fearlessly at the base motivations that have shaped your life thus far, and here you will begin to see your color clear.

## Step 2 Stepping into Spirit

Once you have labeled several of these primary motivations in your life, we ask you to now look at them in a different light. Now we ask you to step out of your physical body and examine each one of these as the Spirit you are. Find ways to re-label each of these motivations to reflect the basic needs of a Spirit in human form. What you may have first labeled as jealousy may be now be relabeled as a need to be loved. The experience of Love is the greatest hope of all souls entering the Game. What may have first been labeled as a need to feed your ego may now be relabeled as a need for basic recognition. Spirits enter the Game for the intent of experience, and that is not possible if they are invisible and not recognized.

What may have first been labeled as wanting more or a fear of not having enough, may be relabeled to simply a fear of dying. All souls are brought into the Game with an inborn fear of death. From the perspective of the spirit, this is actually more a fear of dying before completing your primary life lesson. Those who no longer fear death have risen above that within this lifetime.

What may have been labeled as laziness or sloth may be relabeled as a need to nurture oneself. All Spirits in human form must learn to nurture themselves first before they can accept nurturing from others.

What may have been labeled as competition or a need to reach the top, may be relabeled as a need to experience creation. You are an integral part of God with the same abilities of creation. Those abilities must be utilized, or you will turn the energy of creation inward. That produces the useless human emotion of guilt. Although we tell you that the human emotion of guilt has served you very well in the lower vibrations from which you are evolving, in the higher vibrations of the New Planet Earth, it is the most useless thing that you carry with you. We will offer you instead 'action.' If there is something you can do about something, then do it. If not, release the guilt, for it will taint your color clear more than you know. Each time you find yourself dealing with the "G" word, we ask you to look up and laugh. Enjoy the humor of who you are, for that is the true perspective of the angels. The great laughter is what sets the energy right in an instance. And if ever you are struggling to see the color clear, or if you find yourself wrapped up in a drama and cannot quite get clear, stop and laugh at your situation. This simple action will bring the color clear in an instant, for clarity can only be gained when the energy is aligned. Once you begin working with this, offer it to others, for that is the action of the Human Angels. Reach out, for you are not alone in your experience of playing human. It is also the reason that those of you who hear us also hear the divine laughter.

## Step 3 Adjusting the Color Clear

Understand that as you play the game, you can change or adjust your color clear. Even as a collective of humanity, your primary motivation is shifting as you raise that collective vibration. Primary motivation of all of humankind up to this point has been the simple motivation of survival. In the lower levels from which you came, all actions and dramas could be traced back to the primary motivation of survival. As you continue to evolve, that no longer is your primary motivation. You are not afraid of dying. Is that not wonderful? When the collective belief was that you only had 'now,' you felt as if you were under pressure to use every moment, and time was a precious commodity to be squeezed. Yet because of this advancement, your color clear, and, therefore, the very base of who you are, has been altered. The cosmic wink is that this allows you to make the highest use of every moment and now you have time to just be. It is only when you know the color clear, you have the freedom to make the greatest choices within every second of every day. Your color clear can be adjusted to match your higher vibration as you evolve in human form. Now we will show you how to incorporate those adjustments.

Now we ask you to take a moment to have an inner dialog with your own higher self. See the connection with your higher self and then ask your lower conscious self to join in the inner dialog. With both the higher and lower self present, examine each of these labels you have now adjusted. If both higher and lower self agree, then take these labels as your new color clear. If you have discord between the two, then please return to the theatre and watch these pictures again and place new labels on base motivations. Once the labels have been found to clearly define base motivations in your life, then you can move forward with a base understanding of the color clear. Now that you have identified, without judgment, your wants and needs as a Spirit in human form, you will find that the feelings of being stuck or restricted will dissolve and your forward movement will gain speed. Then you are a clear slate ready for a new script. We ask you then to focus on your highest and best attainment of your base motivations. Dance with your passion, play with your joy. Search out that which makes your heartstrings vibrate the highest. Enjoy the ride and understand your own primary motivations, for some of you will be motivated by attainment, some of you will be motivated by a higher vibration. Incorporating higher truths into a higher reality will motivate some of you. They are all yours for the choosing, for you are the creators. Choose well, dear ones, and if at any time you are not happy with your choices, have the courage to choose again.

All choice is honored always. It is your birthright. Until recently, you have been playing your Game on the only Planet of Free Choice. You have had no predetermination. For God to see God, you took these drastic measures. And now you step to the next level as the Children of the New Earth enter and take their place. You have evolved as Spirit over eons of lifetimes after lifetimes. Your intent was to evolve as a spiritual being just so you could experience the Game in human form, to reach out and touch another hand also in human form. That is the greatest evolution of Spirit. Yet you do not understand its magic. Every time you reach out and you touch another soul in physical form, we applaud you.

## Holding Your Power

Please do not give us your power, asking us which way to turn. Please do not look to us for your answers, for that is not why we are here. The second wave of empowerment is moving from 'follow the leader' to 'follow yourselves.' This is not an easy transition, for you have not been taught to trust your own heart. You look to us and you wish to make the best and highest choice. You say: "If only you will show me which road to take at this juncture for me to reach my goal, then I will find my passion and experience my joy. Then I will be at the highest use of the Universe."

And we say, dear ones, if you ask that question, you have already missed the turnoff, for the road is not a destination, it is a journey. If you wish to see the color clear, you must see it and hear it where you are at this very moment. If you wish to see the color clear, you must understand there is no right or wrong choice. If you wish to see the color clear, you must be here, now. For it is not a destination. It is about enjoying the Game and enjoying the ride. Our work as angels is to reflect your magnificence and help you to re-member who you really are. We are here only to help you see yourselves from a perspective of Home. Then you will find those answers within you. For as each one of you takes your power, you pull the entire Game closer to Home in the re-union that is now underway.

You have no idea who you are. You have no idea what you have done. You have no idea that you are sons and daughters of the King. You are heirs to the throne of forever. Dear ones, you are the chosen ones. You could not be alone if you tried. It is about finding a way to enjoy each day, even if you find that you have to go to work and lower your vibrations for one more day. We dare you to find the one minute of that job that you love. Do that and you will see the color clear.

With your help, we have created sacred space this day. We tell you the entire day, you have been in the energy of Home. This entire day, you have not aged. This day, you have rejuvenated your energy. You have chosen to sit at the front of the class. You have chosen to be here … to be the beacons of light for those who will follow as humanity evolves. We are honored to be in your presence. We are honored to help show you the color clear. In those moments when you lose yourself, in those moments when you cannot find your way, in those moments when you look in the mirror and you cannot see your reflection, let your spiritual family reflect you. Know that you are not alone. As you step into the next stages of evolution that are now in front of you, re-member the color clear. It is the most beautiful color of all. It is with the greatest of love that we ask you to treat each other with respect. Nurture one another. Find ways of making space for the empowered human and play well together.

Espavo

the Group

## Connecting the Heart: The Lost Wallet

## From Barbara

I had mentioned in my most current Lightworker Update that Steve and I spent most of the month of October in Holland with a few days in Belgium. I was thrilled to return to this area. In the past, we have gone there twice a year, every April and October. This time it had been a whole year since visiting our spiritual family in this part of the world. What a grand reunion it was! The second week we were there, I managed to attract germs that brought on a cold/flu and eventually turned into bronchitis. Initially I 'caught' these germs from our host Ingrid who was experiencing similar symptoms. She refused to give it a label of cold/flu, but insisted it was simply a clearing of her body moving her on her path. In my process of sniffling and coughing, I refused to agree with her and felt sorry for myself that I had attracted these germs that were just making me feel miserable and indeed, I proclaimed, "I do have a cold/flu." Even though I was caught up in the joy of our seminars and refused to let these physical ailments stand in my way of our events, this was definitely a physical challenge. I have learned much from the experience. Thank you, Ingrid, for your part of this lesson on my path of understanding. Whatever labels are put on any dis-ease, they are definitely a clearing moving us forward in life.

Although I was very much looking forward to our trip to Europe, my body and mind had not had enough time to catch up to our whirlwind of activities I have been experiencing in our past events. I have learned to know the nature of my physical being. I require 'down time' to process all the wonderful experiences that develop during my spiritual journey.

I experienced inevitable consequences on this trip. The law of cause and effect is the law of perfect balance. I was reminded what ever you put out there is returned to you in many ways. The law of circulation declares that the measure we use in giving, regardless of form, is the measure of what will return to us. Although I thoroughly enjoyed our events in Holland and Belgium, I felt myself being in a weakened state. The last week Steve and I were there, we took some personal time for ourselves. We spent a whole day and night in Amsterdam, one of our favorite places. We spent the day visiting our favorite sights and stores, ending up staying at the Victoria Hotel that overlooks the main street. It sounds perfect to be with the one you love in such a beautiful setting, doesn't it? Unfortunately, my cold became worse and I was not feeling my optimistic self. I went into a negative thinking. I found myself going into shops and being irritated that people were outright rude to me. Steve pointed out to me that they indeed were helpful and not rude at all. In my negative state, I couldn't see that. I was attracting what I was putting out. I just wasn't myself and was circulating negativity. After shopping, we returned to our beautiful room in the Victoria Hotel and went directly to sleep because I was not feeling well. It frustrated me that I couldn't even enjoy this lovely hotel room with the view of the main street of Amsterdam.

I woke up in the middle of the night (yes 3:00 a.m.) to have a good talk with myself. I said, "Okay I will listen to my body. I am not taking care of myself and this causes me to put out negativity." I went to bed confident that I would awake with my familiar positive self and life would be good again. This was not the case. Although I awoke with a positive attitude, the negativity I had placed into circulation was still playing out. The next morning, we were walking down the busy main street enjoying the ambiance of Amsterdam during morning rush hour. Walking into a store on the way to the train station, I reached for my wallet only to find it was missing. I retraced my steps and finally accepted I had been the victim of a pickpocket. I did not have time to report this to the police because Steve and I needed to catch the train just in time to present our seminar that evening. After feeling sorry for myself, I again decided to change my thinking and release the negativity and move on. I was determined to once again refocus on the positive and bring that flow back again into my life.

I was proud of myself how I took charge of my reality once again. The evening event was enjoyable, connecting with special Lightworkers. I explained what had happened to me that day and how I made a shift in my thinking. I could feel the good consequences of my thinking already working as I had started the circulation of the positive. Physically and mentally, I was on the mend. The day after that, we traveled to our weekend event. I again was explaining to this group the story about my wallet. During the next break a woman by the name of Helen came up to me and said she was a police officer in Amsterdam who worked with burglaries. She looked me straight in the eye and told me that she would find my wallet! I thanked her and told her I would not be surprised if she did. I had released the attachment to the wallet and I had created a positive flow in my life again. I know this is when miracles happen.

The last day we were in Holland, we received an e-mail from this wonderful police woman. She said, "I was involved in a burglary raid at a house in Amsterdam and I found your wallet!" As I write this, the wallet is on its way to me from Amsterdam. This reconfirmed the law of circulation for me. I already was beginning to bring back the positive into my life.

Today I choose to be mindful of my thoughts. I plant only those seed thoughts that produce the life I choose to experience.

With all my love and light,

Barbara

# A Theory of Reality

# Reality

## April 2002

Greetings from Home

Dear ones, we cannot tell you the honor we have for you. You hear our words and still cannot understand our perspective. You see us as the angels of heaven. We tell you that with all the might in heaven, it has not been possible for us to do what you have done. Can you see why we honor you so? Can you see why we are so honored to be in your presence? We tell you we have missed you at Home, for you have been gone such a long time. You are such a part of us and we are such a part of you, that you know us. You are in our hearts where Home already exists. Hold that energy. Re-member who you are, and you will honor the connection between all of us.

You have dared to step into the fifth dimension. You have dared to take your Game to the next level. There are no rules in the fifth dimension. Ahh, but that should not have been a secret for you, for there were no rules in the third. Oh, but you did a really good job of making some up, did you not? The field of polarity is so thick and so difficult to see around. We watch with such humor as you make your games more intricate than they need to be. We understand that complexity is a part of human nature, and it is necessary for you to complicate things just enough for you to understand. We, and many like us, are here, not to tell you which way to turn, but to reflect the magnificence of humans. You have taken the step of becoming the Human Angels. You have taken an intentional step toward creating your highest reality, and we are so honored to be here watching you. There are many coming in at different overtone levels to watch as you make the choices ahead. You see, it is not just about you, it is about All That Is.

## Fifth Dimensional Attributes

We wish to speak this day of some of the attributes of the alternate realities, which exist within your own time and space. For we tell you that the fifth dimension is no longer something that you are reaching for. You have stepped right into it. The time lag is very short in the fifth dimension. You hold a thought, and that thought is soon standing in front of you in your reality. There is no problem with this, for in the higher vibrations of the New Planet Earth, all is possible and you are masters of your thoughts and your reality. Oh, but when you are confused by the veils, you reach outside of yourselves for answers. You look for things that are not there. You reach for the mysticism to surround you. Sometimes, you do not give anything any power unless you surround it with mystique. That is no longer necessary, dear ones, for you are holding your power and taking charge of your realities. Fear not making mistakes, there is no such word on the New Planet Earth. We tell you, there is no right or wrong. That is an illusion of polarity that has existed on your Game board. Find the passion of who you are and what feeds you. Dare to create a reality of your own choosing. Have the courage to go after that passion first, for that is where you will find the essence of Home. That is where your greatest success will be on the New Planet Earth.

The fifth dimension you have stepped into has a very short time lag. In the third dimension, you would have a thought and it would hang out there forever, teasing you as you waited for it to manifest. Occasionally, it would check back with you and it would say, "Are you sure this is what you want?" And you would say, "Yes, that is what I want." And the time lag would continue to stall the creation, asking ever so often if this was what you really wanted. This was a necessary part of the Game, for you were not yet masters of your thoughts. Finally, when it reached the edge of creation, it would check one last time and say, "Are you sure?" And if you were the same vibration as you were when you originally set this creation in motion, it would manifest. The process was called co-creation, for you would create together with spirit to manifest things in your world. We tell you even now, you have moved past the process of co-creation for there has been an integration of spirit. You are no longer outside of yourself. You have come together as one. There is a merging of the higher self into the physical form that has never been possible before. You have created it, dear ones, and we stand back and applaud you. The thunderous applause that exists on this side of the veil for what you have created through your own choices is beyond your understanding for it is not about you; it is about All That Is.

## A Theory of Reality

We will share with you this day an important definition of reality that will help you acclimate to life in the fifth dimension. Your problem with understanding reality is that you think it is real. In the fifth dimension, reality is only a theory. A theory of reality is a presumption one makes when attempting to define the infinite. You have been living quite a long time in a theory of reality that is shared by many. Because the collective has supported it, it became what you call reality. Now that you are creating the New Planet Earth in the fifth dimension, that reality changes with your individual thoughts.

So much has happened on your planet, even in recent days and months. For you now have opportunity to take power like you have never taken it before. We do not ask you to hold yourselves responsible for everything or everyone that happens on your planet. We ask you to hold responsibility, and therefore power, for who you are in each moment. This is what creates the new energy and the higher vibrations of the New Planet Earth. That is what you have come here to do … and you are doing it well. Fear not making mistakes. Fear not the energy as you take the power, for it does not serve you to play less than the creators that you are. It does not serve the highest good of all to pretend that you still do not take your power. For now is the time to change that within you, for that power of creation is where your responsibility lies. Take your power as creators. Create first within. You will be known throughout all of history. You will be known throughout all of time as those who sat in the front of the class, for you, dear ones, are the chosen ones.

The veil is so thick that you sit quietly in the dark and you feel the tears as you reminisce of Home. You ask, "Why am I here?" Ah, if we could only raise the veil for but a moment to show you what you really came here for. You would be so incredibly proud to be who you are that you would never doubt yourself again.

As each and every one of you holds your torch high and claims your flame of truth, there will be no more shadows on planet Earth and Home will be re-created.

Each and every one of you has a responsibility. Create the highest and best for yourselves first. Dare to create abundance in your life in all areas. This is the true vibration of Home. No one ever wants for anything at Home. If you are creating Home on your side of the veil, it will be necessary for you to dare to accept all that is yours. Do so now with full connection and honor to all things around you. Understand that when one rises, all rise.

## The Celestial Stream of Light Energy

The energies are increasing everyday as planet Earth moves into a stream of celestial Light energy. This is the third year that the Earth will experience a substantial Light shift in May. This is due to a change in direction of the entire planetary system in which you reside. What you call your solar system is not yet fully defined. There is more than you know traveling around your solar sun. A few short years ago, the Game took a turn. Three years ago, the ascension process began to move your reality. This was the first time you truly experienced the New Earth. To some of you, it felt like an invasion and a shift that you needed to protect yourselves from. At that time, your entire system of planets began to shift its placement in the Universe. Three years ago, your planetary solar system began to move toward a new resting place in the Universe.

You experienced this as your planet traveled through a cosmic stream of celestial Light energy in the month of May. Your planet has traveled through this same Light stream during the month of May for the last three years. The first year, you felt it the strongest because it was new and different to you. You are feeling the effects of this energy shift less now because you are becoming accustomed to energy shifts in general. We tell you that this year you will experience the strongest energy shift from this source than in any year prior. You have a minimum of two more years before your solar system passes through this energy stream. The length of time it will take you to pass through this field will depend on how fast you assimilate and engage the new energy.

Those of you who feel the pulse of the Earth may feel the anticipation of this cosmic event even now. As you move into this stream, you will feel consciousness shifting all around you. Those of you who are empathically sensitive to the Earth will feel this energy change before the others. Some may feel on edge or jittery for no apparent reason. Others may feel energized. The reactions will vary greatly, yet, all eventually will feel the shift in some manner. Some will, as they have in recent times, react in fear. You can hold the Light high by choosing thoughts that create a reality of your choosing. This is what we refer to when we ask you to hold your Light high.

## Release of the Crystal Energy

In addition to the energy field that you are passing through, you will also experience a release of the Crystal Energy on May 19, 2002. This too, is an energy stream that bombards the Earth. This, however, is the Crystal Energy originating from the Central Sun that is stored in the tectonic plates of your planet. The solar winds you have experienced recently are the carriers of this energy as it is redirected through your own solar sun.

Dear ones, you have asked time and again, "How can I make a difference?" We tell you, the opportunities are now directly in front of you. Part of the challenges that you are now facing is the difficulty assimilating the Crystal Energy. Parts of the globe are in turmoil and war as a direct result of this energy entering your world. The Crystal Energy brings with it a new level of human empowerment. Those who have spent lifetimes living with little personal power will take this as a call to action, and, as you have seen, may easily overreact. They naturally think they have been repressed and kept from their power by those around them. They see the actions of revolt as an expression of their own power. Please be patient, dear ones. Know that they see what they are doing as an expression of their powers of creation. Be patient as they try to separate themselves. Do not allow yourself to be segregated even from them, for in truth, you are not separate from each other. When you find ways to take responsibility for your own reality, you set the energy for the many more than you know.

In these times, you easily lose sight of the creation of Home. Instead, you think in terms of stopping all fighting and returning to the peaceful environment you were in only a few months ago. We tell you that it is not possible to return to those times. Your humanness would have you think that peace on the planet is simply a lack of war. It is not. Life on the New

Planet Earth is much more than that and must be handled with the responsibility of understanding.

Connect with others and intentionally take responsibility for using this Light energy on a personal basis. May 19 will be a powerful day to set into motion a turning point. Yet, we ask you not to wait for that time. Start now. In the darkest of times, the most difficult situations, find ways of creating your highest reality. Choose a theory of reality that allows you to be in your passion, and you will be creating Home on your side of the veil.

## Personal Darkness

Most of you reading this now have gone through periods of darkness. Some of you have had an experience known as the Phantom Death. It was the time when you were complete with your contracts. With the exception of long-term commitments, most of you are finished with what you came here to do. Yet, here you are. You stayed, even when you had a chance to go Home. You have gone through a period of darkness so that you can see the light, and here you are. We know the pull of Home is strong. The energy you now feel is not the energy of 'the Group' but the energy of Home, and that is what you feel at this very moment. Breathe it in, and accept what is rightfully yours. That is the re-minder of where you come from. That is the strong pull of Home that you have each of you have felt in the last several years. Re-member it well, dear ones, but do not long for it. Do not pine for it. We ask you to simply hold that energy and create it where you are. You do not need to pass beyond the veil to feel that energy. You now have the abilities to create it where you sit. Feel it often, dear ones. We will help you by touching you with the touch of an Angel until you learn to touch each other.

Dear ones, it is with the greatest honor that we thank you for your work. You have no idea what you have done ... but you will. Make space in your heart for your own energy and you will open the door for the children of Indigo vibration and the children of Crystal vibration as your world begins to shift. Make space on the New Planet for empowered humans. Play with the realities and fear them not. Enjoy dabbling in the magic, for it is magic indeed, and it is yours now. You have only to push the boundaries to find they are no longer there. Hold your flame high. For then, there will be no more shadows on planet Earth. And it is time for you to hold your flame in your own energy. Fear it not. You are the creators. You are the chosen ones. You have done it before. Trust yourselves. If you cannot re-member who you are, reach out and take the hand of the one next you and they will help you re-member. It is with the greatest of honor that we re-mind you to treat each other with respect, nurture one another, and play well together.

Espavo.

## Connecting the Heart

### By Barbara

You may have noticed, we no longer call my words to you the meditation. For many years, Steve wrote the monthly Beacons message from the Group and the meditation. As our work grows, we see changes happening. Steve is so involved with the ever-expanding movement of Lightworker. His heart felt the connection with the monthly message from the Group, but the meditations were starting to change. At first, he asked me to write the meditations. I was honored. For any of you who have attended our events, you know that Steve and I share in this energy of Lightwork. I know my message is a different energy from Steve and the Group's, yet Steve has always encouraged me to offer my work in this space. It felt good to have both sides of us share in this monthly message as we do with our seminars. But still, we felt changes coming about.

I found myself moving away from meditations and gravitating to messages from my heart. This is what I do in our events, connect with the heart. So for those who miss the meditations that were so special from Steve and the Group, we ask you to understand the changes as we now move forward. I know I have had many comments welcoming my input, and for those, I thank you.

Now, we ask you to step into your own power and to create your own monthly meditations after reading the message from the Group. It is my greatest hope that you will continue to enjoy my monthly message to you as well. It is a connection of my heart to yours. From now on my message will be called:

## Connecting the Heart:
### Fifth dimension equals creativity.

Your affirmations, how you envision your life, will determine your reality. Do not doubt your choices as you allow for the rapid changes entering your daily existence. Speak and act from your heart. Trust the inner feeling you have that gives you that inner sense of peace. As you move into your next level, know that not all will understand your truths. Some will be in fear, some in feeling a disconnection. Re-member to trust yourself. Hold all within your heart but know that with movement in your life, comes changes in many areas. These changes may be with jobs, relationship, friends or lovers. Be open to these changes as you learn to practice Unconditional Love and follow your heart.

I look at this with my own life. Never in my wildest dreams could I have imagined the life that Steve and I share together. I followed my heart. I believed in Steve, but more importantly was that I believed in myself. I put total trust in the knowing that my path would be one of the highest good, and that I would create my Heaven on Earth. This path is not always easy. The obstacles that came my way allowed for greater growth.

Imagine your dreams and turn them into you reality. Stay focused on your creation and you will make it happen. Anything you desire is within your reality in the fifth dimension. How exciting the possibilities! Enjoy the challenge! Enjoy this ever-changing theory of reality. You may just surprise yourself as to what you bring into your own Heaven on Earth.

# Dolphin Flow

## The Second Act

### June 2002

This was a live presentation from a seminar in Syracuse, New York. I was saving this message for an upcoming book but when I got it back from the transcription manager, I saw that it really needed to get out right away. The recent energy shifts and re-positioning have made life a bit difficult for many. Here, the Group offers practical tools for moving through life comfortably.

Greetings from Home

You have come in with the most wondrous veils in place. These veils do not allow you to see yourself as you really are. It is as if you have little tags on your forehead that reveal your identity to all that see you. Still, you are unable to see these yourself. Ah, and even if you look in the mirror, you cannot read them for they appear backwards. Everyone else can see who you are but it is you who does not have the vision to see yourself. Those are the properties of the veil as you have designed it. Yet as hard as it is to see your true magnificence, the memories of the magnificence of Home are deeply ingrained in your being. When you feel the longing of Home we ask you to understand that it is one way in which you are able to re-member who you really are. In the time you are with us, we will share with you these powerful vibrations of Home. Breathe them in, dear ones. These are not new to you. These are your memories of a time when you re-membered your true nature and walked every step in that knowledge. These are the memories of Home.

## The Flow of Light from Home

Welcome the energy and connect and, as you walk from here today, take that piece with you. For even as you walk into the grocery store, when you shine those smiles, and flash your eyes to the people you meet, magic happens. For you share with them the vibrations of Home and the memories of their magnificence. That is what we call Lightwork. Spreading Light through empowerment is what many of you have come here to do. Sometimes, it is done in the most mundane places. Sometimes, as you pass another on the street, you smile … and something magical happens. That energy is passed from one to another. In this fashion, the energy is distributed until the collective vibration of Humanity is raised to such a level that you begin to see each other consciously. That is the thinning veil that you are now beginning to experience. You are at the brink of this stage of evolution as we speak. You are such wonderful beings. You have no idea what you have already accomplished. You sit here talking and reading the books and sharing with each other to try and figure out ways to take your work to the next level. We tell you, dear ones, you have already won the Game.

In times past, you have looked so very carefully for the little road markers, and the ideas that you have set in place for yourself. We tell you look no further, for they no longer exist. There is no grand plan in place from this point forward. You are the masters of the Game board and the grand plan is now complete. You are the ones holding the pen in your own hands, for everything you script from this day forward is of your own design. We ask you to dare to script the very best for yourselves for that is the time that you put yourself in your passion and be of greatest use to the Universe. Oh, holding power can be so difficult when you are unaccustomed to it. No one told you this would be easy. You have tried so many times to stand in your power, and you re-member the pain of falling, scuffing your knees, and elbows. There we are with our wings, helping you back up. It is in these times that we hold you and hug you and re-mind you of Home in any way that we can. We know that if we can only spark that memory deep within you, the energy will begin building. We know that, after you feel the energy of Home, even once, you can never go back.

Oh, dear ones, you are never alone. Make space for that part of you which connects to your own higher self, and you find much more of the power held within you. This is when you step into your true work on the New Earth. This is also the time when you walk into the grocery store and make more of a difference than you will ever know. Sometimes, it is the most mundane things on your planet that make all the difference. There are many times that you, as facilitators, do not get to see what you have set into motion. Walk in the knowingness that you are carrying the Light of Home in all that you do. Walk in the knowingness that you may make a difference with more people than you can possibly imagine. And enjoy that.

## The Whole World is but a Stage.

There are no less than two hundred of you reading and hearing these words who are holding modalities yet to unfold, that will transform the face of the New Planet Earth. Ah, you are all thinking now, "How do I come to know that? Where do I find this?" and the one we love so much: "How do I make a living at this modality?" Then you pull out your pens and get ready to write the answers you think will lead you to your passion. Oh, you are such wonderful beings. You are so imaginative and so accustomed to giving your power away. Yet, we tell you that you have had it all along. You have known this in your heart, for this is not a process of taking down notes, not a process of learning, but a process of re-membering. This is a process of simply unfolding for yourselves that which you have known in your heart, for you are back from the days of Atlantis, you are back from the days of Mu. You will be re-membering the magic of those times and incorporating that into your reality. The world you visit now is only a stage. It is only an illusion you have played out many, many times. Only now the play is over; it is complete. And you stand on the stage taking final bows with the most thunderous rounds of encore and applause flooding all of your senses. Each one of you thought your work might be over. There you stand on stage as applause dies down, only the curtain does not fall. From this point on, the play continues, only now there is no script to follow. We wish you to know, even though you cannot see the audience, you cannot imagine the applause from this side of the veil for what you now do. Now you step into the role of Human Angel.

Each one of you thought this was about you. And we tell you it is not. It goes far beyond that. You could have left the stage and returned Home if you so chose. You look for meaning in life outside of yourselves and try to understand your bubbles of biology. Ah, we love when the Keeper does that, for he is still searching for the instruction manual that came with his. Oh, dear ones, you are the spirits of your being. You are your true essence when you smile, when you laugh. That is when you pass it on one unto another. That is when you give the gift of Home.

In your efforts to carry around these dense bubbles of biology, you have forgotten who you are. That, in fact, was the nature of the Game. Yet now, re-membering your nature and your power, and carrying it with you, becomes the next act of the play. That which you call ascension is not leaving the Earth. That which you call ascension is not leaving the physical body. In fact, it has already begun. You woke up in the fifth dimension this morning, dear ones. Previously you have only experienced brief glimpses of fifth-dimensional realities. Some of your dreamtime and meditations have taken you there. And now we tell you, you are firmly standing in the reality that you only glimpsed prior.

## The Timing of the Second Act

Dear ones, as you struggle, you hit the brick walls you think restrain you from finding your higher truth. When you find that the rug has been pulled out from under you and support is no longer there, we tell you there are some keys. Those of you who hold the modalities of higher vibrational healing may have felt like you have hit a brick wall. For try as you might, you have not been able to get this information out. Dear ones, did you not understand that the timing was of utmost importance? You can easily see that, if you were here teaching energy techniques fifty years ago, you probably would not have been accepted. The collective vibration of humanity was not high enough to support higher healing modalities at that time. Ah, now you are beginning to understand. Some of you have been in a holding pattern that is so difficult for you. You have felt restrained, you have felt not supported, and you often wonder if you are on the right path because it seems to be blocked. Oh, dear ones, sometimes a rock is only a rock. Do not give your power away to the rock as you look for a deeper meaning. For if you know in your heart that you have something to give, if you know in your heart that there is something you have come here to do, do not let anything dissuade you. And see that those roadblocks and those brick walls that seem to be restricting you are simply a matter of timing. For you cannot see, from behind the veil, what is being orchestrated behind the stage. Some of you look at yourselves and say, "I am sixty-two years old and I have never done anything before. What makes me think I can be a healer now?" Do you not understand it took sixty-one and three-quarters of a year to get to the point where you could take your true role as a healer? The experiences and difficulties of your first sixty-two years now become your credentials. And, in fact we tell you, you are at a crossroad with your own evolution in biology. Within your lifetimes, you will easily reach three hundred years. If you only live another ten years, we tell you the average life span will increase to one hundred and twenty. Ah, sixty-two may not sound that bad now, does it? In fact, you are wondering, "Does that mean I have to go through puberty again?"

# OverLight

There will be a process where you will be able to move from one level to the next and you will be able to rejuvenate emotionally, physically and spiritually. There will be a process that will allow you to raise your vibration, and, for most of you experiencing our energy, it has already begun. It is the process of OverLight. Please do not place too much into those words, dear ones. You hold the power and, if you choose to go through the OverLight process, it will bring you to a vibration that will equal the Children of Crystal Vibration as they enter. These are the magical children. They have not been supported previously due to the fact that your collective vibration was not high enough to support them. We speak of them as if they are separate from you but, in fact, they are not. They are you, incarnate in the higher vibration. They carry magical abilities for soon you will be in each other's heads, you will know each other's thoughts, you will know each other's feelings, you will know each other's fears. We tell you what a grand place this will be when that happens. For in that state, there will be no room for shadows, there will be no room for war. What you are experiencing is simply the birthing pains of the new energy. Welcome it, dear ones.

# Connecting Passion

Be courageous and know that you have a purpose for being here now. The key to finding that purpose is to look for your passion. Look for that which lights you up when you talk about it. Oh so many of you right away go to thinking, "Oh, but how can I make a living at my passion? How can I do this all the time?" We love the way the human brain works. Some of you will, some of you will not. It is not important to transfer everything into every piece of your life. What is important is to carry the vibration of that passion in everything that you do, in every time that you smile. Many of you have said you cannot find your passion. We offer you a suggestion to begin the process of releasing these restrictions.

We ask you to try an exercise this day. Every time you look at another, smile and just pretend the person you are making eye contact with can see all the way to the very center of your being. Understand there will be nothing hidden from each other. You have no idea the beauty that will be seen in this exchange. Here, you will have the opportunity to see to the very core. You have no idea of the real beauty you will see in each other when you let each other all the way in. There, you will find God.

## Pain and Resistance

You have spent much of your life trying to avoid pain. Pain has been the big motivator. Pain is the part that has caused you to move this way or that. Physical pain, emotional pain, there are many forms of pain. Each of you experiences pain differently. It is not calculable on a scale of one to ten, for each experience is unique. This really frustrates your scientists. We tell you that pain, and especially the emotion of pain, is the connection between the energy tube of your life force and your physical body. So every time you experience some sort of change, some form of pain will accompany it. We tell you, however, misery is completely optional. Understand that this is a choice.

We now tell you something, for it is time you understood the reflection of how you will look when you come Home. Ah, for when you get Home, you will look at each other and you will hold each other so tightly that you will feel the oneness you share with each other. You will hold your arms around each other and you will laugh about the time you passed each other on the street and did not see each other. You will laugh about the time you had a misunderstanding and could not re-member what it was all about. You will laugh about the time you tried to connect and could not communicate, and you will say how wondrous it was. Here, you will re-member the pain as the most joyous human experience. For it is not a negative on our side of the veil, dear ones. Still, when you experience continuous pain, it represents a misdirection of energy. Pain drains energy from you that can be utilized elsewhere. When energy is misdirected, it simply means that its path is altered to less than its highest use. As humans, you often feel energy mis-directions as some form of pain. The pain most often felt in the human experience is simple resistance. When a being in any form, moves through energy, they will experience resistance. The amount of resistance, and thus the amount of pain, will determine the energy available to do one's real life purpose. Therefore, learning to flow through life with Grace can be very helpful in the higher vibrations of the New Planet Earth.

You look outside yourselves as a result of the veil you wear. You do not believe you are whole, so you are constantly looking for things to add to you to make you whole. Connect to the energy of each other, and you will feel whole in that moment. The Children of Crystal Vibration will connect much easier than you, for it is their nature to honor the oneness. We will offer you a suggestion that may help to create that connection now.

## The Flow of Abundance

Let us offer you the suggestion of flow, for many of you have worked very hard at the art of graceful acceptance. You are wondrous givers and you feel great when you can give, yet, many of you do not know how to accept. You cut yourself off and you actually limit the amount you can give because you have not allowed yourself to accept. Part of the challenge of that is that you have been taught a belief that everything is finite when actually nothing is. You hold the belief that if you receive, everyone else will have less. Energy is not finite, dear ones; it is infinite by nature. There is no beginning and no end to anything. It is only an illusion of polarity to set the stage on which you act in your play. You live forever. Your energy is, and that is the secret of I Am. There is no end and, when you accept, everyone can have more. In fact you often block the flow of energy when you do not accept. That is the concept of energy flow. When you accept energy, it does not stop with you, but simply flows through you. When you allow yourself to accept energy, you have more to give others. If you are in the process of creating Home on your side of the veil, you will need to learn flow, for we tell you there is no greater place of abundance than Home.

We use the word 'abundance' and in your mind you envision those funny little squiggles with lines through them. Your illustration of money is only a reflection of energy, dear ones. It is not energy in itself. And it is so humorous to watch you, for reflections can be manipulated and you love to chase reflections. You get very discouraged and then ask spirit to help you. Yet, even when that help is given, it is often not accepted. Just understand that what you call money is only a reflection of energy. So let us go to the true essence of the energy it is reflecting, for that is the essence of Home. That is the true essence of abundance. Abundance is an excess of what is minimally needed. Many have been so concerned with being selfish that they only create what is minimally needed. They have requested only what is absolutely necessary, and then when someone comes in their field and needs help, they have nothing extra to give. Can you see how abundance could play a part in the role of the Human Angels? You have stated that you wish to be a Human Angel, which will allow you to be in exactly the right spot at the right time to help make a difference, to help spread the light. It may be a smile. It may be a hug. It may be a word of encouragement. It may be money. Whatever it is, we ask that you allow the energy to flow through you. Open to acceptance, for it is the flow. You are not the energy that sticks to you, you are the energy that flows through you. Likewise, it is not the destination that you seek, it is the journey.

## The Dolphin Flow

In learning to move through the energy you are experiencing now, we ask you to take a tip from the dolphins. See yourselves as dolphins, which are actually part of your parental race. They are built with such sleek design that they can swim through the murkiest waters and nothing sticks to them. That is not by accident. They have learned to flow the energy through and around them without attaching themselves to it. Their sleek design is actually a product of eons of evolution. As a result of this evolution, they live in the greatest of abundance at all times. Whatever they need is right in front of them in each moment. Because of their evolution, they live in a constant state of abundance. They experience abundance moment by moment, so they need not carry anything with them. By adapting to the energy rather than attaching to it, you learn the flow of energy. With the Crystal Energy infiltrating into the Earth at this time, many are grasping to old ideals and beliefs for assurance. Be the dolphins, dear ones. Know that everything you need is right in front of you, and allow yourself to accept in each moment. Allow yourself to accept everything that flows through your field, for the more that you allow yourself to accept and flow through you, the more abilities you have as a Human Angel. Whatever the circumstances in your life, adopt the role of the dolphin, just traveling through, looking for a place to play. Let nothing attach itself to you. Instead, enjoy the flow of energy as you travel through it and simply enjoy the ride.

You decided to come to planet Earth to put on these veils, to wake up screaming as a little infant and be confused. You have been very successful. You have confused yourselves so well. We tell you, use the laughter, dear ones. For when we find you getting too serious, we will tickle your funny bone to re-mind you that it is only a Game. Play the Game well and enjoy the abundance that is your birthright. Enjoy the Game and play as the dolphins do. Their role as custodians of planet Earth is over. Those dolphins that are choosing to stay are here to teach you how to hold the energy. They are here to teach you how to play.

Do not worry about the next act of the grand play. You are in the process, at this moment, of writing the script as you go. Fear not the change. Welcome it and be the dolphin that swims everywhere and has everything. Allow the energy to flow completely through you without allowing anything to stick to you. For it is those things that stick to you, in the way of your beliefs, that make it so difficult for you to swim to the next level. Some have worked very hard to obtain possessions, only to find that when you have many things, those things own you. True abundance is not about things; it is about having the courage to create a lifestyle that fully supports you to the highest degree. That is where the joy is. Dare to treat yourselves well, for only then can you play the role of the Human Angels. Dare yourselves to have all that you desire now. Dare to create everything in your life that you want and more. It is the 'and more' that allows you the opportunity to play the role of Human Angel, for that is the piece you will pass amongst you. Those are the seeds you will plant in other people every time you smile. That is the joy of the next act.

You are the magical beings. You are the magical third graders who have changed the whole school. Walk in pride, dear ones. Dare to hold your light high and proud. For in that time, there will no longer be shadows on planet Earth. You sit at a critical juncture now, deciding what will be in the next act of the play. Do not concern yourself with how the play ends or who plays what role. That is the act of a Human Angel.

Dear ones, we are so honored to be in your presence. It is only possible because you have asked. We are here with simple suggestions so that you may see, and re-member your magnificence. For you are the angels who do not re-member you are angels. You are the part of Home that we are missing. Take a moment and feel the honor that all of us on this side of the veil have for you, the masters of the Game board.

Dear ones, you cannot see who you are, and yet you are changing your reality, for you are beginning to see God in the mirror. Know that you hold the power. Enjoy the journey, dear ones. It is with the greatest of honor that we sit in your presence. Re-member Home, re-member your empowerment, re-member to treat each other with respect, nurture one another, and play well together.

Espavo.

the Group

# Emotional Intuition

## Creating Reality or Drama

### July 2002

Greetings from Home

We greet you this day with a special message about upcoming events. As you know, it is a rarity for us to speak of events in your future. Our work is designed to re-mind you of your power, and to predict future events will encourage the human practice of looking outside of yourselves for answers. We do so today for the express purpose of explaining your ability to create your own reality.

## The Impetus of Change

Many on Earth would not consider any explanation without scientific data behind it. That is somewhat of an enigma in these times, for in the higher vibrations of the New Planet Earth, you create reality with your thoughts. Therefore, we tell you, even the most controlled scientific experiment is tainted from the beginning by the intent and beliefs of those conducting the experiment. Some of you love to blend scientific validation with what you feel in your heart to be correct. Please understand that at this stage in your evolution, there is a balance that must be maintained between the two. You are stepping from a cold hard factual world into the fifth dimension where, for a time, some things must be felt rather than thought. Therefore the divisions are beginning to close between feelings, thoughts and reality. But where are you exactly when you are between your emotions, thoughts and reality? Here, you are in a heightened state of creation, where all is potential. In this heightened state, a balance must be maintained between the emotions and the thoughts. In the fifth dimension, when one falls out of balance on either side, a vacuum is created that must be filled. More often than not, that vacuum is filled with some form of drama.

Your human attraction to drama is unsurpassed throughout the Universe. It is for this reason that we can hardly wait to see what you will do next. From our perspective, humans put on such a wondrous performance. In the beginning of your Game, art imitated reality, only to have those roles reversed as you grew into higher vibrational status. You must understand that never before have humans reached the levels of vibration you now hold.

## The End of the Game?

Many times we have spoken of the doom and gloom prophecies around the year 2000 that helped motivate humanity to awaken. Those predictions of the end of reality and the First Planet of Free Choice were real. Yet, here you now are on the other side of these prophecies. The reality they held has now changed as, through your own power of choice, you have changed these events. Yet in some small way, you miss the drama and excitement associated with these stories. The need for drama even pulls you to fear-based predictions. If there had been even some cataclysmic events that would have allowed you to start over, it would have fulfilled the need you are now experiencing. As a collective of humanity, you are looking for a fresh start. This is what you are now seeing as a resurgence of end time predictions. What you see now are more stories of the end of life on planet Earth. We tell you that this anticipation of change has made the space for this to surface. Time and again you have looked to drama to supply you with a reason to change. You now have another one in front of you. We tell you that, as you look to the sky to watch the mysterious hidden planet that is to return from its elliptical orbit to turn your planet on its side, this is actually a replay of a very old event. It is reminiscent of the day when you saw the waters entering the city from the hilltops to which you had retreated. It is reminiscent of the final days of Atlantis. So the question has been put to us: "Will the world end in March of 2003?" Very simply put: No, it will not.

In fact, we can see that there will be many who watch the night skies in anticipation of the return of a long, lost planet, only to watch a beautiful but empty sky.

## The Balance of Emotional Intuition

Can you see the patterns re-emerging that we see from here? First you must be supported in your work. You see a restriction in the money flow as you move into your passion, and cannot see that it is a direct result of the changes that have been set into motion on a larger scale. You feel the changes are needed for you to move forward with what you came here to do. Yet, you feel blocked and not supported by the systems in place. Let us tell you, the need to be supported is real, and if it is not addressed, you will eventually fill that void with drama. You see that, as more people fall into the same drama, it becomes more real. The challenge is that as creators, you have the natural inclination to create that which you think about. Now in the fifth dimension, this is truer than ever before. In the higher vibrations of the New Planet Earth, you no longer have the tolerance for lower vibrational thought patterns that you had only a short time ago.

So how do you know what to trust and what to believe? The reality is, there will never be a single source that will be a direct match for you at all times. Truth is not stationary but rather, an evolutionary process. We ask you to take in many flavors of the truth and watch for the sparks of passion. At the center of this process is what we have labeled Emotional Intuition. Your emotional state has also evolved as you step even further into the fifth dimension. Mental intuition has been a part of your growth for some time. Empathic connections with souls who have passed, and the basic intuition connection is a form of this mental intuition. The connection you experience with Spirit and your own higher self is actually a form of Emotional Intuition. As the human evolution continues, the differences will become more apparent. For now, know that it is this inner emotion or knowingness that is at the center of your being as creators on the New Planet Earth. Becoming comfortable with this inner emotion is the next important step in human evolution.

Emotional Intuition is when you take in all the information from outside sources, blend it with inner guidance and distill all the input down to an emotion. The singular base emotion is Love. It is the highest vibration and all other emotions are experienced only against their relationship to Love. Fear is the opposite of Love and is actually not an emotion but simply a lack of Love. All emotions fall between the spectrum of Love and Fear. Here is where your actions as creators become more discriminating. Using Emotional Intuition to see where things fall on that scale between Love and Fear is an important tool for the higher vibrations. This will help you determine what you choose into your thoughts, as your inner truth will allow you to create your highest reality.

Practice employing Emotional Intuition in your own life and see the inner peace it brings. You do not have control over what enters your thoughts, as you are part of a Universal stream of consciousness. You do, however, have complete control over what stays in your thoughts and therefore, what you create. Please understand that, in the higher vibrations of the fifth dimension, there are no longer the polarity concepts of right and wrong. Please understand that Love is not good, nor is fear bad. As you fall away from a polarity consciousness, you will see that they exist simply as one. Therefore, it is a matter of choice. Choose the vibration that allows you to feel the most inner peace. In the state of inner peace, you are the Love vibration expressed in human form. You deserve to feel good, to be fully supported and to experience Love. This is your divine right and necessary for you to move into your true work on the New Earth. This is underway.

Know that in the human experience, there is an innate desire for drama in your reality. Make space for that experience. Dramas entertain you and actually have a part to play in the Game. Play out those dramas well and enjoy those which you choose to experience. Enjoy being scared if you like, for fear allows you to feel more human and therefore, more Love. Yet, when the lights come back up and the credits roll on the screen, pay close attention to your own Emotional Intuition. Do you feel the inner peace? If not, please have the courage to choose another script.

Know that you are never alone. The connection to your own higher self is getting stronger each day. That connection is your own direct link to Home. We are all here watching in amazement as you strengthen these connections daily. Even though you cannot hear it, the applause from this side of the veil is deafening. We are here in the greatest of love, holding the energy for you, helping you to re-member your magnificence, helping you to re-member who you are. It is with the greatest honor that we ask you to treat each other with respect, nurture one another and play well together.

Espavo

the Group.

# The Breath of
# GOD

## Connecting the Infinite Self

### August 2002

We can all tell that something big is about to happen. There is something on a cosmic scale that has never before been equaled. About a year ago in Holland, the Group talked for the first time about the fabric of the Game board. They talked about how this Game board is a stage on which we are all playing parts. They said in that message that there was a mathematical equation upon which the Game is based. They said it was the Golden Mean. This is the mathematical equation: $f = (1 + \ddot{O}5)/2$ or more simply stated: 1.618 (actually 1.6180339887499). This equation is replicated throughout all of nature. It is the base of the Fibonacci series and the Fibonacci spiral that can be seen in all things. The Group says it is the base of everything in our reality. The Flower of Life, the Merkaba and most sacred geometry are based in this simple equation. The Parthenon and the Acropolis in ancient Greece are standing today as a result of the builders' application of this simple equation.

In the days when Barbara and I first started doing seminars, the Group had me make a Scepter. It was a full walking staff length with a huge crystal mounted on the end. Beneath the leather wrapping, they suggested that I coil a copper winding from the crystal to the tip that hit the ground. It was coiled in seven segments all different widths apart, and all according to the Golden Mean. As many of you know who have attended a Scepter of Self Love seminar, the crystal started off completely cloudy. After the first two seminars, the crystal cleared completely. Today it is still clear. Is this 'magic' or applied science? The Group says this goes much deeper than we know. It might just be time to pull the veil aside and take a look.

Greetings from Home

We are honored to be in the presence of the masters of the Game board of Free Choice. Yes, we know you do not always feel like masters. Yet, when you begin to see yourselves as you really are, you will see why we call you that. The advances you have made through the power of your own free choice have made possible a grand cosmic event.

## In Search of Universal Answers.

In your own understanding of the cosmos, you see that the Universe is ever-expanding. You can see from your study of the stars that this can be proven from your own sciences. From this, you have deduced that there was a cosmic event you call the Big Bang. We love your human expressions so! Please understand that you are, in fact, the finite expression of the infinite. Therefore you have no real comprehension of what it is like to be infinite, even through your spirit carries those exact attributes. As an infinite being, you would never ask questions you feel would lead you to a better understanding of the true meaning of life. In finite form, you have a prede-termination to search for answers. This is a part of the human attributes we love so much, for this does not exist here in what you call Heaven. Here, in an infinite reality, we simply allow, and everything comes to us. As finite beings, you are under the influence of polarity and therefore do not see yourselves as a part of the whole. This is why you are constantly 'in search of.' As we discuss this point, please understand that the infinite reality is not better than a finite reality. They both serve as an important part of the whole. They are simply different expres-sions of Universal energy from which everything is made.

## The Golden Mean

Your reality is changing as a result of your advancements. Your reality is now coming closer to Home and, as a result, we can tell you more about how the inter-dimensional reali-ties interact with one another. You live in a reality of polarity. This was the needed component of the Game that allowed you to carry the attributes of being finite. In order to create the illusion of separateness, polarity consciousness was intro-duced. Now, as you move into higher vibrational status, you no longer need the same polarity. You are learning to see unity through glasses that are still tainted with polarity. As you do, watch for the keys and signals along the way. One of these is the factor known as the Golden Mean. The Golden Mean is the mathematical expression of the conversion of infinite to finite. Understand an important truth here, that the reverse is also true. It is this simple expression that makes up all of the fabric of the Grand Game you are playing. Like the props on the stage of life, everything you see beyond the curtain is fabricated from this simple expression. Even in our communications with you, there are certain phrases we intentionally use to stir memories deep within your soul. Here, we use this same mathematical formula in the words we send through the Keeper. These vibrations invoke the memories of Home deep within your being for they re-mind you of the time the Game was first created. This is similar to a person who smells freshly cut grass and re-members a special time in their childhood. They know that if they wish to re-member the people and the feelings of their childhood, they only have to find a freshly cut lawn. Similarly, we often use words or codes in the words that invoke memories for you to re-member Home. One of these is the word 'Greetings.' This word carries a pure vibration. Imagine the gates of Heaven swinging open when you hear that word, for that is why we use it. You will also note that as we speak either in spoken or written words, through the Keeper, we use a rhythm and syntax in our expressions that is very carefully chosen. This is all designed to help your stir your own memories of Home and gently awaken you from the dream.

## The Big Bang?

It is your own need for searching, in finite form, which has created what you call the Big Bang theory. This theory explains the current condition of All That Is in terms that fit within your finite reality. This allows you to contemplate the concept of All That Is. If we told you that all that lies out there always was and will always be, you will not fully be able to comprehend the nature of the Universe. Your own conception and what you call scientific evidence lends itself to searching for a point of origin. We will not argue that fact with you but we will offer another perspective.

Imagine that what you call the Universe, and all Universes, exist in many dimensional realities simultaneously. Even your own existence can be said to have several concurrent dimensional realities. There are actually many of 'you,' all existing side by side in slightly different dimensional realities. In each one, you may make slightly different choices, therefore, each of your dimensional realities may lead you in a slightly different path. Up to this point, all dimensional realities have been kept from crossing each other. This was necessary due to the strong influence that polarity has on a reality to create the illusion of being finite.

'All That Is' exists within a rhythm. The beat of your own physical heart determines your base vibration. All human hearts that beat within a complementary range of vibration make up the humans who exist within a dimensional reality. The Earth, as a living, breathing being, also exists within a vibrational range complementary to yours. The ocean, as a microcosm of the Universe has ebb and flow that sets the base vibration for all that it contains. Everything you see in your reality is actually a living being that is vibrating in a harmonic resonance to your own vibration. If anything were vibrating at a rate not complementary to your own, it would simply exist in an inter-dimensional reality and would not be a part of your Game.

On a grander scale, All That Is also has similar ebb and flow. From a cosmic perspective, what you see as a point of origin of the Universe is the point where that reality began as a finite expression. You, as finite beings, see this as a point of origin that you call the Big Bang. We tell you that there have been many Big Bangs, for they are actually a part of the process of the ebb and flow of the Universe. See that each beginning is actually a new beat of the grand heart that sets the base vibration for All That Is.

## The Heart Beat and Breath of GOD

The Universe, as you know it, has been expanding as far back as you can see. Yet we tell you this is only half the story. The Universe expands until it reaches the point where all realities intersect. As it reaches this zero point, then it continues with the same motion and collapses upon itself. It collapses until it reaches zero point again, then, continuing with the same motion, it begins its expansion again on the other side. Please understand that astronomers will not discover this fact until well after the event. In reality, as you look to the stars with your telescopes, you are actually looking into a time machine. What you are seeing is long in the past. There will come a time when you will be able to look through this time machine in reverse as you discover the nature of Light. This will happen as you discover new applications for the Golden Mean.

The ebb and flow of the Universe expanding and collapsing is the base vibration of the Universal Energy. This is the heartbeat of GOD that gives expression of the infinite in finite form. We tell you, this has happened many more times than even your own heart has beaten. Every time the heart of God beats and reaches this zero point, the realities blend together as one and, for an instant, the finite blends with the infinite once again.

## Intersecting Realities into Unity

There have been times when alternate realities have crossed paths. When this happens, they blend together for an instant and leave permanent impressions on both realities. These have been the origins of many of what you have called myths and stories that have been passed down unaltered from generation to generation. The story of Camelot is such an intersection of realities. These stories live as strongly today as the first day they were channeled through the imagination of a single human mind. We tell you that other than these momentary intersections, alternate realities have never blended together permanently. Can you grasp the excitement that exists within all dimensions of reality as, for the first time, the blending of dimensional realities is about to happen? The best way we can describe what is about to happen is to say, as the heart beat of God breathes in and out, all life begins anew. Never has a conscious manifestation of God in finite form made the transition from one breath to another. That is about to change.

Once again, we tell you that we cannot predict the future, for you have yet to write it. Yet, there has always been a time loop based on the Golden Mean. If we told you that we, as the Angels in Heaven, were actually channeling your future selves, it would give you a glimpse of the different realities that exist within the same time and space. You could easily see the difference between the reality of your current selves and your future selves, and us as the intermediaries. Now, if those realities were to blend, even slightly, you could see that each one of you would have the inner guidance of the future 'you.' We tell you that this is a good example of what is happening, as more divinely inspired information is coming through each one of you every day. Your job at this point in time is simply to learn to trust yourselves and your own inner guidance. How many times have you said to yourself: "If only I would have listened to myself!"

## Channeling Your Future Self

This is a good example, for it is one that you as finite beings can easily comprehend. Now we will take this a step further. If you will take that example and change it to see that the 'you' in finite form is actually connecting to the infinite 'you,' the connection will be more completely understood.

Again, we as the Angels in Heaven are the intermediaries and are here to re-mind you that there is an infinite 'you.' The infinite you also has full range of time, so it is able to move both backward and forward in time. These are the realities that are about to blend together as one. As this happens, you will have guidance from your own infinite 'you' available at all times. Your own evolution as the finite expression of the infinite will now take you to a deeper contact with your infinite self. This is what you have known as your own higher self. The veils that you wear are crucial to the Game of Hide and Seek. They keep you separate from your infinite self and are indispensable. At the same time, they are thinning more than ever before. This is the blending of the two realities that will open the door for the greatest event. The next breath of God is closer than you know. This is why all the eyes in the Universe are upon you at this time. You are the masters of the Game board. You are the honored ones throughout All That Is.

What lies ahead is beyond description. Approach it with excited expectation. Expect a miracle! Please take your time and keep your balance, for the times ahead are filled with wonderment and joy. Connect with others of like vibration in the days ahead, for it amplifies and heightens the collective vibration. Know that you are never alone, and that we are one step behind you, always wrapping you in our wings with each step that you take. We hold the energy for your infinite self until such time as you hold that energy on your own. We do this with the greatest of gratitude and love. We ask that you do not take life too seriously and learn to enjoy the ride. It is with the greatest honor that we remind you to treat each other with respect, nurture one another, and play well together.

Espavo.

the Group

# Awakening the Crystal Children

## Becoming Crystalline

### October 2002

The Group was the first to identify and label the Children of Crystal Vibration in a channel in May of 1997. Here they spoke of their attributes and said, "If you can make the planet safe for them, they will come." In November of 1998, the Group spoke further about the Crystal Children in a live channel at Sudbury, Ontario. This information later appeared in the chapter, 'The Children of Crystal Vibration' in our first book Re-member ~ a Handbook for Human Evolution, which was published in October 2000. On that occasion, the Group provided more details about them, and said that they would be entering soon. I must say that when the Group first spoke of the Crystal Children, I thought they were talking about the Indigo children. However, they quickly corrected me and said these children have different attributes and identified them separately. They also said that the Crystal Children will only be identified as such in the beginning. When the majority of children carry these attributes, we will simply call them 'children.'

Lee Carroll and Jan Tober are the authors of the Indigo Children books and are wonderful people and personal friends. Lee and I have discussed this point. He and Jan say that the Crystal Children are a sub-set of the Indigo children, whereas the Group says they are markedly different. The word 'Indigo' comes from Nancy Tappe, who sees energy fields in a very unusual way. They use this word to talk about all the new children entering the Earth including Star children, Psychic children and more. This seeming discrepancy has caused confusion among many people, as we can attest to by the number of e-mails we receive regularly. In any event, there is one only important point we need to bear in mind – that none of the labels are important. This is not about labels or semantics; it is about the children, and about how we can make this planet safe for the evolving human race. So please understand, if you hear opposing views or different definitions, within just a few short years, none of it will make any difference.

Many authors will soon be bringing in even more information about the new children. Let us be careful not to allow ourselves to fall into the trap of spiritual competition. By the same token, let us also not forget that there also are many children currently on the Earth who are neither Indigo nor Crystal. We can only do them, and ourselves, a great injustice by getting sidetracked by labels.

We hope that the information provided below helps you to see what the Group says is directly ahead in the evolution of mankind. We offer the following with love.

### Greetings from Home

Many of you have felt the recent shift of energy. Like a breath of fresh air, the energy has recently reset. You may feel a relief in the air as you prepare to move forward on your paths. This energetic shift will continue and be complete early next year. This is an evolutionary step to integrating the crystal energy. Have you ever wondered why you have such attraction to crystals? It is no co-incidence, as the crystals themselves have been communicating with you on an energetic level for hundreds of years. More than that, your own evolution is changing your own biology to a crystalline form. That is the reason crystals call to you so. In fact, we tell you that all of what you call nature and all things upon Earth are now in the process of shifting to crystalline form. You are beginning to discover these changes as you find that most of the Earth is crystalline in nature. You are currently carbon-based beings. Yet, we tell you that the base of the carbon atom is only a slight shift away from a silicon atom, which is the crystal element. Even your own scientific periodic tables show only a slight difference between the two. The effect of Earth's pressure on carbon is what causes the evolution of that material into the crystals you know to be diamonds. From our perspective, we are watching as you, and all around you, turn into the most beautiful diamonds. We are honored to be even a small part of this process.

## A History of the Information

You will soon begin to see the effects of the Children of Crystal Vibration as the scouts who are carrying some of the advanced attributes are now making themselves known. The process of OverLight will allow those of you already here to raise your vibrational bodies to the higher attributes of the Crystal Children. This process will stretch over the next 50 years or more and will help you to carry more of the crystalline form in your biology. Light interacts with crystal in very unusual ways. As a result, you love to watch light dance within the facets of a diamond. It is this same interaction with light on your crystalline form that will bring the higher attributes of humanity to the Earth. We are watching this development with the greatest expectation.

Several years ago, we presented information on the return of the Children of Crystal Vibration. At that time, humanity was only beginning to embrace the concept of evolutionary children entering with higher attributes. At the origin of the messages, we spoke of the Crystal Children returning, carrying a new vibration that would appear to have magical abilities compared to present day human attributes. At that time, we described these children as the next stage of human evolution, embodying an important link between the physical bubbles of biology you now inhabit, and your ultimate return to what you now call 'lightbody.' The Crystal Children have two primary attributes. Firstly, they are extremely powerful, with abilities that you would often see as magical. Secondly, they are extremely vulnerable, with exceptional sensitivity to lower vibrational energies.

Much to the dismay of those of you searching for details, we described their attributes to you in somewhat vague terms. This indistinctness was intentional, as we foresaw a potential problem associated with introducing this information. One of the lower vibrational human characteristics you often wrestle with is that of spiritual competition. Since spiritual competition is a lower vibrational concept based on the illusion of polarity, it can be challenging to the Children of Crystal Vibration as they enter. Therefore, we simply planted seeds in the beginning. Now, however, the need for information about your own evolution outweighs any potential challenges. The last several months have brought a new energy shift to all of humanity and the attributes of the Crystal Children now need further definition.

## Crystalline Attributes
## Psychokinetic Abilities

The Children of Crystal Vibration have the ability of multi-level communication. They not only know what is in your thoughts, but, importantly, they will know what is in your heart. When their numbers grow on the Earth, you will see instantaneous communications between them. Their own understanding of energy and the way they refract light within their being will give them psychokinetic abilities. They will be able to move things with their minds. More importantly, they will be able to rearrange matter with their thoughts, with little or no time lag. To us, this is quite amusing, as it was not that long ago that you invented stories for your own entertainment of outer space beings with great powers of the mind who would take over your world. Now you will find that this is true, but that they are, in fact, your own children.

## Potential Challenges

As we have mentioned, the Children of Crystal Vibration have a crystalline structure that allows them to carry more light within their physical being. It is this crystalline structure that causes them to reflect back those things for which they have no reference. Being as powerful as they are, they not only reflect back energies for which they have no reference, but in the process they will also amplify that energy. In as little as 150 years, these attributes will be commonplace, yet those who are the first to carry these in physical form may experience considerable challenges.

Autism or Crystal?

Let us explain some of the immediate challenges these higher vibrational beings may encounter. Having a base of crystal form, they have what you would consider to be loose ethereal bodies. This is what you will first see as hypersensitivity. This is the second attribute that we described as extreme vulnerability. Once mastered, this sensitivity allows them to travel inter-dimensionally. Ultimately this will lead to inter-dimensional movement and what you currently envision as time travel. At present, however, those entering with even small amounts of crystal energy may find themselves unwittingly being pushed into other dimensions. There are currently instances of what you call autism. These are actually Crystal Children who have been pushed into other dimensions and are unable to recover. These gentle beings are extremely sensitive to their surroundings and to outside stimuli are not in harmony with the higher vibration they themselves hold. This actually gives them the appearance of being weak, when in reality they are advanced, powerful human beings. We ask that you begin to observe and to question all outside stimuli, even those that may have been previously used to promote health.

## Vibrational Hypersensitivity

You will also find that the Children of Crystal Vibration are sensitive to all vibrational input. Vibration in all forms such as sound, color, ambient electromagnetic fields and environmental pollutants can have unsettling effects on the Crystal Children. Their hypersensitivity to vibration can be felt on many levels including magnetic, electromagnetic, environmental, aroma, sound, color, and various other forms of vibrational energy. These Children are hypersensitive to their environment and are particularly vulnerable to pollutants. Even today, you are finding that certain color combinations are having strange effects of some Crystal Children. We tell you that even what you have referred to as 'gang colors' was an unconscious attempt to control this input to lower levels of vibration. It is these lower levels of vibration to which the Crystal Children are ultra sensitive.

One form of vibrational energy that the Crystal Children are having difficulty with is electricity. Electricity is a form of energy that occurs naturally in nature, yet your adaptation of it, and particularly your use of alternating current, will take some time for the Crystal Children to adjust to. This is humorous, as this form of electricity was actually developed by one carrying a tremendous amount of Crystal energy [Nicola Tesla]. The Crystal Children must learn to adapt to this form of vibrational energy. In the interim, if they come into contact with an electrical device when they are off center, angry or confused, it is highly possible that they will not only reflect back the energy, but also amplify it as they do so. This will effectively melt most electrical devices in use today. With practice, the Crystal Children will adapt to this man-made waveform of energy. In the meantime, typical home life may be rather interesting.

## Crystalline Connection to Earth

The Earth, as a living sentient being, is also undergoing transformation to crystalline form. You have recently discovered the crystalline nature of water. What we share with you now is that this is not simply a recent discovery; rather, it is a recent evolutionary step. The magnetic grid adjustments of the planet are almost complete. The work of Kryon with the preparation of the magnetic grids on Earth will be complete within the next few months. This will make it easier for the Earth to resonate at a higher frequency and help all humans hold their true power in physical form. Additionally, it will allow the Crystal Children to take their place. This cosmic event alone will set the energy and open the door for the

Children of Crystal Vibration to take the next step in human evolution.

## Emotional Empaths

The largest area of adjustment the Crystals will need to make is with their hypersensitivity to human emotions. Much the same way Indigo children have no reference for the human emotion of guilt, you will find that the Children of Crystal Vibration have no reference for the human emotion of fear. Fear was an important emotion for humans in the early stages of development. Along with the ego, it has helped to ensure your survival. Fear has served you well. However, its usefulness is now reaching an end. The emotion of fear is rampant within the hearts of humans. This is the very reason you are facing so many fears as a collective at this time in your history. Even that which you see in your world as terrorism is an opportunity for you to move beyond fear as a collective.

## 'Allergic' to Fear

Those of Crystal Vibration will easily feel the fear within the hearts of those around them. The challenge comes when they feel the fear and unconsciously reflect it back as amplified emotions. This causes strange reactions to lower vibrational humans. For this reason, those of Crystal Vibration walk lightly, choosing not to invoke fear. When this fear is reflected back, it can cause reactions detrimental to all humanity, as it simply brings out the very worst in humans. For this reason, the early Crystal Children will often take refuge in hiding. They will assume low profiles and not generally show their abilities publicly. At first glance, this will make them seem meek and mild. Do not misinterpret this to mean that they are not powerful. Parents of the first Crystal Children will seek to hide them and keep them safe at all costs. This will change as humans release their need for fear. This was the original message we gave to you many years ago when we first spoke of these children. We said, "If you can make the planet safe for them, they will come." You have listened … and they are coming now.

## Crystal Walk-Ins, Crystal Elders and You

The awakening of the Crystal Vibration within your own physical bubbles of biology is causing changes within each of you that will need your attention. Even though the first Crystal Children will not enter your world for several years, there are many now on Earth carrying varying degrees of the Crystal attributes. These are the bravest of souls who agreed to enter first and test the waters. Working with them to find the greatest possibilities is something many of you immediately feel drawn to. Yet there is much more still to do.

The next several years will also bring Crystal Walk-ins, who will incarnate quietly as adults carrying the Crystal Vibration. As we speak of the Crystal Children, there are many of you who are now identifying yourselves as the Crystal Elders who have been holding these attributes all along. Those who choose to do so will now come out of hiding and share their stories with the world. Also, due to the changes in energy that you have recently moved through, many of you have begun developing some of these attributes to which you are unaccustomed. We see this as an awakening of the Crystal Child within each one of you. As these adults and children continue to enter and use their power, it will awaken these attributes in all of humanity. You are becoming crystalline.

The energy shifts on the Earth at this time are preparing you for further connection to the crystalline vibration. In the days directly ahead, many of you will notice a form of clearing that you did not expect. There will be further pulls into polarity that may seem like separation, rather than unity. Fear this not, and walk forward knowing you are on the path. You will also find your physiology is changing rapidly during this time, with changes in your eating habits, sleeping patterns and general likes and dislikes. Your own internal connections will grow stronger, although most of you have yet to learn to trust those intuitive connections. Relationships may be stretched and re-stretched. Some will break beneath the strain and some will find new levels of communication and love. Those carrying repressed anger may find it surfacing at inappropriate times. During the next few months, please give yourselves and those around you the latitude and room to grow. There will be times when you feel your world is upside down, and times when you equally feel that all is right with the world. During your centered times please take the role of Human Angel and reach out to others to lend them a steady hand. When you yourself are feeling off-center, have the courage to reach out and take the hand that is offered to you. You are becoming crystalline and when you hold hands together, the process becomes magical.

As we watch your evolution unfold, the excitement on this side of the veil is beyond description. You are creating Home on your side of the veil. There are no words to describe the love we have for you. You do not understand the magnificence of who you really are. We ask you simply to feel it within, and hold that truth. That will bring you Home again. It is with the greatest honor that we ask you to treat each other with respect, nurture one another and play well together.

Espavo.

the Group

We have heard a lot from people going through the stretch into polarity that the Group predicted in last month's Beacons of Light. Even in this message, the Group has said that this may be a time to re-evaluate and stretch relationships and personal limitations. Believe me when I say that if this is happening in your life, you are not alone. If you have been feeling stuck in your life, you may want to consider stepping out of your comfort zone now. The

Universe and Spirit will support you more than you know. These are also the times to reach out and touch the wings of another human angel.

## Connecting the Heart

## New Kids ~ New Ways

### From Barbara

I was glad to see Steve and the Group focus this month's Beacons on the Crystal Children. This message is so important. It seems everywhere we turn we are hearing information about children in all areas. The energy of the children is calling our attention. It is time to listen and to be aware of the lessons they have to present to us.

As we see the children with so many new attributes entering our world, we can also see ourselves developing new attributes. Old ways no longer seem to fit our lifestyles. It may be very subtle changes or marked differences. I no longer have a tolerance for certain things that used to be a part of my life. I am feeling a change in the many areas. I am feeling drawn to eating lighter, more toward being vegetarian. At times I find myself slipping back into the familiar old patterns and regretting it because of the way my body feels. I am more aware of color, sounds and scents in my field. Communication is changing. I have the need to say what is on my mind so others know exactly how I feel. At the same time, I am seeing communicating happening more without words but simply with thoughts.

I have always felt children are our greatest teachers. This is why I enjoy being a parent so dearly. Steve and I have two wonderful sons who are now in their twenties. When we first became parents, we were fairly young. As our children grew in life, so did we. We learned from each other. I use to think it would have been better to wait to have children, when we were a little older, wiser and more mature. I thought I might have known how to better handle two very energetic sons, especially with one being a strong Indigo. Reflecting back, I now see it was a perfect time for us to have this magical experience. I can say that we all learned many lessons and have many more in the future. I will look forward to someday having grandchildren if we are blessed with them. For now, I see the light in all children's eyes, the natural curiosity and their excitement for life. I welcome the new children. All children are a reminder to recapture that child within myself and to enjoy with great anticipation the interesting times ahead.

   With all my love and light,

   Barbara

# The Gift

## Secret of the Magi

### December 2002

In many parts of the world, December is traditionally a month that includes the giving of gifts. I remember the excitement of opening gifts on Christmas morning as a child and the wonderful anticipation as I opened each present. I also remember the special excitement as I watched someone open a gift that I had carefully picked out for them.

The giving of gifts is a long-honored tradition that goes back to the beginning of recorded history. The Celtic-Teutonic Druids used to make a gift of their holy plant mistletoe at the beginning of each year. In ancient Rome, gifts were exchanged during the New Year's celebrations. The gifts of those days were simple, as it was common to give a symbolic gift of a tree branch from a favored tree or gifts of food from your garden. Among the Romans, such gifts were called strenae, a word said to be derived from the goddess of luck, Strenia. The idea was to share something you had in abundance, which was touted to bring good luck to the giver in the coming year.

As Christianity gained popularity and began to spread, the early church leaders believed that the custom of gift-giving did not fit into these teachings. In fact, they attempted to prohibit the custom, calling it 'pagan.' Nonetheless, it was too far ingrained in daily life at that point and people continued in the customs of those times and gave gifts behind closed doors. Later the church leaders realized that this was not going to go away and accepted the custom. Shortly thereafter, they embraced the custom of gift-giving, citing the gifts of the Magi to the infant Jesus as the first Christmas gifts.' Similarly, many religions of the world have adopted the giving of gifts into their official traditions.

While most giving was done on a voluntary basis, many leaders throughout history actually enacted laws to ensure they would have plenty of gifts to open. One year, Emperor Caligula of Rome declared to all that he would be receiving presents on New Year's Day and that gifts he deemed insufficient for his stature would be publicly ridiculed. Then there was Henry III, who closed down the merchants of England one December because he was not impressed with their monetary gifts.

Today we are more accustomed to giving gifts at Christmas or Hanukah, rather than New Year's Day. In the United States, this is traceable to the German and Dutch settlers. The English and French dominated settlements continued with the tradition of New Year's Day gifting for many years. The idea of New Year's gift-giving was to greet each other and, though the exchange of gifts, to celebrate one's abundance, with the intent of extending that abundance into the New Year.

We have all been given gifts in our lives, some of them physical gifts and some gifts of opportunity. According to the Group, gift-giving is actually an emulation of the motion of the Universal Energy, which blends all things together. But what is the secret of giving and why did it catch on and stay with us so long? What did the Magi know that we do not know? And how can we use that principle as we move forward into the next stage of evolution? Last month, the Group talked about the 'Color Clear,' showing us ways to uncover our true base motivations in life. If we look for the Color Clear in the tradition of gift-giving, we may uncover an important truth. The Group suggests that we may even uncover the secret of the Magi.

Greetings from Home

Dear ones, we are so very pleased to be with you at this time in your history and evolution. You are sitting at the very brink of the evolutionary edge of mankind at this very moment. Motion is just ahead. From our perspective, this is one of the most exciting events ever unfolded.

## Preparing for the Downhill Slope

As the final work on the magnetic grids is being completed, many of you are beginning to feel the anticipation of what is ahead. Your long hike up the hill is nearing an end. You are feeling the steep slope beginning to lessen and are anticipating the journey with the wind at your back as you start down the other side. It has been a long time since you felt the wind at your back. Before you begin the increased forward movement, we offer you an opportunity to prepare yourselves to make the most out of the journey down the hill. Many have been clearing and cleaning their past to prepare for the most effective movement. You have been clearing yourselves of excess baggage that can hold you back. That is an important part of the work you have been so effectively doing, yet there is more preparation that can be very helpful in the days ahead.

As you have experienced in the past, rapid forward movement has the ability to jar loose even some of the wonderful attributes you have earned. There have been times when your human experiences have been so intense that you have doubted yourselves and even your own connections to Spirit. We see the potential of such movement just ahead and wish to help you find ways to firmly cement in the wondrous gifts you have been given thus far in your journey.

## The Universal Energy in Motion

The Universal Energy has the motion of blending or pulling back together that which was separated to create the illusion of polarity in which to play the Grand Game. In the higher vibrations of the New Planet Earth, all actions that are in accord with the Universal Energy will be supported, and all actions flowing against the motion will find great resistance. The motion of the Universal Energy is the motion of blending. One manner in which this has manifest in your Game has been in the act of gift-giving. The underlying idea of gift-giving is that when you share a part of yourself in any way, you are actually strengthening that part by honoring the Universal Energy. In effect, you are blending your energy with theirs. This has been an honored tradition for millions of years. As one in a tribe wished to interact with another family or tribe, they would approach first with gifts, showing their intent to give of themselves and to blend energy. If the gift was accepted, the giver was no longer considered an outsider and had certain rights within that tribe. Successful world leaders have followed this tradition and continue to do so even today. As you walk into a friend's home and see a gift that you have given them, you feel more at home yourself. Similarly, a bond of unity is formed when a gift given from the heart is received and accepted with grace. Giving gifts to a perceived enemy can shift that perception and therefore shift that reality.

The art of giving is also a powerful expression of abundance, for it places into motion the action needed to transform intent into reality. This is a truth that you have used since your earliest days. To express your abundance to those who are important to you raises your own levels of abundance.

Ah ... but what of the gift itself?

## The Two Parts of a Gift

We tell you there are two parts to the gifting process and both are equally important for the magic of gifting to take place. The first part of the gift is in the act of giving itself. There are many reasons for gift-giving. The way you play the Game now, many of you feel that you are expected to give gifts to certain people to celebrate specific events. The most effective gift that can be given is a gift that is given unconditionally. At first thought, this seems an easy concept, yet putting that into practice may be more difficult than you at first imagine. To give a gift unconditionally means that the gift is given with no anticipation or expectation. At this time in your human experience, all gifts are given conditionally to some degree. We ask that, instead of judging yourselves, you simply and honestly identify the Color Clear, or your base motivations, in the gifts you give. It may just be that the expectation attached is simply that the gift is accepted and coveted. Once you are CLEAR on your expectations of the gift, then it is easier to allow the energy to flow full circle. Understanding the Color Clear in the gifting process helps you to advance toward unconditional giving.

This brings us to the second part of a gift, which is the act of accepting the gift, or that which we have termed 'the Art of Graceful Acceptance.' A gift that is well received is then released to complete the full energy circle that was the highest intent of the gift when it was given. As that energy circulates, it builds and becomes more than it was, even when the gift was originally given. This is easy to understand when you see that a ring on your finger has more value than the individual components because it was a gift from someone you love. We tell you that all gifts increase in value when they are accepted gracefully. Learning and practicing the Art of Graceful Acceptance will be critical to your continued movement into the higher vibrations. The act of acceptance is an acknowledgment of Unity and a statement that you honor and are a part of each other. Your evolution is bringing you closer to experiencing Unity consciousness, and therefore, the Art of Graceful Acceptance will be most helpful as you move forward.

## The Secret of the Magi

See yourself for a moment as someone is receiving a gift you have given. A smile comes across their face as they receive the gift. In that very moment, your heart and your entire being are elevated. If the gift is particularly useful or especially touches their heart, the elevation of your spirit as the giver is that much higher.

Gifts are often used to even the score or pay back some great favor that was given. This actually makes the gift or deed more ingrained in their reality. Important events throughout history have been marked with gifts for that very reason. Gifts are a way to immortalize an event or a deed, and the giver actually becomes a part of the event through the gifting process. All of these are true, yet the important part to re-member is that the act of giving itself increases the value of the gifts and the vibrations of the giver. This is the secret of giving held by many wise men upon the Earth throughout history. The value of the gift given does not compare to the rise in vibration achieved by the giver. The secret of the Magi is, simply ...

## The Gift belongs to the Giver

There were times in your past when you believed that giving gifts would bring you luck in the coming year. Here it is clearly seen that the gifting process will bring a return that will last far beyond the original gift. As in all creations, what you hold as beliefs quickly cross into reality; therefore, the process brought its desired results. Combine that with the fact that the gift itself was a physical representation of the flow of abundance and it is easy to see why this custom became so entrenched into the fabric of societies. You celebrate the day of your birth with gifts and allow those around you to express their abundance as they celebrate your spirit. Humans are so imaginative!

## The Rite of Gift

You will soon sit atop the hill, poised in anticipation for the journey ahead. Most of you are joyfully anticipating the wind at your back once again. It has been years for some of you. As you prepare for the forward movement that is now before you, we offer you a way to add value and stability to the many gifts that have been given you throughout your life thus far. We offer you a time-honored tradition, as this is a practice used here at Home. Many of you will have faint memories of this as we speak. Here at Home, this process you would see as a custom is simply known as 'The Rite of Gift.'

In order to use the Rite of Gift, you must first emulate certain attributes of Home within your reality. Therefore, for the purposes of this rite, we ask you to release the concepts of good and bad, and right and wrong. For the time it takes you to complete the Rite of Gift, we ask you to view things from a perspective of energy and know that positive energy is not good and negative energy is not bad. Know that they are only different expressions of the same energy and that one cannot exist without the other.

We ask you to set aside time for review over a four-day period, reviewing your life thus far in the clear vision of a neutral observer. Please refrain from judging or regretting actions, and the useless human emotion of guilt must be released, or it will taint both your vision and the Gift. Over a period of three days, search for every event that has shaped your life in some way and list them. Even if you only spend 15 minutes each day, by the third day, your head will be filled with the events that have helped to make you who you are. Prepare a list of these events as you re-member them, placing the more important events at the top of the list. On the fourth day, review these events one by one and look for how they have helped to shape your life. As you go down the list, re-member each of the people involved as you make your final adjustments to the order of the list.

Once the list is complete, review each event, reliving each and every one. As you do this review, search for gifts you have received within each of these events. If there are no immediately discernible gifts, then go on to the next, returning to it later. Search fearlessly for the gifts that have come into your life in many forms, and imagine how your life would have been different had you not received those gifts when you did. As you relive these events, identify the people, groups or organizations that were the givers of these gifts and form a new list of those names. Now we ask you to reduce this list to twelve people, groups or organizations that have enriched your life.

Each week for the next twelve weeks, take a name from the list and give them 'the Gift.' Find a way to touch them in some way and thank them for the role they have played in the shaping of your life. Through this gift, you are engraining the original gift into your own cellular memories. If you feel it appropriate, you can tell them how their gift was received by you and the ultimate effect it had on your life. If you can, contact them personally, write them a letter or send a physical gift. Explain how much their gift to you meant and why. Please understand that many will not even be aware they have given gifts. Tell them how they have made a difference in your life and the gifts you received as a result. If you feel the gift may not be well received or accepted, then send them an anonymous gift. If the person, group or organization is no longer in physical form, then give the gift to the closest person, group or organization to them in their honor. Gift from the heart as an expression of your own abundance and the gifts they originally gave you will gain even more value as it integrates fully into your soul.

Do this for twelve consecutive weeks or as long or short as you wish to make your final list. Acknowledging these people and their gifts to you enables you to move forward and use their gifts to the highest potential. Understand that when you make any movement within the Universal Energy, a vacuum is created that will be filled. When you acknowledge and fully accept the gifts they have given, you return the gift to the giver. This action in itself will create a new vacuum that will return to you amplified. This return may take many forms but return it will, for that is a simple Law of the Universal Energy. As these gifts begin returning to you, please accept them with grace and the true honoring of the Unity within all.

Using 'the Gift' in this fashion will allow you to utilize to the fullest extent the wondrous gifts that have already been given to you. This action will allow you to master the attributes you have gained from each event that has shaped your life thus far. The shift from Human to Human Angel is a large step. Stabilizing the gifts you have already been given with the Rite of the Gift will set the stage for the next step forward.

What we have just described to you is the Rite of Gift applied to those who have given to you in the past. Soon, with your new attributes, you will see applications to use this rite to set the energy for those who will gift you in the future. This was the true secret of the gifts of the Magi.

## The Michael Crystal

Within the Rite of the Gift, you will once again see the uses for the Michael Crystal, so we wish to re-mind you of it. The Michael Crystal, by definition, is always received as a gift, although it can be given to oneself. The mark of the Michael Crystal is that it is always given to one who has made a contribution to your life in some way. The intent of the crystal is to share your gratitude through sharing your vibrations held within the crystal itself. It is an excellent tradition and a way to gift from the heart.

Here is how it works: First find the crystal to give. It may be natural crystal, a gemstone, diamond, manmade crystal, or any form of crystal. Then, infuse your energy into the crystal by placing it in liquid crystal (water) overnight, along with a Michael Crystal that has been given to you. This action will charge the new crystals with your intent and the energy of the family of Michael. If you have not yet been given a Michael Crystal, charge the gift crystals with a crystal that has great personal meaning to you. Then, gift each crystal to a person who has made a difference in your life as a Human Angel. Explain to them that the gift is theirs without condition. In the event that they choose to activate the crystal, it can be done by placing it in water overnight with two other crystals that will be passed on in a similar manner to Human Angels who have made a difference in their lives.

We give you the following words to include with your gift as you so choose:

You have just been given a Michael Crystal. Upon receiving a Michael Crystal, please accept it with the highest grace and love, for that returns the gift to the giver and completes the cycle of energy of this gift. This crystal is yours to keep and, even if the physical crystal is lost, it will remain with you on a soul level forever, for it was given on a soul level. It carries the blended energy of you, the giver, and the entire Family of Michael. It will be a constant reminder that you are a part of an important family. Receiving a Michael Crystal means that you are being acknowledged as a Human Angel, within the family of Archangel Michael, who has made a positive contribution in the lives of those around you. Please accept it with the honor in which it was given. Once accepted, this crystal will bring beauty, passion and joy into your life. If you wish to activate this crystal to its fullest potential, find two or more crystals to gift to two or more people who have made a difference as Human Angels in your life. Place them overnight in water with the crystal you have just been given, charging them with your intent and the Michael energy. Then gift these crystals to the Human Angels who have touched your life, along with this message.

It is with honor that we ask you to treat each other with respect, nurture one another with wondrous gifts, and play well together.

the Group

from the very Heart of the Family of Michael

# Harmonics

*Grace in Turbulent Times*

*February 2003*
*Seventh Anniversary Edition*

Greetings from Home

We greet you with the memories of Home, for it is our highest potential to help you re-member your magnificence and take your power. The ascension grid is now taking its final form as the final connections are being made. This is being felt by all of you at this very moment and will be clearly seen as you look back at this time from the overall history of mankind. Please understand also that some who believe they are in charge feel themselves losing their grip and can easily overreact. Please do not judge them, or you, as they all are simply working under a belief system of the lower vibrational realities from which you are evolving. Instead, we ask you to take this opportunity to examine and clear your own house and your own heart of the illusions of three-dimensional thinking.

## Fifth Dimensional Attributes

The reality is that you are fully in charge of your own reality in every moment. If you watch the daily news and think you are a part of what you see, your power as a creator instantly creates that very reality. In the higher vibrations of the fifth dimension, all of your powers of creativity have drastically increased. Even as the ascension grid now connects and moves into its new location, it does so only to help you hold your true power as creators while still in the bubbles of biology that you inhabit. Please be aware that all of your powers of creation have been enhanced in recent days. Please also be aware that all powers of creation of all humans have been raised as well, for it is not possible for one to move without the others. It is, therefore, that we tell you that your intentional use of your abilities as creators is needed now. This is your call to Light. As Lightworkers, you have intent the ability to intentionally spread the light of Home at every opportunity. That opportunity is now before you in a big way.

We ask that you create first the reality of your own heart within your own heart and radiate it outward into the world around you. Start first by creating the highest and best for yourselves, for it is then that you become of highest use to the Universe.

## Blending Realities

Please know that now is a time like never before to understand the flow of the Universal Energy. The Universal Energy is the energy that permeates all things and is even present when all forms of energy are removed from a vacuum. Being energy, the Universal Energy is by nature in constant motion. By observing the motion, you will realize that in all things you have choice as to when you place yourself in the flow of Universal Energy and when you oppose it. In the higher vibrations of the fifth dimension, the flow of Universal Energy and your alignment with it will become more important than you now know. We ask, therefore, that you begin to observe it and compare all of your actions, personally and in collectives, to the Universal Energy.

The Universal Energy is infinite; therefore, since you are in finite form, it is not possible for you to fully comprehend something as simple as Universal Energy. It is because of this fact that we will complicate it just enough for you to understand. The Universal Energy is the base of all things in your world and your game. It is similar to a sheet hanging on a line: if you poke your finger into one side of the sheet, there will be an equal and opposite effect, seen simply as a bulge on the other side of the sheet. This is the mechanics of what you call the 'Law of Cause and Effect.' The cause was that you poked your finger into the sheet, and the effect was the bulge or protrusion on the other side. Likewise, when your game was created, you, as Infinite Beings, took form in finite bodies. This caused a reaction in the Universal Energy that will be in effect as long as your game is in existence. The Universal Energy is, therefore, always in a motion to blend together, that which was separated in order to play your game in a field of polarity. Therefore, from your perspective, the action of the Universal Energy is the action of blending.

In the field of polarity or duality in which you play your game, you see yourselves as separate from one another, when, in fact, you are not. Every action of every person on the entire planet has an effect on every other person. You are actually one Being acting as individuals. This is the nature of the game, for it is this individuality that allows for God in infinite form to see itself. It is this individuality that gives what you call "God" definition.

Please understand that you have a problem with reality: you think it is real. You are, in fact, all part of each other and not separate, as your eyes tell you. As you have now moved into the fifth dimension, that is becoming more evident that ever before. Therefore, actions that flow against the blending motion of the Universal Energy will cause more of a bulge or reaction than even those same actions only ten years ago. There is less tolerance for misdirection of energy because of your evolution. We tell you that right now, more than ever, the thoughts held within your own heart make more of a difference in the collective consciousness than anyone can foresee.

The Crystal Energy has been infiltrating your reality for the last two years. It has helped to provide a base for you to move into higher vibrational status. To many of you, it has helped a lot. It has also threatened some who desperately try to cling to the old ways. Currently some are showing resistance in very public ways. Please understand that even though this is going on around you, you do not have to play this part of the game.

## Harmonic Resonance

Hold the connection to all others first and foremost in your personal reality, and your individual actions will place you firmly in the flow of Universal Energy. This we call the 'Art of Harmonics.' People in accord with your thinking are vibrating at the same rate as you. To put it another way, they are on the same level. Those who are not on your level are different than you, and a human's first reaction is to find fault with them so that you have a reference for the experience of being on different levels. This also serves to justify one's own level. Rather than attempting to change their vibration or yours, it is much easier to find a harmonic resonance between the different levels. Once this single strand is in place that connects your level of vibration with theirs, you both begin to see the similarities rather than the differences.

Placing yourself in harmonic resonance with other people places you in the flow of Universal Energy. Then, even if the world seems to crumble and fall, it will not touch you. You will walk through the falling debris and not be touched because it will not be a part of your reality. We therefore ask you not to believe all that you read, see or hear. Create your highest reality by working with harmonics, and it will spread to all those around you.

In recent days, many of you have been coming together to pray for peace. We tell you that this is admirable and that, any time you come together in combined intent, you make a difference in your world. We will offer you some suggestions for doing this in the higher vibrations of the fifth dimension. Please understand, the universe does not understand negatives. That is an illusion created by the veil, useful for living within a field of polarity. Negatives do not exist outside of duality. As much as you love the word, we tell you that in some ways Peace itself is a negative concept. Peace is a lack of discord or a lack of war. Lack itself is an illusion of polarity, and inside the fifth dimension, where you now reside, the concept of Harmony could be more useful.

The concept of Harmony is honoring the connection to all things and all people. This relates to the highest primary life lesson of Grace. When one masters the life lesson of Grace, it means that they walk in full harmony with all things around them. These are powerful people indeed, for they draw from the harmony of everything and everyone they encounter. Practicing harmony and Grace also places you firmly in the flow, as you honor and emulate the blending motion of the Universal Energy.

## Action Activating Intent

The other challenge is that, when you pray for peace and demonstrate for peace, there is no action behind it that keeps that commitment in motion after the initial action. Therefore, in the higher vibrations of the New Planet Earth, a peace movement will never seem to gain momentum the way it did only a few years earlier. To demonstrate and stand and be counted for peace will not have the same effect as it had in the past. We ask you, therefore, to practice the art of harmonics on an individual level by intentionally finding ways to achieve harmonic resonance with those you are having difficulties with. If there is discord in your world in any area, take it upon yourself to study the ways and lifestyles of those who seem to be in discord with you. Study them and gain an understanding of their beliefs. Even if your level is different and your beliefs are different, this harmonic strand can bridge a very wide gap. By adopting a global attitude towards humanity, you will quickly understand that you are, in fact, much closer than you know.

The joke is actually on you. With as much war as you have experienced during your Game, we tell you that if contact were made by what you call an alien race of beings from another Game, the humans of planet Earth would instantly bond together as one and readily erase all of the imaginary lines you have placed in the sand that you so proudly defend. Then, proud earthlings would stand tall, shoulder-to-shoulder, brother next to brother, and the lines would dissolve.

Practice the art of harmonics and study those on the Earth whom you do not understand. By educating yourselves, you will raise the vibration. As the Lightworker named Einstein once channeled: "It is not possible to solve a problem on the same level on which it was created." First raise your own vibration, making better use of the fifth-dimensional attributes that currently surround you. Do this by educating yourselves on the beliefs, habits and needs of those who seem to oppose you. Then you will find the resonant harmonics and you will find the strands of Light that connect you to them. Once these harmonic strands connect, everyone will begin to see the beginnings of true unity-consciousness develop on planet Earth. As this progresses, there will be no place for war ever again.

The work of Lightworkers is more important now than ever before. Many of you have gone through great difficulty and tribulation just to place yourselves here at exactly this intersection of time and space. You are here to make a difference on this planet. We remind you that the best way to begin is by creating harmony within your own heart and your own reality. It is in our greatest reality to remind you to treat each other with respect, nurture one another, and play well together.

Espavo.

the Group

# Magic Hugs

## April 2003

Greetings from Home

We have been teasing with you all the last few days, attempting to get you to enlighten up. We have been touching you with our wings, grasping you from behind and holding our hands over your face so that you cannot see who you are or who is touching you. We have been attempting to play your game from our side of the veil. In this time that we now spending together, we have created an inter-dimensional time hole. While you are in these vibrations, whether you are reading or hearing these words, you will be fully immersed in the vibrations of Home. Welcome Home. Welcome Home. Welcome Home.

In our time together, we wish to tell you the next step as Human Angels, for you are now taking the process for yourselves. We have told you there is a Second Planet of Free Choice that has already begun. You have moved to graduate status and that the Planet of Free Choice is no longer in the same collective lesson it was only a short time ago. You have stepped firmly in the fifth dimension. You have seen the rules have changed. You have changed them yourselves. You are becoming accustomed to carrying the power within yourselves; still this is a new attribute. Each and every one of you is learning how to carry that power, yet the veils remain firmly in place. You wonder if you are you doing it right. You wonder if you are making mistakes, and we say yes, you are doing all of those things. Fear not the mistakes you make. We ask you to get good at making mistakes for those mistakes will lead you Home.

## Steps into Human Angel

We wish to take you back to the time you were one year old, from the time you were born as an infant to the first graduation period of your first anniversary on the planet. That is the second stage of life and is a very important time for, in that time, you learned lessons that you will remain with you always. In that time, you pick up attributes and energy stamps that you can carry with you from lifetime to lifetime. For each time you do, your own energy is stamped. Each time you do, you carry the energy of that stamp with you evermore. We tell you that if ever there was a human on planet Earth who got through the first year without being touched, they left very shortly after that, for it is a necessity of life to be touched by other human beings. And now you are learning to stamp each other intentionally with the vibrations of Home through your touch. A baby is born into the world and a very wise person looks that newborn in the eye and says with an open heart: "Welcome to Earth. There is no players' manual to read for this game and even your parents will not have all of the answers. The secret of the game you have just begun is to trust yourself, for all of the answers are within. Enjoy your stay, make lots of good mistakes and know that you are never alone." This is followed with a simple but magical hug.

Can you see our excitement? Can you feel the joy we feel, as we see you understanding a concept we have tried to share with you for so long? You are learning to do what we do. Like parents watching their children mastering a life attribute, we watch with excitement as you take the next step forward in your own evolution.

We are in such honor to be in your presence for you are truly the masters of the Game board. Walk tall in that power. Walk tall in that knowledge and make room for the other masters. Side by side, each one of you carries the power within and the inner guidance. Ah, we love it so much that when you make a mistake and you go, "I knew that. Why did I do that? I knew I felt it in my heart." And we say, "Yes you did."

Learning to trust that gentle nudge within your own heart is the hard part for humans. You have agreed to wear the veils of forgetfulness, and that makes it difficult to trust the whisper of spirit as it passes ever so quietly through your own imagination. If you believe a voice to be from the highest of high, you will trust it implicitly and shout it from the rooftops. Yet if you believe it to be your own imagination, then you will disregard the messages as something less than perfect. You can now see our frustration as we most often speak to you through your own imagination. Learning to trust that gentle nudge within you, and then helping each other to trust that with themselves, is the role of the Human Angel.

We sit in Heaven and we try to reach you with our message. Yet most of the time, that message is cast aside. Yet we cannot enter your world and interact in the way we once could because, in the higher vibrations of the New Planet Earth, that would take your power from you. So we will not do that any longer, as you now hold the full power of your own divinity and we are teaching you to use it. We are telling you these things because you are learning to what we do and now you are doing it with each other. That is the secret of the ages, for you are learning to become Human Angels for each other and, when you see an angel falling, you rush to help them up. You are needed more than you can possibly imagine at this time. There is much that is happening for, as more people move into the fifth dimension and experience the new attributes of the higher vibrations of the New Planet Earth, there will be much fear on planet Earth. You have seen a lot of it already. And yet you in the front of the class will be very quietly holding your vibration and holding your light and, when you are asked, you have the opportunity to reach a hand out and be the Human Angel to someone else. You look to us for guidance for we have been the angels who have been working with the humans on Planet Earth all along. And we tell you, never before has this happened. You are writing the books in your minds as you read these words, for we are planting seeds of Light in this message. There are many of you who will write the books. There are many of you who will help to be the Human Angels to help others touch each other. We ask you to find each other and share your experiences and resources with each other, for that will speed the evolution of the Human Angels more than any other act. We are going to give you one important suggestion for being Human Angels this day.

## Magic Hugs

We tell you there is an action that you do that is magical beyond your understanding. You do not understand the power of a simple hug. This is the magic of angels that can only be expressed in human form. When you can come together with physical touch, you have the ability to activate and awaken other human angels. Try as we might, there are times we wrap you in our wings and hold you and hold the energy of who you are, and we cannot have the physical touch you have. With all the might in Heaven, it is not possible for us to touch you the way each of you can touch each other. We reach into your world and we try to help you re-member who you are, and we give you the cosmic winks, and we brush your face with our wings. We hold you in our embrace when you cannot re-member who you are. Even with all of our power, all you feel is the hair rising on your arms or a gentle breeze against your cheek. We cannot touch you the wonderful way that you can touch each other. That is the first and most magical tool of the Human Angel.

## Touch of an Angel

You have the ability as Human Angels in physical form at this stage in your development to make a difference and plant the seeds of peace on a physical level through your own physical bubble of biology. You do so through touch. We have given you the touch of the angel and we will re-iterate it here because this means more than you can possibly imagine. Hold the middle two fingers on your hand together straight with the outer two fingers raised slightly. Touch another's heart with the middle two fingers and you are using the touch of an angel. This act calls the angels of Heaven into action and their energy is then funneled through your fingers into the person's heart. The touch of an angel is a way for the angels to interact with you on a more personal basis.

The real magic happens when you combine the touch of an angel with a magic hug. While in the embrace of a hug, reach around and touch their heart chakra on their back with the touch of an angel. The Keeper uses this technique with every hug for it is a very unobtrusive way to give the touch of an angel. Because of this, he is now known as the 'Keeper of the Hugs.'

## The Second Planet of Free Choice

For you to intentionally touch someone, to find a way to empower them, to give them the gift of their own energy reflected back to them, is powerful beyond your belief. That is the true essence of the Human Angels, and you are doing so well. There are also many of you who are saying, "They cannot be talking about me. They cannot be speaking about me, for I am not a facilitator." We tell you that every one of you reading receiving this message has done work to touch people as a Human Angel in some way. Every one of you has a contract as an awakening master healer if you so choose it. You have been doing it so long, you are wondering if there is something else in store for you. Where is it going? What is the purpose of this? Are we going to now only help other humans on the planet? Ah, not quite. You are in training, dear ones. For as you see an angel falling, help them up. You will work with other humans to become the Human Angels, but that is not where it stops, for there is a Second Planet of Free Choice. You will now become angels to the Second Planet of Free Choice. And that has been the intention of the portals all along, for they will become the pathways for the Second Planet of Free Choice that you will use and you will experience the same frustrations we do as we try to brush your face with our wings or wrap you in our embrace.

There are some of you here who wonder how you are going to take this energy to work with you tomorrow when you go back to work. Oh, it is so easy being amongst the Lightworkers. "But how am I going to do that with a problem boss that I have? How am I going to do that with someone who pushes all of my buttons?" We tell you, start small. If you work from the heart, in that area, holding the energy of who you are, you can do it first with a smile. You can plant the energy of the Angels in front of you before you walk into the room, by touching yourself with the touch of an angel. You can plant the energy of the Angels in the path for yourself before you pick up the phone, before you type the e-mail in the same manner. Please re-member the call of a Human Angel: "There Before the Grace of You Go I." Place yourself first in the energy flow and re-member that you are here also to help other people. As you pass someone in the hall, if you cannot hug them, put your hand on them. If you are talking to someone, reach out and take their hand. If you have the opportunity, touch them with the touch of an angel, and you will leave a lasting impression. Some of your attorneys will argue with us and yet we tell you to do it anyway. Understand that you are not taking their power from them nor creating something for them or changing them in any way. With this act, you are creating a space of pure energy for them to walk into if they choose. You are creating the space of Home, which is something you all share with us and in doing so, they then have the choice of whether they wish to use that or whether they wish to simply let it flow through them unhampered.

## Sharing the Touch

Is a truth unshared really a truth? No, it is not, for you are an integral part of each other. Share your energy with others. Share your heart. Share your hugs. Share your touch. There are so many of you on the planet who are tactile in nature and do not get enough touch. You may have energy stamps that make you hide. Many have frail angelic energy structures, much like the Crystal Children, which makes them vulnerable and sensitive. For some physical touch may be difficult.

You may have beliefs about your physical body that make you think you are untouchable in some fashion. Ah, we love your ingenuity. You come up with some wonderful excuses. Do it anyway. Reach inside and stretch your boundaries. Touch each other with the touch of an angel whenever you can. Hug each other in our name. Take yourselves back to the day you were born and you cried until you were touched. We have all the might in heaven but it is not something we are able to give you. Take your unique gift and use it. Touch one another often. Re-member us when you do, for we will be with you experiencing your touch. Whenever two or more come together with angelic touch, we are there. We are part of your energy. We are pulling you together so that you may blend your energy through touch.

There is much work to do, dear ones, for it is not easy being an angel. There is a reason you have been sitting at the front of the class. There is a reason that you chose to be here in exactly this time and many of you have jumped in without ample rest in between incarnations just so you could be here. Some of you have been carrying the energy so much that you feel like you have been gasping for every breath, that everything has been a struggle. And some of you have had energy disorders and reverse polarity situations because of that. And to you we say thank you, for you have dared to be here at exactly the right moment in time to make a difference on planet Earth, to become the Human Angels. To change the outcome of the Game, sometimes even through your own healing. You have stepped into the fifth dimension. Welcome Home. Welcome Home. Welcome Home.

You are the magical masters of the Game board. You are the Human Angels who are now moving to the next level. We are so honored to be in your presence. All eyes are upon you, dear ones. They watch with such love. We watch with such support. Support each other now. Find ways of helping each other move to the next level without taking their power from them. What can you do to make space on this planet for the Crystal Children? You can make space for yourselves to be empowered. That is what we need the most. Take your place as a Human Angel. Stand up proudly. Hold your light high and there will be no more shadows on planet Earth.

It is with the greatest of honor that we have spent time with you. We tell you during this time, you have not aged. We tell you that during this time, you have felt the vibrations of Home as they are reflected through biology. Take the energy of that. Take the heart of that and create it in every area that you can, and you will make space not only for yourselves but for all those to come. And we thank you for having the courage to do it. Your work and training has begun. Please re-member the magic of a hug for when you were one year old and prior, that first year of life was incredibly important for touch. The touch of an angel is incredible especially if it is applied to the heart chakra of a human. Reach out and touch someone with that. Touch an infant with the touch of an angel, and watch the magic happen. We ask you to reach out and touch someone with that touch, for it honors us and the entire angelic realm every time you do. Oh yes, you get so hung up in where you believe you are in a particular moment that you do not understand that in order to take twelve steps forward there are times when you may take four steps back. Bless those steps, knowing that they lead you forward eventually. Dare to take other steps forward, placing one foot in front of the other. Dare to hold your power within, for that is where you will find us. That is where we live, in the gentle nudges that you feel every day. That is where Home is. Welcome Home. Welcome Home. Welcome Home.

Dear ones, it is with the greatest honor that we ask you to re-member these three simple tools: Treat each other with respect, all of you are one unto another. Nurture one another and find ways to make space for the empowered human and re-member the "E" factor, And most important, play well together.

Espavo

the Group

# Relationshifts

## Somewhere O ver The Rainbow

## May 2003

Barbara and I had just landed at home for two weeks. Whew! Since mid-Jan we had been home a total of 21 days. That sounds like a lot of traveling, but in fact, we both love our work and the awesome opportunities we have to connect family all over the globe. I have always wanted the type of job where I couldn't wait to get up in the morning. I am happy to say that I have it now.

Of course, like anything, there are the times, for example, recently, when the airport shuttle was picking us up at 5 a.m. and I had only three hours before then to pack for a three-week stay in Europe and file our income tax returns. Then there was the time we were leaving the country and had already shut off our mail delivery. Paying our personal bills in the middle of the night is now the normal course of events, but this time, we found ourselves taking our bills-to-be-mailed to the airport, since our mail had been stopped. We arrived at Los Angeles International, only to find that it was no longer possible to mail from any airport in the US due to increased security. So there we were, at the American Airlines Admirals Club, begging the clerks to take our mail home with them and put it in their mailbox the next day. They took pity on us and did.

When talking to other people, they all ask, "Aren't you tired of traveling so much?" When I stop to think about it, since our boys moved out on their own, we have spent most of our time on the road. I'm really not tired at all. I love it! I really think that is because I am blessed to have a supportive relationship and a partner who travels with me. That makes all the difference in the world.

Those of you who have been with us in a talk, seminar or training know that Barbara is a very big part of the work. She is not just someone on the sidelines or behind the scenes. She stands on stage with me and presents the feminine part of the message. I'm very proud of her and the entire dimension she adds to this important work. In fact, we often receive comments about the balance we have in our relationship, as it really shows in our presentations.

Many times, we have walked into a television or radio studio where they only had one microphone and chair set up for an interview; but that doesn't happen anymore, as I won't allow our viewers and listeners to be robbed of the opportunity to experience both of us. Yes, I may be the one who is channeling the

Group, but it would not be as easy to live the life of an empowered human without her standing beside me; and living as an empowered human is just as important as telling others how they can find empowerment.

In my private sessions, I get a lot of questions about relationships and how to create one. The Group says that it isn't possible to create a relationship; it is only possible to attract one, and you can only do that by being aware of the vibrations you are sending out. They disagree with the concept of 'soul mates' and that there is a special person perfectly matched for each one of us. What they say is that all relationships must be 'built.' And that means change.

Last year Barbara and I celebrated thirty years of marriage. I don't say that to impress anyone but to illustrate that during those thirty years, we have had to 'grow' our relationship to keep up with our growth as individuals. Many times it was stretched to the limit. A lot of growth came when I moved into this work. After all, she didn't marry a 'channel.' We see this over and over, where someone 'explodes' into this energy and their relationship does not survive the shift. Not all relationships are meant to survive, however; in fact, the Group has shown me many relationships that were originally set up only so that one person could define themselves enough to leave.

The issue of relationships continues to be a big one as we move forward into our evolution. We have just started a new series of seminars that include a whole section on relationships in the new energy. They are the relationships that are built on the ability to grow together. We call these 'relationshifts.' Here is the latest on what the Group says to watch for.


Greetings from Home

The Earth today is evolving faster than anyone had ever imagined. You have been creating Home as you reach for higher truths to support your higher vibration. Because of the questions you are now asking, you have opened the door to a reality that you have only dreamt of to this point. The new Planet Earth has begun, and you have one foot firmly in both worlds.

You have been worried so much about where you are. "Am I still in the third dimension? Am I in the fourth or am I in the fifth?" Ahh, we love it when you attempt to apply human attributes to our side of the veil. Humans are so imaginative. Some of you even say that the actual dimensional level on Earth at this moment is 4.4324. We think that is so wondrous of you. Although we tell you there are no measurements that can gauge your collective evolution, it may also be helpful to know that all of these concepts are true in some way. Please know first and foremost, the important point to remember is that you are evolving at the speed of love and that is substantially faster than the speed of light.

We do tell you that you have opened a door and are now stepping firmly into the fifth dimension as a collective of humanity. You felt the resistance of some of those who were not ready to step forward. In any event, your advancement is now ready to begin anew. A favorite song of the Keeper is entitled 'Somewhere Over the Rainbow.' We are honored to tell you that you have just taken the first steps 'over the rainbow.'

## Sex As an Expression of Duality

Let us back up and tell you of your history so you will understand where you are going. There was an interesting process that took place as you began the Game of Hide-and-Seek. The Grand Game of Free Choice started within a field of Unity Consciousness, for you were one and an inseparable part of each other. The Grand Game of Hide-and-Seek began as you decided to put on the veil of forgetfulness and walk through the second dimension to find a resting place in the third dimension.

As you passed through the second dimension, you split off into parts of yourself and you gained illusions of duality. In that field of polarity or duality, you found things you labeled 'right or wrong,' 'up or down,' 'black or white,' 'left or right,' 'good or bad,' 'fear or love.' You then chose to enhance the illusion of duality further by splitting into a sexual division for each incarnation in physical form. This was necessary to create the complete illusion of duality within your Game. It has also been the source of great confusion for you as you have evolved.

Effectively, you have divided yourself with the illusion of being two: one male and one female. This lends itself to the belief that you are only half a person, not a whole being, and has caused you to believe there is an exact match for each of you waiting magically somewhere just out of reach. The entire concept of 'soul mates' and 'twin flames' is based on the illusion of duality. This illusion of separation has been important for your primary life lessons.

Please keep in mind that when the Grand Game of Free Choice was set into motion, you were the ones who determined how thick the veil would be. In fact, it was your greatest desire to enter into physical form thinking you were only half a person. That is one of the reasons we laugh loudly and often. The joke is on you, for as you can now see, your creations have been more successful than you first imagined.

The illusion of duality is now thinning, and a new reality is being seen. The trinity will have a deeper meaning as you move into your next phase of evolution.

## Relationships = Harmonic Attraction

It is for this very reason that we tell you the key to moving comfortably into the higher vibrations of the new Planet Earth is balancing the male and the female within each one of you. The concept of your 'alter' energy is not on the outside but rather on the inside of your being. Balance the male and female within you, and you will then attract a complementary harmonic relationship into your field or enhance the one you now have.

It may be helpful to know that it is not possible to create a relationship; it is only possible to attract a harmonic vibration to your own. When you become fully aware of the vibrational pattern you are sending out, then you can easily understand what is returned to you in response. The Universe has only one answer to all requests: "And so it is." Now you know the answer, perhaps you might care to rephrase the question. This process is harmonic attraction, and is the basis of all creation. The first step in harmonic attraction is to balance male and female energy. This process of harmonic attraction is now becoming an important part of your evolution at this time.

The Crystal Energy continues to enter from the Central Sun and flow through your own solar sun, as it provides the new energy needed for the evolution of humankind. The Crystal Energy has been prophesied for many years, and although its return has been misinterpreted by theologians, it is well underway nonetheless.

Please understand that this is the reason some of your world is experiencing war, aggression, confusion and severe lack at this time. This is the very first reaction to feeling the Crystal Energy. As the Crystal Energy is perfectly balanced with male-female energies, it is felt as a threat to those most out of balance within themselves. We find it very interesting that there are very few female leaders on Earth. This is a perfect example of your collective imbalance in this area, and we can promise you that as your collective vibration rises, this too will change.

## Love Relationships

Even though each one of you feels alone to some degree, you are not. In fact, you are each an integral part of each other. Therefore, it will be helpful to understand that all relationships are personal. Also understand that relationships in any form are actually a way of reaching beyond the veil and connecting to the Universal Energy that binds all things together. This Universal Energy is the source of all creation, and all connections to it enhance your rise in consciousness.

All experience as a human is transmuted back into Universal Energy, ultimately finding its way back to Unity Consciousness as an experience of God in human form. This experience is what allows God to see himself-herself. This takes you back to the age-old question: "If a tree falls in the forest and no one hears it, did it really fall?" The answer is "No," for it was not connected to the Universal Energy through shared experience. Therefore, an experience unshared is an experience ungrounded in the collective of the Universal Energy. That is the real purpose of relationships of all types. The act of sharing experience inside a relationship connects the experience to Unity Consciousness by connecting it to the Universal Energy. The most difficult relationship to maintain and the most effective in this process is a relationship of love, for it grounds all experience in a base energy of love.

On a more personal note, because of the energy infusion of the Crystal Energy, many will now experience drastic shifts in their personal relationships. Again, those people with imbalances in male-female energy will see the first and most pronounced change. As you evolve, raising your vibrational level as an individual, you naturally lose the tolerance you once had to vibrational mismatches. Intolerance in the area of unbalanced male-female reaches a critical level, and many relationships will feel this stress. Some will succumb to it and fall apart. The Keeper likes to say: "As you evolve, your tolerance for bullshit goes way down."

## Communication: The Key to Growing Relationships

Now, more than ever, there is a need to consciously work on growing relationships. If you wish to move the relationship to the next level as you evolve, it will need to grow. This can be done with an extra effort to use communication from the heart, placing yourself first in all things. Communication on all levels becomes increasingly important, as this is the first step in balancing the male and female energies within each one of you. Work on increasing communication through words, deeds and the magic of touch. Do this before it becomes critical in a relationship, and there will be little stress when the relationship begins to move to the next level.

Humans have the uncanny ability to convince themselves that they do not need to change, even in the face of great pain. Unlike many other games that exist throughout All That Is, humans have total free choice in every step of their experience as spirits playing a game in human form. Because of this relationship to free choice, you often find comfort in not making any choices at all. In fact, even in the face of great pain, you can seemingly convince yourselves that to change is worse than the pain itself. This is when you miraculously become comfortable with pain.

You are such an interesting race of beings! Please know that this strange ability to be comfortable with your pain will not be as easy as it once was, due to the decrease in tolerance. You are in a wondrous state of evolution, and your higher self deserves so much more than many of you have given it. Now is the time to step into self-love and allow your light to shine, even if it means confrontation or drastic change. In reality, you deserve to be happy.

## Attractive Light

Know that for some of you who choose not to change, the rise of vibration you are experiencing will send out a call for a harmonic match even without your knowledge or your intent. To put it simply, your light becomes stronger and you become more attractive to those around you. Even though it may not be your intent, it will be quite common to attract someone who is a harmonic vibration quite unexpectedly. In this situation, it can be quite stressful if your commitment to another prevents the relationship from happening or taints either or both relationships with the most useless human emotion of guilt.

We ask you instead to prepare for your evolution now, knowing this is a strong possibility. Release your comfort with your pain and know that when you stay in a relationship past the time when it adds to you, it only serves to intentionally dim your light and lower your vibration. This does more damage than you may ever know to all those who are in your field. The children for whom you are willing to sacrifice your own happiness receive a tainted impression of what a relationship really is. They can then be doomed to repeat your same misdirection of energy time and again until they learn to override this energy stamp. If you love them, please save them these painful experiences and give them permission to find happiness by fearlessly reaching for happiness yourself. If you are in a relationship that no longer serves you, make a commitment to shift it to the next level or release it in love and dare to move forward.

## Attracting New Relationships

For those of you who have experienced challenges in attracting harmonic relationships in the past, this is a time when these patterns can easily change. Please know that no one needs a relationship to be whole. In fact, if you are working under that assumption, you are doomed to a 'leaning' relationship from the very start. With this belief, you can only attract one who needs to lean against you or be leaned against. However, if you are choosing to share your life with one who can walk side-by-side with you and share an experience of love, this can be beautiful beyond description. If this is your choice, please start with yourself, checking the vibration you are sending out into the universe instead of looking for someone with this attribute or that quality. In place of looking for vibrations entering your field, first examine and shift the vibrations emanating from your field.

Again, a conscious effort to balance your own male-female energy will set the stage for a change in your experience of the heart. Stand brave and tall, and hide your light from no one. Dare to let all see you in these times, and feel your greatest strength by allowing yourself to be completely vulnerable. Your true strength in these higher vibrational relationships comes from your ability to be vulnerable. Allowing someone to see completely inside is the greatest gift one human can give to another. Do this without reservation, knowing that there truly are no more secrets, and your perceived weaknesses will quickly become your greatest strengths. Your real beauty will shine for all to see, and a harmonic relationship will align itself magically.

## Sex in the Higher Vibrations

There is much happening as evolution begins, for the fifth dimension contains different attributes than those to which you have become accustomed. Much of what you will see in the days ahead is a blending of the energies. Even the sexual energies will blend more than before, for there is much here that is misunderstood. The magic of touch is an expression of divine love only available in finite form such as a human body. With all the love in Heaven, even the greatest of angels cannot touch each other the way you can. Use this as a divine expression of love and communication, to heighten your relationships. Your challenges with sex have come mostly from its use as a device for control. Use it as an expression of unconditional love, and you will discover its highest return.

As you take each step 'over the rainbow,' many of your paradigms will change in regard to sexual expression. We will speak of a few of those now, for they are important for you to understand. In the days ahead, you will see more blending of male and female energy in all areas. This means there will be more understanding of each one's needs and desires. In this state, a heightened sexual experience will be more commonplace as a deeper level of communication is possible in this way. There will be times of change in relationships, when your minds can no longer speak, yet your bodies will have the ability to communicate beautifully.

In the days ahead, you will see an increase in same-sex relationships and multiple-partner relationships. You will see more expression of unconditional love inside committed relationships and in open relationships that will be truly open and not just those avoiding commitment. There will eventually be much less fear of these beautiful expressions of love, as the true beauty of all relationships becomes more understood and coveted.

Please understand that sexual expression is not necessary for a successful life in this Game. It is a finite tool to help re-member the vibrations of Home while in physical form. During experiences of sexual expression, you raise to a vibratory level that we live in all of the time. Although it is not a necessity, we ask that you do not discard this effective tool without consideration. Experiences of self-love through self-sexual expression can be used as a tool of creation that you have yet to fully discover. Some of you believe you will evolve to a heightened state where sex will no longer be a part of your experience. Please know, as long as you are in finite form, you will have this valuable tool available to re-member Home and who you really are.

## Over the Rainbow

As you step 'over the rainbow,' there are magical things you are about to experience and uncover. Will you make mistakes? Of course, you will. Will you learn from them? Absolutely! Play with them now, dear ones, for you are in a new dimensional reality, and as you start stepping over the rainbow, it is imperative you take your power and create your own reality.

Dear ones, the road has not been easy. You have not been able to see who you are, and yet, you have worked so diligently, having only that little spark of something deep inside calling you, guiding you Home. You have felt the pull from Home, felt the deep sadness, felt the fact that you have been separated from your true Home and have not been able to find your way back. Know you are right on the verge of stepping over the rainbow and that you will not be returning Home; you will be creating Home where you are now. Welcome Home, dear ones. Welcome Home. Welcome Home. Reach out and touch one another with the touch of an angel, and dare to make a difference in your reality, starting first with your own happiness in relationships. Hold your light high, and there will be no more shadows on Planet Earth.

You have just taken your first steps over the rainbow. Now you will see that dreams really do come true. It is with great love that we ask you to treat each other with respect, nurture one another, and play well together.

Espavo.

the Group


Big Hugs and gentle nudges
Steve Rother

## Connecting the Heart

## Listening to Love

# By Barbara Rother

I have always said, when it comes to relationships, communication is the key to success. Whether it is a one-on-one love relationship, mother or father with child, friendship or casual acquaintance, communication is imperative.

The most precious thing we can give the ones we love, or anyone who comes into our lives, is our presence, our full attention. Steve and I have an on-going joke with each other: I accuse him of not listening to me. I will have told him something and later he swears he didn't hear it, so I teasingly accuse him of not listening! To some extent, this is true, of course; I have been guilty of this, too. I know we both have a lot on our minds and are not always fully present with each other. This is especially true when Steve is connecting with the Group. I have learned to watch him to see if he is fully with me when I wish to have an important conversation.

It makes a person feel unimportant when they feel they are not being listened to. When a person speaks, it is a sharing of thoughts, many times coming from the heart that should be honored. It is an insult if one feels that their thoughts in words have not been heard. It feels as if what they have said is not of importance. This is taken very personally. Usually it is just a matter of the other person being preoccupied with his or her own thoughts. They may very well honor you in every way, but by not truly listening to you, it may not seem that way.

So often, we are living in the past or future and not fully being in the present moment. When Buddhists talk about mindfulness, they refer to a state of awareness that is fully in the present moment. Focus on the present moment and truly connect with the person you are with. That is true communication. If you are alone, connect with yourself and honor the conversations that play in your own head. This is what I like to call "inner listening." When we honor the importance of our own words or thoughts, then we can honor what all around us are saying. Namaste. The

God in me honors the God in you.

I have made a vow to listen more attentively as an act of love, not only with those I have some type of relationship with but also with all of those I encounter in my life. When someone speaks to me, I practice the act of true listening. Instead of focusing on what I will say when it's my turn, I attempt to truly listen to the person who is talking in that moment. I sometimes fall back into old patterns, and then soon realize I have not truly honored this person in what they are saying. When this happens, I take a deep breath and look into the person's eyes, down to their soul, and deeply connect. Then all my attention is given to what this person is saying. I then am giving this conversation my full respect and attention and, in return, expect the same honoring when it is my turn to speak. With this we both benefit from the conversation.

This is what true communication is all about. We all have so much to offer each other, whether it's in a love relationship or a person we meet on the street. Often at our seminars, I look out to the people who have joined us and say, "I wish I had an hour with each one of you to see what we could share and learn with each other." I mean this from my heart. All of us have different experiences that we can learn from if we listen.

So often a person does not feel they have the gift of expressing themselves, whether it's because they are shy, or they don't have the courage to speak and acknowledge that what they have to say is of importance. The well-meaning people around them may shift into judgment and decide they know where the other person's thoughts are going. So often they are not able to tune into this person's thoughts and energy but, rather, reflect their own truths onto this other person because they haven't heard the communication. Although we are developing the gift of reading each other's thoughts, too often we go into our own thoughts and decide to label them as the other's. Speak your truth so others may clearly hear you, and dare to disagree if they misunderstand you. Be strong in your power, and dare to have others hear what you have to say with love. This is when the flow of communication begins.

Relationships are all about sharing. We want to connect in so many ways, from trivial thoughts to the most important details of our lives. It comes down to honoring each other's space. It is important to read another's energy and know when that person needs to be alone with their own thoughts or if they are open to sharing at that moment. It is important to share thoughts, but know when both people in the relationship are ready to connect the mind totally together; at this stage is when true communication can happen. Practice the art of listening and then be willing to share from your heart. Connect with your body, mind and soul. This is the art of communication. This is what relationships are built on, whether it is a relationship with yourself or with all the wonderful people around you.

With Love and Light

Barbara

# True Beauty

## Experiencing Home

### June 2003

In June, 2003, the Group spoke about the month of May 2003 and how it had been one of the most difficult times for Lightworkers. Some felt their emotions stretched to the limits while others were scattered and unable to focus. Manifestation seemed to be blocked and the path to passion became unclear. Communication that normally gets us through these times was also difficult. There was a practical reason for this, according to the Group. First, we experienced the lunar eclipse and, more importantly, the intense energy of the full moon, which pulled at our hearts before and after. Then, as this crazy energy began subsiding, we had a huge increase in the "Crystal Energy" entering our Earth through the solar flares on our sun.

The Group had been talking about the "Crystal Energy" entering our planet since October 2000, and we had a presentation of the science behind this from NASA in our one-day seminar, Welcome Home. This is the energy that will support our higher vibration in physical form. Normally the Crystal Energy is not felt as it enters our Earth and is stored in the tectonic plates; it is felt as it releases into our atmosphere. But the pull of the full moon left us with a sensitivity that made us feel the energy as it came off the sun. From May 22 to May 28, we had a series of "X-class solar flares" that pelted us with a huge infusion of Crystal Energy. Then on June 9 and 10, we got hit big again.

Everyone was feeling this energy, and that's why were seeing people acting out their fears. The events in Israel showed what these reactions can be like. The energy we felt was a big catalyst for us in many ways. People were being pushed into change like never before as this energy infiltrated into our world. Eventually this energy would support us, but the timing was right for a big infusion then. The Group hinted that August 2003 would be the last time we would need to acclimate to this new energy, as it will shield us from another cosmic energy of some sort. In the meantime, they also said that steps into your real work will pay off tenfold. The actual words the Group used were, "Now is the time to step off the cliff, knowing that the bridge will form magically under your feet."

In this channel, the Group spoke of one of our deeper meanings in life: the search for "true beauty." Sometimes being stretched and pulled can leave us in self-defense mode and not thinking about the important things. Here they took this opportunity to re-mind us of what is really important.


Greetings from Home

We are pleased to be with you as you take the next steps now in front of you in the game of Free Choice. We begin each of these messages with the three words that most accurately reflect the pure love from Home. The phrase "Greetings from Home," and particularly the word "Greetings," is a vibrational signature that all beings in all dimensions recognize as having the same meaning. These words are a trigger that brings back the memories of your place of first origin. When you hear or read these words, please allow yourselves to feel the full impact, as they unite all of the time lines in which you live, and instantly place you in the state of Now. Once again we say, "Greetings from Home."

## Semitransparent Veil

The veil you have worn for so long that keeps you from seeing your true nature is n now beginning to thin. This is an event you have been working towards for a very long time; yet now it is beginning to take place, the immediate effect is somewhat different than you first imagined. As you see the veil thinning, your tolerance is growing short to vibrational mismatches and lower-vibrational ways. The more disturbing effect of the veil-thinning is the sense of inner sadness you carry after re-membering Home.

We understand your sense of missing Home. Even as children, many of you found yourselves inside a physical bubble of biology only to cry out, "I want to go Home." Please know that as your evolution continues, you will begin to see into other dimensions of time and space. There will also come a day when you will walk with a semitransparent veil. You are in training for that now, and that is the reason many of you feel the cloud of sadness that overshadows your reality. The first glimpses of Home, as seen through the semitransparent veil, bring back a flood of long-hidden memories of true beauty.

## True Beauty

Upon entering your game, it was necessary to hide from yourselves the memories of Home and the true beauty that permeates everything here. This was the most difficult decision for some of you to make and the ultimate sacrifice; however, it was a necessary decision to enable you to play the Game of Hide-and-Seek. What happened in the very first incarnations of Earth was that you hid the beauty within the Game board. You knew you could not exist without regular infusions of true beauty, so you carefully placed openings in the veil that you could find as you played the Game. These were like crystals you placed on your own path to find later. In fact, many of you are actually motivated entirely by the search for true beauty. You knew from an early age in your evolution as humans that the preservation of beauty was an important part of bringing Home to your side of the veil, or Heaven to Earth. This is the reason you discovered the importance of the preservation of the arts in your societies. The arts are important crystals that you have placed in your own path to find at the exact moment you need them. The search for beauty throughout history is something shared by all cultures.

What we share with you now is that all beauty is a direct reflection of the memories of Home. Time spent in creating or appreciating beauty in any form is one of the most spiritual experiences of mankind. It rejuvenates the spirit within because it re-minds you of Home. It was a way for you to ensure you would never completely forget Home. Much of what you see as the Earth is designed as a direct reflection of Home, just the way you are a direct reflection of what you call 'God'; therefore, finding beauty in the spirit of the earth is particularly rejuvenating.

There are many levels of vibration that exist upon the Earth. For the sake of this message, we will limit this discussion to only some of the levels you perceive. The minerals, the plants and the animals are all different levels of vibration that exist within the same dimensional reality in which you play the Game. Each vibrational level is actually a different reflection of the true beauty that exists within the unified vibration of Home.

Since the true beauty in your world is a reflection of Home, you have emulated that action by reflecting it further. How many poems have been published in attempts to describe the beauty of a tree? How many landscapes have been painted to capture the true beauty that is available to each of you upon looking out the window? How many songs have been written in attempts to capture the beauty of love? Since all experience makes its final connection to the Universal Energy through shared experience, these are effective ways to reflect the beauty of Home in the human experience. Likewise, since "beauty is in the eye of the beholder," here you not only see the reflection of the beauty of Home but also the true beauty of the person who reflected it.

## The Gift of Reverse Eyes

If you understand that your emotions are the conduit between your higher self and your physical being, you will understand why you feel emotions every time you perceive beauty in any form. This is also the reason we encourage you to 'feel,' as it is the quickest way to move you to a higher state. Everything that you feel when you see anything that is beautiful in your world incites the same vague memory of the true beauty of Home that each of you holds hidden within. When you take in beauty in any form, your emotions are activated and stirred.

Since the day the Keeper awoke, he has noticed a phenomenon that he calls 'reverse eyes.' He has always perceived himself as a 'manly man,' yet since his awakening, every time he is touched with true beauty in any form, his emotions express through tears. He calls this 'reverse eyes' because he does not cry when he feels pain or is sad; he cries when he sees something truly beautiful. He still attempts to hide this at times, but we are working on that.

In the fifth dimension, the human attribute of emotions will play a bigger part than ever before, for true beauty cannot be seen; it can only be felt. This is the balance of male-female energy within each of you. Know that when your heart leaps and you feel the beauty flooding through your soul so strong that it brings you to tears, you are actually seeing Home. As the veil thins even further, this beauty will be felt and can either flow through you in a powerful expression or can be resisted and held within, only to be expressed as frustration. The creation of Home is now dependant upon each one of you feeling and expressing this beauty within yourselves.

## Balance and Kundalini

As you move into the higher vibrations, there is a need to balance the male-female energy, as it encourages this flow of beauty throughout your being. If you fall too far into the feminine energy, the flow of true beauty will overload the emotional circuits and make this shift far more difficult than it needs to be. If you are too far into the male energy of the powerful warrior, you may never see the beauty and miss the opportunity altogether. Here we ask that you balance your raw power with your sensitive emotions and watch as the magical transformation takes place.

These are also ways in which sexual energy can be most effectively utilized. The Kundalini energy is activated when all of the chakras are open and flowing. That is also when the soul can most easily balance your physical energy. This is felt as the sexual energy in most humans, and is largely misunderstood because of old belief systems. The intent of a soul taking form as a finite being is to experience the beauty of Home in ways that can only be done in that form. The challenge comes from the fact that your experience of time is linear; therefore, you often live in the past or the future and find it difficult to be in the Now. True beauty can only be experienced in the moment of Now, for in fact, it is the only part of linear time that is not illusion. The experience of sexual energy grounds the soul instantaneously within the physical body and pulls all the inter-dimensional aspects of one's self into the experience of Now. When a soul experiences orgasm in physical form, it is instantly centered in the Now. This is an experience of the beauty of Home, as Now is all that exists on our side of the veil. This experience also allows for a natural balance of male-female energy to be reset.

Above all, when attempting to balance your energy, it is most important to not take yourself too seriously. As with all spirit, you have an internal balancing mechanism that will activate when needed if you are not intentionally overriding it because of a belief system that you are attempting to sup-port. When you feel the beauty in any situation, simply allow yourself to fall completely into it and fully experience the passion of the expression of beauty as it flows through you. Then bask in the balance and the experience of Now. The expression of true beauty through your being will set you into a higher state of creativity. You will then find ways of express-ing true beauty with every step you take and in all situations. That is the creation of 'Heaven on Earth' and is underway at this very moment.

## The Quadrant Shift

The truth is, many of you have moved vibrationaly but are still living daily life in the lower vibrational pattern that you set up for yourselves. That is the reason you will now see much change in your personal lives over the next three years. You passed the final marker to end the great planet of free choice approximately three years ago. You are now setting up a new collective pattern for all of humanity. The staging for this shift is divided into four parts and extends from the year 2000 to the year 2012. You are now completing the first quarter of the initial staging process.

Know that when the Game of Free Choice was first set into motion, the year 2000 was to be the pivotal time when the final outcome of the game would be determined. The highest outcome possible was to drastically shift your vibrational pattern and to step into a new dimension of time and space, while remaining in the same bubbles of biology that you inhabited. At the beginning of the shift, however, an interesting event happened – you began to move more quickly than anticipated. This created great excitement throughout all dimensions, and the shift to prepare a new road ahead began. You will note that very little of your prophetic writings extend beyond the year 2012. Even now you will find that many of those prophecies are no longer valid, as they have been altered to reflect the drastic vibrational shifts.

It was this unexpected move into higher vibrations that brought so many beings that are here now watching you from inter-dimensional realities. No, they do not control you, although some of them would like you to think that. Please do not give your power to the drama they create, for it effectively takes your true power from you. Understand that no matter what you see in the immediate future, there are no beings anywhere who can control you in any way unless you give your permission to play that game with them. You may wish to reevaluate your natural human attraction to drama if this enters your reality in any way.

You have dipped the quill in the ink and hold it firmly over the parchment, ready to write your next script. We think it quite humorous that you read these messages, looking for hints of what is ahead when we cannot wait to see what you write next. The excitement on our side of the veil is greater than you can imagine, as we watch with love as you take each step. Because of your advancement, we no longer enter your Game to move you into position. You are now in the Second Wave of Empowerment, and here, it is up to you to create for yourselves; therefore, to continue those interactions now would only serve to take your power from you.

The change in the way that we interact with you is the reason so many of you feel you have temporarily lost your way. Your guidance seems to be gone, and you do not know where to turn. Even when you know where your passion is, it seems to be blocked or hidden from view. Trust that these feelings will soon dissipate and leave you in a heightened state of creation. All change leads to something better and is part of your evolution at this time.

Now we show you the magic and stand back as the sorcerer's apprentice plays with the magic wand. It is our deepest desire to see the magicians take their place as creators on the Game board of Free Choice. Find the beauty in every moment and in all things you experience, and all the unimportant things will fade from view. For in the moment when you find the true beauty, you will find yourself Home again. It is why we now share with you another phrase that is a vibrational signature. We now ask you to find the true beauty in these words:

Treat each other with respect, nurture one another and play well together.

Espavo

the Group

# Connecting the Heart

## Beauty Within and Around Us

## By Barbara Rother

Steve and the Group talk about the beauty all around us. We cannot begin to be aware of the true magnificence before we connect with the beauty within our own beings. I have found that when I am truly centered and at peace with myself, I am open to appreciating all around me. It is when my confidence is high that I truly like who I am. Colors seem a little brighter, people a little nicer. The entire world seems at its best; my excitement for life comes alive. When I am not connected to myself – rushed, stressed, feeling judgmental about myself – everything appears to be just a little off. Our perspectives affect how we view the world around us.

When we become still and open to our true selves, only then can we see the beauty within our very being. It is the centering of our soul. When we quiet our minds and relax with the natural rhythm of our breath, we can be centered. Enjoy your own company. Enjoy time alone, and celebrate the person you have become.

When we honor the physical person who we have matched with our spiritual selves, then we can honor others. Recognize the beauty in yourself and then see how easy it is to be aware of all the true beauty around you. In our seminars, we talk about putting yourself first. Please remember, this is not being selfish but only taking care of you. When you give to yourself, you have more to give to the world. Take the time for you.

In this hectic life of ours, we so often forget to pamper ourselves. Steve and I have had a very busy schedule so far this year. It has been wonderful traveling and connecting with Spiritual Family; yet, for July 2003, we will take the whole month to be at home. This will be my rejuvenating time. I will be busy with all the details of Lightworker, but it will also be a time for me to ground. I will take time to walk along the beach, exercise more, read, connect with family, and do things I enjoy while at home.

This will be my time to center and enjoy the 'Now' time. When we start traveling again in August, I will have more of myself to give because I will have given to myself first.

I wish for each and every one of you some special time just for you. Take the time to revitalize. Honor the person reflected in the mirror everyday, and find the beauty there. Appreciate who you are in every moment. Those around you will see you as you see yourself. See your inner and outer self as one. Then you will truly be open to all the beauty around you and perhaps begin to see all Selves as One in the beauty of the Light!

With Love and Light,

Barbara

# The Phantom Death of Planet Earth

## July 2003

I was sitting at my computer in our new Lightworker Family Room talking to people from the US, Ireland, the UK, Holland and Turkey. It's great to be able to communicate with family all over the globe like this. I had just mentioned to people in the room that I was going to have to leave the Family Room to finish writing the Beacons when someone asked what the Beacons was about this month. I proceeded to tell her. I became aware of the faint laughter over my shoulder. By the time I came back 90 minutes later, I had to tell her that the whole thing had changed. So many times, I think I know where they are going only to find that they have different ideas. Such was the case with this message.

In the private sessions I do with the Group, we talk to a lot of people who have experienced the Phantom Death. Basically this is the original time that we scripted to leave. Now that we have the opportunity to stay, many of us choose to stay instead of dying. In all instances, when I talk to someone who has experienced the Phantom Death, it's easy to see that their entire lives took a drastic turn at that very moment. Now the Group says that the same phenomenon is happening with our relationship to light. They say that from a cosmic perspective a big sign is hanging on the Earth that says: **"CAUTION - Phantom Death in Progress."**

## Greetings from Home

We are so pleased to be with you at this time to watch as the magicians of the Game board awaken from the dream. We see you from a perspective that we love to share with you, for that is the view from Home itself. Our greatest hope is to guide you in the new ways. You are not the same people who you were only a very short time ago. You are now stepping fully into the second wave of empowerment, and that is changing everything that has gone before. The first wave of power was 'follow the leader' and the second is now 'follow yourselves.' Yes, this sounds simple, yet it is not. For you to function in the second wave of power, it is necessary for you to totally re-evaluate every paradigm you have created thus far.

## Dawn of the New Light

You now emanate a new light. We have called you Lightworkers, for you spread the base energy of love through the light that you share. Even as your advancements lead you to a new understanding of your purpose here on Earth, your advancements in the area of science will also begin validating even more of the higher truths you have only been able to prove in your hearts thus far. The energy we have called light will soon take on new meaning, as your sciences are now right at the edge of great discoveries about light. This will start a shift in the scientific community that will have far-reaching effects on the way humans perceive themselves.

For those of you with scientific curiosity, we will give you some hints here, and the rest of you can skip this paragraph. That which you have seen as light is only a small portion of the energy band that carries the full energy from Home through the Central Sun to you. The spectrums of light for which you have no perception exist over a band of other dimensional realities that you cannot see yet. The way to access these dimensional realities is through a series of 90-degree turns. Even the ancient Egyptians knew that to enter the afterlife, as they called it, a 90-degree turn was necessary. We have planted seeds of this ancient wisdom within earlier messages and now those seeds are taking root. What your science is on a path to discover is the relationship of light to magnetics. That relationship is exactly 90 degrees.

Recently we showed the Keeper a new color band that he had not seen before. We tell you that he was very excited when we showed it to him, until he realized that the words necessary to share this experience with others did not yet exist. Yes, there are many other spectrums of color beyond what you call the four primary colors. The point to remember here is that the other bands of color do not exist outside of those four vibrational bands but, rather, within them.

It will not be long before you begin to understand how simple light really is. And even though you may not see the other bands of light with your eyes just yet, you will be able to see the evidence and the reaction of this light. You may not know it, but we tell you that you can see this even this very day. That is the important message that we share with you now.

## Welcome to the Fifth Dimension

You have stepped fully into the fifth dimension and are just now acclimating yourselves to this energy. Even as we say these words, many of you find yourselves getting excited, looking forward to the possibilities of new power and new abilities. Yes, that is true, yet with this same advancement comes a new, sobering responsibility to use those abilities to their fullest. This is the importance of utilizing the second wave of power.

## Phantom Death of Light

Many of you have experienced the Phantom Death, when you had a specific opportunity to leave and return Home. These exit points in your linear time line were placed there in the first stage of life during your planning session. Those of you who have experienced at least one Phantom Death know that after that demarcation point, your life took on a new focus and turned the equivalent of 90 degrees. Ahh, yes, now many of you are recognizing that you had a Phantom Death after all. We tell you today that it is the light itself on planet Earth that is experiencing the Phantom Death. When you look back at this time in your history, you will see a new relationship to light from this day forward. This is truly the Phantom Death of Planet Earth and a new starting point.

## The Crystal Energy

The Crystal energy has been filtering in from your Solar Sun and is being stored in the tectonic plates of the Earth. The recent infusion of energy has caused much stress to those of you sensitive to it. In fact, most of you who call yourselves Lightworkers are sensitive to this energy as it enters your world. Many of you have felt lost and disconnected. You may have found your emotions erupting at the most inappropriate times. The sensitivity you have to this energy is the same gift that makes you a Master Healer, so fear it not. Yet, understand that you will acclimate to the energy as it enters your world. Continue to watch the solar flares for signs of this energy and this new light entering your world. It is here to provide you with the magnetic base in which empowered humans will thrive. The energy infusion was needed, for you are about to turn an important corner. The 90-degree turn will now begin this next month. August 2003 will be seen throughout the cosmos as the Phantom Death of the old light. Even as little as two months ago, the times directly ahead were uncertain. It was not known whether the strong infusion of the Crystal Energy would serve the highest good, or tip the delicate balance as it has in the past. Know that you have done well and the stress you have dealt with has served a much higher purpose in acclimating this energy.

Ah, but you are not the only ones feeling this energy. Those advanced children of Indigo color are feeling this energy most of all. They will feel disoriented, confused, anxious, and in discord as this new light enters your world. It may seem to them that their magic has disappeared and this may cause them even more stress as a result. Be patient with them during this time, dear ones. They are here doing a very difficult job and deserve your love, guidance and respect.

## The Secret of the New Light

There are two ways to work with light in your Game. One is to reflect the light and the other is to be the light. You have so often thought that it was best to reflect the light, for it was very difficult for you in the first wave of power to see your true magnificence. Without seeing your true self, it is not possible to be the light, only to reflect it. Although there is no difference in the outcome, and one way is not better than the other, by not having both options, you are limiting the amount of Lightwork you can accomplish.

We tell you now, there is a direct correlation between the acceptance of your true power in the second wave and the ability to emanate the new light. Take responsibility for your own happiness and your own reality, and have the courage to choose again if your circumstances do not support your spirit.

Now for the secret, for humans love secrets … The light is not outside of you; it *is* you. You are the light. Even the light entering as the Crystal energy is actually a reflection of your own. That is the reason you feel it so strongly as it enters your reality. This new light in the form of the Crystal Energy is interacting with and changing the magnetics of Earth as it enters. This is why science may now see the connection between light and magnetics. At first, you did not feel it until it was released from the tectonic plates into your dimension. Now you have acclimated to the energy to such a degree that you feel it even as it enters from the Sun. That is the reason your times have been filled with amplified stress. The challenge is that you are not accustomed to being the light and allowing this energy to flow through you, igniting your higher light within. We ask you to find ways to let your light shine, for that holds the key to feeling comfortable as the changes to the Earth magnetics proceeds. Dare to stand in the most difficult situations and allow your own light to emanate from you. For that work, we offer you a valuable tool.

## Spiritual Confidence

Yes, we have watched you and know it is most difficult to be God in human form. Your egos that have served so well to ensure your survival have also kept you from taking your full power. Now, even as you are advancing past the need for an ego, it still haunts you, overshadowing your every move. Yet, when you understand that your true selves are Spirit and not human, the ego holds you no longer. Therefore, we ask to you to find the spiritual confidence within all of you at every moment. Access that Spirit within for even a moment, and feel the confidence that lies dormant deep within your soul. Then you have a tool that can be utilized in the most stressful times. Stop, breathe, and feel the Spirit within. Simply feel the smile of spiritual confidence easing its way to your face. It is a subtle smile that can be carried with you throughout your day. Re-membering it is there is the most difficult part. That is all that is needed to face every moment of every day with the confidence that is your soul birthright. That subtle smile gives birth to the full spectrum of light that is yours alone. That subtle smile is the most effective way for you to be the light in the days of change that lie ahead.

Take that knowledge and intentionally share your special spectrum of light with every person willing to look your way. Stand fully in the truth and beauty of your light and own its power fully. Touch others with your light openly and freely when it is accepted. Then you will find it becoming stronger with each application. This is the full power of Home expressed through the most beautiful beings who have ever taken finite form. You are Lightworkers ... but even more, you *are* the light ... and we love your light more than you could ever know. We know your times are challenging, we know there are times when you cannot clearly see where you are going or what is happening. Please do not live your lives in anticipation of some magical day when everything will be right in the world. Please know that you have the ability to create that world in your own field this very day. Start by accessing the spiritual confidence that lies within you and you will see the new light upon Earth.

We so enjoy the time together with you in this fashion, for you invite us to play in your game in this special way. Ah, but it is more than that, for you invite us into your very hearts and we honor that invitation more than you will ever know. That opening of your heart gives us the unique opportunity to plant the seeds of light that will help you re-member who you really are. Like proud parents watching with the greatest love as their child stirs from sleep and opens its eyes to make soul contact with the parents, we too are deeply honored to be here watching as you are now stirring, awakening from the dream. Know you are never alone. We ask you to re-member, this is a wonderful Game you are playing so treat each other with respect, nurture one another, and play well together.

Espavo.

the Group

## Connecting the Heart

## Awakening to New Light

### By Barbara Rother

Steve and the Group talk about the Phantom Death of the old light. They say this will be felt beginning in August 2003. I know the energy of this shift will be high and we can anticipate it with excitement and maybe with a little hesitation because, as with any change, it may be a little uncomfortable. Stepping out without our safety net and daring to fly high in our own energy can be scary, but yet quite exciting.

I feel I experienced leaving my old light almost four years ago. However, I am sure I am ready for another shift soon. This was when I chose to trust Spirit and leave my career that was my safety net of twelve years. I dared to trust myself that I was to join Steve in our Lightwork on a full-time basis. This was a huge leap of faith. I have never regretted that choice.

Last night, I joined co-workers from my past job for a reunion and celebration of one of their birthdays. Once in a while in the past few years, I had been in touch with some of these people, but last night was an awakening moment of looking at my past – who I was then – and seeing my present – who I am today. It was like stepping in and out of two different dimensions. How happy I was that I could return to be in my reality of my present life where I have created my new light!

The people I reconnected with are special, warm-hearted souls, especially one dear friend who will always be in my life as a friend and sister, Jean. They all helped me on my path of self-awareness, mostly in positive ways but at times in negative ways. Duality very much played a part in that experience. For twelve years, this was my reality of daily existence that my world revolved around. For the most part, this was a rewarding job. How often we get caught up thinking our jobs are who we are! I see people who have lost the sparkle in their eyes. They appear to be existing in life instead of creating. I so encourage people to: "Dance in your passion and play in your joy, every day of your life," as Steve and the Group say.

As I sat enjoying the conversation, in which we were catching up with each others' lives, I felt myself falling back into who I thought I was for so many years. Then I took a deep breath and began celebrating who I am today. It was almost as if my spirit was lifting me above my body to look down on my past and present. With the exception of a few of these people, nobody understood exactly who I have become in my new life. They commented that I have a glow about me and about how happy I looked, but it was clear that my new reality was not theirs. And I know that is okay.

I drove home with thoughts spinning in my head. I felt as if I had just revisited my past. I know in order to create a new life, you have to come to terms with the one you have left behind. This is the Phantom Death of light that I can see that I just experienced. I was feeling mixed emotions about who I was all those years. The job served its purpose, but it had its moments when I allowed others to take my power and to feel less than who I know I am. One of the happiest moments was when I was leaving the old job and I told my boss how I really felt. I told her. "I feel so connected to who I really am when I'm doing my Lightwork with Steve, and so disempowered when I come into the office." This was the beginning of my communication I have developed with others and myself. I must speak my truth. This is my empowerment. Even though it may have been something she did not want to hear, I think my boss understood. She wished me well, as did all my co-workers. I am now able to step back and feel any negative emotions from the past and know they were crystals on my path of awareness. I am thankful for all the wonderful, joyful memories I experienced during that time of my life, too.

It is exciting to want to reinvent yourself by creating your new life, your new light, but it is important to never forget your past. Each day we have experienced is a stepping-stone to who we are today. We can do a partial or total makeover with who we are, but remember to connect with your center being—that is the Spiritual Confidence that the Group just spoke of. This is your core personality no matter how many levels of growth you go through. Access it and you will find your power.

Every day I discover different, new areas of who I am and who I am becoming. I thank my past, I embrace my present and can't wait to see how brightly my newfound light will shine in the future!

With Love and Light,

Barbara

# The Grey Zone

## Birth of the Spirit-Body

## August 2003

I do a lot of private Re-member sessions on the phone where people can view themselves from the perspective of the Group. Recently in these sessions, people have been talking about the shift of energy being felt all over the globe. The most common complaints are anger and frustration coming up and old issues returning that were dealt with long ago. These are signs of advancement, according to the Group, and they even talked about them in last month's message (July 2003). Even knowing that is not enough to keep us from being overwhelmed by it at times. Here, they offer practical advice for taking the next step forward. They watch with love as we get wrapped in our dramas. They say, simply, enjoy the dramas, just don't take them too seriously. The good news is that this may be a time when our physical bodies can catch up to the changes and stop resisting the shift. For many, this will be an easier time to lose weight.

Last month's Beacons was all about the Phantom Death of Planet Earth. Now we are in the process of moving into a higher state, something we have been anticipating for a long time. It's obvious to most of us that we have not made it there just yet, so where exactly are we? What is the door that is in front of us and how do we open it? To answer that, the Group reminded me of the words of Rod Serling at the beginning of each Twilight Zone TV episode: "You unlock this door with the key of imagination. Beyond it is another dimension, a dimension of sound, a dimension of sight, a dimension of mind. You're moving into a land of both shadow and substance, of things and ideas. You've just crossed over into the 'Grey Zone.'"

Greetings from Home

We greet you with the love of Home, for that is the one energy all beings everywhere recognize and feel deep within their being. Dear ones, your courage as spirits masquerading in human form is once again at an all-time high. The energy entering into your world at this time is far beyond anything you have ever before experienced. The next few months will be times of change and introspection as you realign your energy fields.

## Adjusting the Matrix

Please understand that, as you step into higher dimensions, your own energy matrix must adjust to accommodate the higher energy you carry. However, this adjustment is causing you great stress at this time. We remind you that from a higher perspective, your work as a spirit in human form was to define the indefinable, to give form to the formless and to define the very essence of God. You do this by disguising your infinite form as a finite being. This is a frustrating experience in itself, but then add to it the agreement you made to place the veils over your eyes to keep from seeing Home, and you have created an environment full of internal frustrations. Here, your heart knows there is a higher truth; yet, try as you might, you cannot see it.

Many of you awoke in physical form saying, "What did I get myself into?" After a while, most of you made your peace and adjusted to the restraining form of the physical body. Now your greatest dreams are being realized. You are changing the physical body and the energy matrix. Yes, we know, it is not what you were expecting. Be patient, dear ones, as you know from your history, these advances will only be seen in hindsight. Your physical changes have been advancing rapidly over the last ten years. When you look back at this time in the evolution of mankind, it will seem as if these changes happened in the blink of an eye. Yet most of you are asking when something will change. Look behind you, dear ones, for a gauge on your advancements and you will readily see that you have moved more in the last six years than most of you have in the last six lifetimes.

## Relax the Physical

Although not everyone is on the same cycles, we will nevertheless address the shifts that are affecting the majority of you at this time. Even if these attributes do not affect you directly, they will affect many of those whom you facilitate. At this time in your movement, you are moving out of the field of duality. Your first reaction to this was a physical one. In most cases, the physical body felt threatened by this change and attempted to stabilize this growth by gaining density. At this current stage of evolution, the physical body is now stabilizing. As your emotional body now stretches to accommodate these higher energies, the physical body can reset its matrix. The next several months will be a good time to effect change in the physical form for most of you. Please understand, you are not your physical being, and making it smaller or more desirable in your way of thinking may not make you any more at ease with being in physical form. For the time being, the pressure is off your physical being as the emergence of the spirit-body begins. Therefore, your physical body no longer needs to react by protecting itself with density. We tell you that when you do return Home, you will see what a perfect container your physical body was for your energy. You will also see how sometimes your judgment of that same body creates the conditions you think you must alter. Humans are so ingenious; we would never have thought of that part of the Game.

## The Emotional Realignment

The emotional template is now shifting drastically for many of you who are leading the way in this new energy. This brings to the surface the emotional frustration you have stored in your emotional matrix since birth. Frustration unexpressed will give rise to releases of anger. Most of you will aim these anger releases toward safe, but generally inappropriate, targets. We ask only that, in these times, you purposely move away from judgment, as that is an illusion of polarity and will effectively trap you in the old energy. As your emotions arise, you will also find the need for different emotional stimuli. This is the realignment of the emotional energy matrix, which houses you in physical form. Dare to reach further and try new things, as these stretches can lead to a new emotional dimension of your soul. Embracing your dark side during these times can help to ease the frustration many of you have experienced since birth. Many of you have already found yourselves erupting in an intense wave of sadness and tears. This is an expression of your dark side that is beautiful beyond your understanding. Are you aware that, even as you feel completely alone in your tears, we are standing right next to you, cradling the very essence of your being as you make these adjustments to your emotional energy matrix? This is the process of balancing the male-female energy within you that we have spoken of so often. The realignment of the emotional structure will enable the emergence of the spirit-body, for emotions are the link between the spirit and the physical being.

## The Pull into Light

In balancing the new emotional matrix, you will begin shifting your basis out of duality. You will adopt the attitude, there is no real good or bad, right or wrong, up or down or black or white. The illusions begin to fade and a new perspective – that of balanced emotional beings – begins to emerge. That can only take place in a very special place you have created. Your fascination with Light will soon bring a new understanding of the reality in which you live. The seeds of Light you have planted have been sprouting for the last twenty years. Your fascination with Light has resulted in "lite" potato chips, lights in your shoes and even "lite" beer. This has served you well to draw your collective attention to reach for the Light. As Lightworkers, your commitment is to spread Light on your planet is some way. This has served you more than you know, for it has motivated you to define Light. It is that definition of Light that will lead you to define that which you call God.

The next step is to embrace the whole. No, we are not asking you to now swing into darkness, for that was the way of old and an expression of polarity. Now we ask you to blend the light and dark, for that is where the real beauty is held. Embrace both parts of yourselves, for that is where you will find truth. Only by embracing the dark can you see the real beauty of Light.

## The Grey Zone

Between Heaven and Earth, there is a magical place. Between Light and dark lies a reality beyond description in your current terms. We will call it the Grey Zone. Sounds drab, does it not? Believe us when we say the Grey Zone is the most beautiful combination of all colors and all combinations of Light and dark. It is a blend of Heaven and Earth. Ah yes, now we see that you are imagining what you believe to be Heaven. You have images of beauty where everywhere you look there is no resistance to any movement, and where you think and everything manifests the moment you grasp the thought. You imagine a place where everyone is in total harmony in every moment. Sorry, that is not Heaven but only your illusion of it. In reality, that would be intensely boring for us. In your field of duality, you naturally believe that you are going toward a better place, where only intent exists and no purpose or action is necessary. You are enlightened seekers and your nature is to seek something better. Many of you live with the greatest hope of returning Home. We also tell you that at this time on Earth, more of you are thinking these thoughts than ever before. Please be patient, dear ones, for your perspective will change. What if we told you that when you return Home, you will look back on these days right now as the most wonderful parts of a Game that you were playing? What if we told you there will come a time after returning Home when you long for the simple beauty of a leaf on a tree or the radiant smile of a loved one, or the comfortable energy of your easy chair? We are not attempting to disillusion you about Home, dear ones. It is all that you re-member and more, but what you don't understand is that the same veil that keeps you from seeing your own magnificence also keeps you from seeing that Home is being built all around you at this very moment. That vision can only be attained by divine intent activated through divine purpose.

## Divine Intent + Divine Purpose = Divine Service

One of the most difficult parts of being human is the veil that you wear. There is a dark spot directly over your third eye that keeps you from seeing your true nature. It has served you well in the human experience thus far, only now it is helpful to begin understanding the veil and its attributes. On this side of the veil, you are one with all things, and that is what you have referred to as divine. It is the veil itself that causes you not to see the divinity within yourself, for that would instantly connect you with all things everywhere. This is what you call 'unity consciousness.' For the moment, let us simply say that divinity equals unity. At this stage of your evolution, it is not possible for you to experience true unity, for that would be pulling the veil aside completely and this would quickly end the game. One way the veil can be quickly thinned is to tap into divine intent. Trusting yourself to utilize the divinity within you means tapping more fully into unity consciousness. This means being one with all things and following the natural flow of energy as it pulls you into balance with everything. We have spoken of this before as the pull of the Universal energy.

Your divine purpose is generally so simple that you can rarely see it clearly. If we were to tell each one of you what your individual divine purpose was, you would reply with, "Isn't that everyone?" Humans must usually complicate things in order to comprehend them. Divine purpose is the larger picture as it reflects your place in unity consciousness. It is where you fit into the big picture.

The magic happens when you combine divine intent with divine purpose. This places you in divine service, which is what your soul came here to do. During the readjustment times you are now experiencing, divine intent with divine purpose can help you to clearly see your own next step as an individual. Do not be concerned if you do not immediately know your highest good or if it is not clear how you will be in divine service. Taking even small steps in that direction can ease the challenges of being human and give your life meaning. Here we offer you three simple tools for mixing divine intent with divine purpose to be in divine service.

## Honoring the Spirit-Body

You are not body alone, nor are you spirit alone in the form you now inhabit. The ways of old within a field of duality taught you to believe that it was necessary to separate the physical from the spiritual self in order to advance. To become spiritual, you found it helpful to denounce the physical desires of the body. That was your truth in the lower vibrations and it worked well. Understand that truth is an evolutionary process and, as you move to higher levels of existence, it becomes helpful to reach for higher truths to support your higher vibration. With the evolution of humans now at hand, you will see the emergence of what we will call the Spirit-Body. In the lower vibrations from which you came, it was necessary to place some division between the Body and the Soul. As you now move closer to Home, that division is fading. At this time, you will see the new importance of treating the spirit-body as one. Honoring the spirit-body as the perfect vehicle to carry your energy is an area of grounding that will become more important as your evolution continues. This can be done by honoring the spiritual desires of the body and the bodily desires of the spirit. This action will help to balance your male and female, your yin and the yang, and your Light and the dark sides. This is the reason you will now find a different connection to what once was your physical bubble of biology. Grounding has always been important as you walk in physical form. Now you will also find it helpful to ground the spirit-body as one. The emergence of the spirit-body is the reason you will find changes in weight and dimension more effective than even a short time ago. This is also why we are asking you to get comfortable with sex as the physical expression of the spirit. The spirit-body is the new vehicle that will take you to the next level of existence and it is beginning to surface at this time among those leading the way in the evolution process. Honor your spirit-body as the physical and spirit united. You have only to listen, as it will tell you what it needs. It now speaks to you through your spirit. These are the new connections we will help uncover in coming messages. This blending motion of the physical and spiritual self also emulates the blending motion of the Universal Energy. This is the next step toward Lightbody and it is available now.

## Finding Paths of Service

Embracing the divine purpose is easiest when you follow your own heart and activate the next step of evolution. Yes, we know, you do not trust your own heart, and that is the most difficult part of working with you as angels. Still, you have planted important seeds of your own divine purpose deep within your own cellular memories. If you allow yourself to experience these, then you will find that your searching for things outside of yourself will cease. Since the beginning of our messages as Re-minders from Home, we have told you time and again that your heart knows the way. Find your passions and step into them in any way that you can.

There is a deep inner peace with one who finds and acts on their own divine purpose. Find ways of being in service. This is an action that can set up the energies to place you into full unity consciousness. Placing yourself in service alters your perception of yourself and therefore alters your reality. Being in service in and of itself will move you to a higher level of existence. These are generally small steps at first, but they put action behind divine intent and therefore lead you to divine purpose. If you are unclear where your passion lies, then begin only to step into service and watch as your passions surface.

## Re-membering

Dear ones, you are here playing a grand game of your own design. The biggest challenge is that you take yourselves way too seriously. Are you aware that all hunger, war, sadness, anger, loneliness and despair can be dissipated with a single laugh heard around your world? Are you aware that you can change your world and help others to change theirs with just a smile? When you find yourself longing for Home, feeling completely alone or intertwined in your own dramas, can you take a step back and see that you are a player in the most wondrous game? That simple fact is the secret of life, as you know it. Re-membering who you really are is as simple as smiling or laughing. When you allow your own spirit to surface, it is magical. Now, allow that spirit to be in service in some way and the magic takes form. That is why you are here now. It is so simple that we implore you to not think this through; rather, feel it in your heart … and smile.

It is our greatest honor to be in the loving service of touching your hearts and reactivating your memories of Home. You have given us the opportunity to touch you with the vibrations of Home and have therefore allowed us to be in our divine service. We ask you only to treat each other as the Gods that you are, nurture one another and play well together.

Espavo.

the Group

# The Out Breath Has Begun

## October 2003

Last month, the Group began speaking about the portals opening on our Earth and what that means to us. They said to watch for electrical storms that, at the time of this writing, have already spread across most of the areas of the globe. They spoke of the electrical adjustments needed to bring in the portal energy and that this was the reason for the major blackouts we have experienced. They specifically said to watch for two more major power blackouts, which have already occurred, as a huge power surge took out major parts of Denmark and Sweden only a week after the channel was published; then, last week, there was another major power outage in Italy.

I do believe these were the two major blackouts of which the Group spoke; still, they say we are in a time of further adjustment to our electrical equipment as it adjusts to the changing magnetics of the portal energy now on Earth. Now we can look forward to further adjustments to our computers and other more sensitive equipment. In most cases, this will not mean that these items will need to be replaced; they will just need adjustment. We are going through a similar rewiring process in our own physical beings. Here, they say, these changes can be very challenging; yet there is one thing we can do to best ease this transition: connect with original spiritual family.

Greetings from Home

Lightworkers of Earth, gather and unite as spiritual family, for the next stage of evolution is upon you. You have earned the right to call yourselves "Workers of the Light," and we proudly dub you "Lightworkers of Earth."

## Discernment: the First Tool

You are seeing major changes in the energy field in which you play the Game at this time. We will now speak more of what is ahead and why, for we are here to help each of you re-member your true empowerment. As always, we remind you that your first expression of power is in your own choices. Choosing the thoughts and concepts you allow to reside in your own head and heart is the first and foremost choice you will make.

In the near future, you will see major changes on the Earth as these portals now open. You will soon see beings among you who you will admire greatly. Many will enter your reality quietly, offering help with your evolutionary steps. These will be the quiet masters, who will be the greatest addition to your world.

Although most of these newcomers will stay in the shadows, it is the Game of Free Choice, and that applies to all who play. Most likely, some of those who will now enter through the opening portals will attempt to take your power from you in very discreet ways. Some will come who claim to have all the answers. It will be very easy for you to look at their advanced levels and freely give your power to them. Your natural love of drama can easily draw you into wanting something to be true so much that you actually create it. It is here that you are most likely to quietly give your power away.

This is the next major event of humanity you have been in preparation for. It is the reason you have stepped into the "Age of E" (Empowerment). We ask you to please get comfortable with feeling the energy within, and choose only those thoughts and feelings that resonate within your heart. Even as you hear or read our message, please take only those thoughts that add to your being and resonate within your own heart. Leave the rest, without judgment, and you will quickly master the art of discernment.

## Dynamics of a Vortex

You have become accustomed to the attributes of vortexes in your world. A vortex is simply energy moving in a circular motion. Many of you have been called to specific places to be guardians of the vortex, and special contracts with the Mother herself may be the reason you have been irresistibly drawn to live in a certain area. We have even given a special message addressing the guardians of the vortexes (dated April 2001 on our website). Vortexes are anchored to Earth only through the intervention of pure love. The guardians of each vortex have been entrusted with the care and feeding of each individual vortex. Some of you have felt so in love with the areas in which you reside as a direct result of these contracts.

Once the vortex is sufficiently anchored and the collective vibration of Earth reaches a level high enough to sustain the energy, the evolution begins. The natural evolutionary cycle of a vortex is to become a door through time and space, called a portal. Your new relationship to time and space has made it possible for you to observe and interact in this evolution. Portals have existed on Earth from the beginning. In fact, it was the early portals that spawned life on your planet. Some of these portals have magically drawn people to them as the high-energy locations on Earth. Yet, now these portals are growing in size and number, and even some of the portals that have been in place for some time are changing.

## Dynamics of a Portal

Portals are essentially a hole through time and space. The easiest way to identify a portal is through its effect on what would normally be a stationary object of time or space. Falling through a time hole will become common, as people will now accidentally fall through portals. It is here that you may find yourself driving down a road you have traveled many times, only to find yourself 40 km further down the road than you thought you were. This phenomenon has already begun to be commonplace among those leading the way vibrationaly. It has begun.

Another way in which you will learn to discern portals is through your advanced sense of smell. Your nose has been rapidly changing to accommodate higher evolution, and in most cases it will be able to discern portals through an odor. Previously, these same phenomena were experienced when spirits that had transitioned Home entered your world to visit the living. They would open their own portal, and you would often smell a familiar scent when the spirit was near you. Pay attention to your nose; it will lead you well.

## Portal Attributes

These portals actually connect all dimensions together. When the collective vibration of humanity is high enough to support it, these portals will be used to travel into other dimensions of time and space. In the meantime, they will be used by visitors, who will travel to watch the Grand Show as the first Planet of Free Choice moves into ascension status. Planets have previously graduated into this higher realm, but never before has it happened without major guidance from a hierarchy of overseers orchestrating the moves. The Grand Game of Free Choice has no such infrastructure, as your overseers (we, the Group) from the angelic realm never violate the prime directive of free choice. Now, the greatest potential of God becoming self-aware is underway on Earth, to the total surprise of many of those in the hierarchy, as well as observers.

## Portals Move

Your familiarity with vortexes would have you believe that they are stationary, yet we tell you that once a vortex evolves into a portal, it is no longer bound to be stationary. Even many of the vortexes that have created the high-energy spots on your planet are now beginning to turn into portals and move. Much the way that magnetic poles of your planet can shift as much as 80 km per day and permanently drift an average of 40 km per year, so can the energy form known as portals. This movement may create confusion for some migrating animals, as the portals interact with the magnetic field from which they gain their sense of direction. The confusion of some of the whales in recent years is due largely to the increase of vortexes and portals on Earth.

At this time, more portals will open on a steady basis and you will become accustomed to the new attributes of living in the higher vibrations of the new Planet Earth. Much the way that the Crystal Energy can create an environment for humans to live in higher energy and reach ascension status, the portals will work with the Earth to help her reach the same higher status. You must move together or no one moves at all.

## The Out-Breath has Begun

Recently we spoke of 'the Breath of God,' where we explained that the universe expands until it reaches a point where it speeds up and enters another dimension. Here it continues the same motion, yet is now collapsing upon itself. When it reaches the center, or zero point, it again continues the same motion and once again begins expanding. This is called 'the Breath of God,' and is the natural motion of the universe. We tell you now that the Out-Breath has begun. As this Out-Breath gains momentum, more and more portals will open. Believe us when we say you are just at the very beginning of this energy shift and things will get very interesting soon.

As the portals continue to increase in number and size, eventually they will reach a critical mass and envelop the earth. At that point, the earth itself will be a portal through all dimensional realities. That is the conclusion of the energetic shift now underway. That is the point at which you will become the angels to those brave souls who agree to put on the veil and play the game on the second Planet of Free Choice. Can you see why there is so much excitement in the universe about what you are now doing? It has begun.

## Activation Teams

The portal activations are now growing. This is a time for each of you to open portals when you hear the call. This can easily be done through ceremony and intent. Earth does hear when you talk to her, and she is waiting for your actions now. Many of you will find clear direction to open portals with ceremony and even form sacred teams that will travel to accomplish this exact task. Please follow your heart here, dear ones, for many of you came in with the highest hope of doing this work. Know that you are honored beyond your understanding.

## Reassignment

The dear people who have been holding the energy of the portals will now find that many of their roles are changing. Some that were drawn to areas to live may now find themselves returning to where they began as their relationship to the land and the vortexes they guarded changes. These are also the people who will most feel the energy shift within their own physical being.

On the other hand, many people may suddenly find themselves being drawn to new areas, as there is work to do within each opening portal. Some portals will attract many, yet others will only need a few. Some entire cities will drastically change energy due to those suddenly feeling drawn to move there. This is a way in which the Earth herself can draw together original spiritual family. Many people from an area may also be drawn to new areas very suddenly. It may seem like an exodus from one location to another. It has begun.

## Finding Original Spiritual Family

Above all, there is one simple action that can help each of you find your balance more than any other: reuniting with your original spiritual family. When you first came in to play the Game in your first incarnation, you came with family and those you trusted implicitly. Time and again, you incarnated with these souls, and they became your family and soul group. Over periods of time and many incarnations, you completed karma with your soul group and drifted into other groups, forming new soul groups. Now that Earth is reaching ascension status, it is most helpful to reunite with your original spiritual family. You will find them whenever you place yourself around others of like mind. These are the special people you recognize the moment you connect with them. Find them, connect with them, and let them into your heart, and your adjustments will be much easier. Help them, and allow them to help you.

## Electrical Rewiring

As these portals begin to open, many things will acclimate. You have seen major adjustments to your electrical power equipment, and now you will continue to see further adjustments to many levels of electrical equipment, including further power outages. Much the way Crystal children must adjust to electricity, we must also adjust to the new Crystal Energy. The portals create an opportunity for the Crystal Energy to enter our world completely. The Crystal Energy now shifts the base magnetic structure in which you live. This has been seen as the magnetic grid blending with the crystalline grids of Earth.

These are unique times indeed, dear ones. You have set into motion events that have never before played out in All That Is. We ask you to reach out to each other, find your original spiritual family, and gain your own balance first. Then, when you are feeling centered, reach out to touch others who will be searching for answers as they experience this change. You are the workers of the Light, and we are proud to call you "the Lightworkers of Earth." It is with the greatest honor that we ask you to treat each other with respect, nurture one another, and play well together.

Espavo,

the Group


Barbara and I recently returned from the ESPAVO Conference in Mt. Shasta, California. At this weeklong event, we presented three live channels. The first was at a magical place called Glass Mountain. This mountain of natural obsidian (volcanic glass) is a true fifth-dimensional space. We had to be very careful where we sat and what we touched, as the obsidian was sharp as razors. Additionally, we also had to be very careful what we held in our minds during that time, for those thoughts surely would create in an instant in that fifth-dimensional space. Here, the Group actually took us on a visual journey into a portal inside the mountain itself, to let us know what it looked like from there. They made several key points about portals to help us understand the phenomenon now happening on Earth in many places at once. This was the first time the Group told us that portals move and change places. We experienced a beautiful day as all of us bonded very close, almost as if we all had just emerged from inside that mountain.

The third channel was presented on the last day of the conference and will be a cornerstone channel for future information from the Group. They told us what to look for as these changes now unfold in this magical time. This channel is titled "The Age of E." In this message, they told us to watch for several key indicators, including changes in economics, alien contact, and other events that will now begin as these portals open and we make use of them. The Age of E (Empowerment) is now upon us. Now it is up to us. (Both of these channels were recorded and are now available on video tape and audio tape in the Lightworker Store at our website.)

The second channel was given on Mt Shasta, where we found a special valley to gather. Everyone took a seat on a rock as the Group led us through an opportunity for each person to share their wisdom. Even though we took all of the recording equipment, the Group said it would not record. They were right; the camera shut down shortly after the channel began.

At the end of the channel, they told us to be sure to leave the valley by going around one side of the main rock. They told us we had been inside a portal the entire time we were experiencing the channel and that the portal had moved even during the channel. I have to say that it really didn't feel like being in a time portal. It felt normal to me. But out of the 50 people who were there, about four did not listen and wandered out of the valley without going around the big rock as instructed by the Group.

A few minutes later, we found ourselves back in the parking lot, and I became aware that while we had been down there, about 20 to 30 people had entered that same parking lot. We had been totally undisturbed while we were there and didn't see a single hiker on the many trails in that valley. Yet the moment we started out of that valley, several people came over the hill into the valley as if on cue. We also found that the four people who came out on the wrong side of the rock actually got lost in a relatively small parking lot and could not find their cars. Once another person touched them, they got their bearings and found their way. Since they had not exited the portal correctly, they had become confused as to what dimension they were in.

The next day, we found that very few of our people were aware of all the new people who had shown up while we were in the valley. Also, on the last day, two guests came to the channel who had not been with us prior. They told us they had been on the mountain that morning and had watched us from a higher elevation where they had a great view of the entire valley. They said that while sitting in their folding chairs with binoculars, they had seen us enter the valley and promptly disappear from view. More to come…

Big HUGS and gentle nudges

Steve Rother

# The Harmonic Concordance

## The Second Step

## November 2003

This was presented as a live channel on the day of the Harmonic Concordance, November 8th, 2003. This is the beginning of a new energy connection where we can have more direct access to the new energy the Group calls the Crystal Energy, which they have been taking about for the last two years. This new connection marks a new beginning of the way we use this energy. And although these new beginnings are exciting they can also be quite stressful. For some, this energy shift will be a trigger for change and for others it may be an opportunity to leave. For those dealing with this stress, know that this alignment is temporary and reaching out to those around you can make this transition much easier. Here at Lightworker we offer the message boards, chat rooms and the Lightworker Family Room to help make these connections globally. We are at a grand junction in our evolution as humans. These are exciting times and we can expect many changes very rapidly for the foreseeable future. Adjusting our attitudes to accept this change can make this transition much easier. New abilities are ahead for all of us and we are at the very beginning. The whole idea is to enjoy the ride and not take life too seriously!

Greetings from Home

Your energy is here this day, for you have gathered to celebrate an event that is extending far beyond your understanding. You know what is happening here this day, you understand there is a magic in what you call the Harmonic Concordance. But we tell you it goes far beyond your understanding as humans, for this is a specific day that is here to work with you, to help you, to connect all the alternate realities as a single one. That is why you use the word 'harmonic,' for these vibrational ranges exist within the same space and time at different levels, they overlap each other at regular intervals that add to the overall strength of the harmony. For that is what harmony is. That is the reason that all of the energies are aligned this particular day: to start a series of events into motion, which will create a higher reality for all of you.

## Higher Technology

You are the masters of the Gameboard, you are the ones who have chosen to be here at exactly this time to make a difference, and here you sit. Yes, we tell you there has been much happening on your planet even recently as much of your technology has needed adjustment. It is not quite there yet, but it will be soon. Be patient, dear ones, for you are working together to use technology in new ways that you have not before. That is going to be one of the gifts of living in the higher vibrations of the New Planet Earth. For as the greater good is served, you will see new uses of technology. You will see the use of technology to spread light. That is the part that is only now beginning. This technology needs acclimation, for it was not originally designed to carry such energies. Yes, some of you have had challenges with your computers, telephones and other devices. Please understand that this energy is taking everything to a higher vibrational state, including your technology.

## Opening to Channel

We have told you since the very beginning of these reminders from Home that there will come a time on this planet when more and more people will begin channeling. Ah-hah, you have noticed it, have you not? Much of what you are starting to see now is to create that opportunity within yourselves, for even as we speak many of these channels are opening. Can you imagine a time and a day where the word channeling will not be used at all? We tell you that it was not that many years ago that your own energies and your own selves made up words to describe phenomena that you had not used before. You called it ESP. We tell you now that it is so commonplace you do not even use that word anymore. For it is simple intuition, a basic human attribute that each one of you has, and you now understand it. Ah, but only a few decades ago it was very strange and very unusual and it attracted a lot of attention. It is the same with channeling at this time.

For you are only reaching to a higher part of yourself as these energies align, especially in times like these. You will see the opportunities to reach through that harmonic alignment of energies to contact your higher self. When that happens, the magic begins. That is the beginning of walking fully in your power as creators. Many of you, even in the past few weeks, have opened to channel. Many more are coming soon. We tell you this will be a magical time, for much is opening now to allow this to happen. For as this unfolds everyone will start connecting in different ways. No, it will not be called channeling, for it will be a very normal form of communication. And much of what you call Lightwork, which is something that many now call woo-woo, will no longer be woo-woo. It will be everyday language. That is where the magic begins, dear ones, for that is where the creations of your own energies take form. That is when you understand that you are the creators walking behind veils inside bubbles of biology.

Even now as many of you gather in rooms to hear the Group, the Kryon, or Archangel Michael, we tell you the real magic is actually within you. There are many who come through alternate realities to observe the masters of the Gameboard even as you sit in these rooms to hear us, they watch you with the greatest expectation. Do you understand the magic that you hold? You are the ones who have created this energy. We wish to tell you that things will now change upon your planet, for you will see things in a new light. Now as these energies move forward you will understand that there are opportunities for you to create energy for yourself. As these changes enter you will feel this energy tapping on your shoulder ever so lightly. Yes, being human we know perfectly well that you will not be able to accept it, for it will not be something you will understand in the beginning. You will see that it is not fully acceptable to you because humans do not trust themselves. It is an innate feature of your ego. It is part of what you have put there as a safeguard to ensure balance.

So when this stream of consciousness begins flowing through you, the first thing you do is think that you are making it up. And we tell you, you are! Please make it up, dear ones, for that is the flow that will eventually bring Heaven to Earth. Please feel the freedom to do this, because now you are going to connect to your higher selves more than ever before.

## Stronger Connection to Spirit

Oh yes, we know that many of you walk out into the front yard and you expect to have a sign in the sky so clear that you know God is talking to you directly. We tell you it does not happen. It always sounds like you. It always feels like you. The reality is that it is another aspect of you. Still, this time it will be stronger, for now there will be times when you will know something deep within your being. In those instances if you allow yourself to follow it through and lean into it, you will begin discovering the stronger connections to your own higher self. No, this is neither special nor unique, yet it may seem so, for only those who have dared to lean into it up to this point have been able to fully use this connection. So we tell you that not everyone on planet earth channels at this point. But it is only a matter of time and trust. That is now changing. That is what is taking place this day.

You now have the opportunity to step completely into your own divinity. Yes, now let us go back to what you call the Harmonic Concordance, for we wish to tell you the larger perspective of this event. There came a time only a few years ago that you labeled the Harmonic Convergence. It was a very unique time in history, for you had set up the Game to be finite. You had originally set up the Game with a beginning and an end. The beginning is what you refer to as the Big Bang. It was then that ethereal beings came to earth, although they were not yet in physical form. That is the reason that much of your history predates physicality on planet earth. But you have been here for a very long time working with biology, figuring out ways to evolve it into a higher-vibrational status. And as you are moving forward, things are changing, things have started. You set the original point up to have a stop date at which point you would check your own vibrational status of the planet earth to see whether you could possibly step into holding power while in physical form.

Ah, no one expected it. No one. Everyone who had a part of the creation of this Game said, "Oh, let us give it a try, we have got nothing to lose." And there were many who stood by and said, "That will never work; you cannot have total free choice. Free choice will never work, for humans will not choose the higher good. They will become selfish because of their own egos." It did not happen. Here you are after winning the game. You are now figuring out ways to help each other. You are now trying to figure out how to become Human Angels. That, dear ones, is taking power as creators on planet earth. That is very unique and wonderful. We cannot tell you the joy on this side of the veil as you step into it. No, you do not sit back saying, "We have come this far, now let us go Home, let us relax." Instead, you say, "Okay, we have been through this turmoil; now what can I do? How can I help? What can I do to help other people to higher vibrations?" That is the greatest winning of the game that you can ever imagine.

## The First Vibrational Measurement

So along comes the date you originally set to check the vibration and to see whether it was possible to carry this power of creators in human form. Along came the Harmonic Convergence and even though no one expected it, no one ever thought that those of the gold ray could actually be winning the Game. It was checked and surprisingly announced throughout All That Is that the human vibrational rate had reached a level that could hold empowerment. Ah, but that was not the end of it, for now a whole series of events began to see how you would deal with your own empowerment. It was to see whether it was possible for you to take this power and responsibility and use it in your daily lives. Yes, it is one thing to read about it, it is one thing to talk about it, it is one thing to hold these higher concepts in your brain, but to actually use them is where the magic is. And that is what you did. You began the process. You started raising the collective vibration of humanity and the entire vibrational state of All That Is. As a result, a whole new set of events has been placed into motion. We tell you something: you did not script where you are today. There is no grand plan in place, dear ones. Yes, we can tell you the direction it is heading, for we have a very good view from this perspective. But what we cannot tell you is your own future, for you have yet to write it. And as much as you would like to think there is a divine plan and a divine collective consciousness that will lead you in that plan, it is not there. You are it.

What you do not see is your own magnificence. But we are here to work with you on that. We are the ones who have chosen the job of being the Angels of the planet of free choice, for we are the ones who have been allowed to spread our wings to reflect the magnificence of humans. It has been a great task indeed. It is not easy helping you remember who you are, but we are making headway. And now we are training you to do the same thing. That is true empowerment. When you can help each other more than you can help yourself, when you can make the space for each other to become empowered around you, that is where the magic begins. You are entering the "Age of E". It has begun.

Because of the measurement of the vibrational rate at the Harmonic Convergence you have set into motion a whole new series of checkpoints. One of them begins this day. What you are calling the Harmonic Concordance is a series of alignments of vibrational status that reach throughout all the cosmos. One of the places that we tell you that you know little about is the Central Sun. And even though the Keeper has said before that it is not a physical place, we wish to correct him, for it is. It is the first physical place you experience as you come from the other side of the veil as creatures of infinite form. The first stopping place of a soul becoming finite is the Central Sun. From that point on you are spread out into rays of vibration. That is why we call you those of the golden ray. You resonate between the range of yellow-amber and gold.

## Crystal Energy from the Central Sun

You are the most beautiful gold light, and the crystal energy coming from the sun is your origin. That is what you remind yourself of as you wear gold bands with crystals to symbolize the union of two souls. It is a reminder of where you come from. So as you emanate from the Central Sun we tell you that after that connection is made and you split out into those bands of color, you do not have the same connection with the sun after that point. You do not have connection with the Central Sun after that. Everything after that point must filter through your solar sun in order to reach you.

You have seen what is happening with your solar sun. It is erupting. Many of your scientists are quietly wondering whether the sun is at an end. We tell you in some ways it is, although it will not end life on earth. The sun as you know it is changing and it will never be the same. It is evolving as well, for you have set into motion an evolutionary process that will now spread throughout all of the cosmos. It is magical indeed and that is what is taking place as we speak.

The second connection point after what you call the Harmonic Convergence is happening now. The alignment of energy known as the Harmonic Concordance reconnects you directly to the Central Sun. And now you will feel energy coming directly from the Central Sun. It is a different type of energy from what you have been feeling. For many of you know that you have been feeling the energy coming in from the sun; you feel these solar flares as this energy filters in magnetic form and envelops all of the earth as it alters the very structure of the tectonic plates on which you walk.

## Rampant Emotions

Many of you have felt a disconnection and space between you that was not there previously. You feel this separation in your emotional body. It has caused quite a lot of turbulence throughout all of humanity, in many forms. It has upset many and has made many feel like they are no longer in control, which, of course, makes them act out and try to grasp control one more time. You have seen it. It will continue for a short time, for these things need to play out and they will only be heightened in the short run. Be patient, dear ones, for you are in a final clearing mode. You are in a process. Can you imagine a day when war does not exist upon your planet? We hope so, because you have stepped into that reality. You have stepped into the possibility of creating that right now.

That has begun. No, we did not do it; you did. You are the masters of the Gameboard. You are the ones who, through your own caring, through your own tears, through your own emotional upheavals, have opened the door for this to happen. And now you take it forward from this point. The Harmonic Concordance is a checkpoint, and much like the Harmonic Convergence it will live on in your memories for a very long time. You may not know exactly what it is and you may not understand the words but you will understand that there is a change on the earth. A whole new energy will now breathe into the planet very quietly, for you have made space for this to happen and that is where the magic truly is.

## Six Checkpoints to Heaven

Now it is your responsibility to take it from this point forward and create the opportunities. Create it through your technologies, create it through your energy, and create it through your passion. Find your passion and move into it. That is when you become the highest use to the universe that you can be. As you step forward, you will create new realities throughout everything that is, as you connect yourself to your origins in the Central Sun. We tell you, so many of you have been working to open up the memories of Home. We have helped you with reminders from Home occasionally to help you remember the energy that you are creating here on earth. Ah, but now something magical is happening, for it is going far beyond the original connection. We tell you that after the Harmonic Convergence there are six more checkpoints. This day is one. From this day forward there are five more checkpoints, and then what? Ah, yes, we cannot wait to ask that same question, for you have not scripted it. But we tell you that at that point, it is very clear that the direction you are heading is that you will step into the Angelic realm . What you know of as the Angels—oh, yes, you have your images of wings and flying beings who go around loving each other all day—we tell you that image, to some degree, is true. We love the those images that you have of the dark Angels and the cherubs and how everything works together and how all the grand Angelic names end with "el." We think you are imaginative in the way you describe us. You will understand it completely soon, because you are becoming us. That is what is happening. And after the other five checkpoints you will know what this whole game was about. For you will be the Angels of the second planet of free choice at that time. Right now many of you are taking out pen and paper to try and write down exactly when those are. When are they going to happen? What does it look like? We will ask you the same questions. For we are not scripting this, you are.

You are the magicians of the Gameboard, dear ones. You are the ones who are creating the energy every day of who you are. We cannot tell you how proud we are that you are doing this. Can you imagine us as proud parents looking over your shoulder, trying to help you make the highest choices and the highest steps that you can? You can only imagine the great opportunities that we see for you and the highest hopes we have that you will find yourselves making those choices. Now, can you imagine those same proud parents, as they look upon their children moving past the highest point that we thought we would dare hope for? That is what is happening this day, for this is the second checkpoint. Five more remain between you and the Angelic realm, and we tell you something else. The distance of time between the Harmonic Convergence and Harmonic Concordance will not be a constant distance between the checkpoints from this point on. These events will happen more rapidly. If you stay on the path that you are on, you will set into motion a whole series of events that will start the new planet earth immediately.

## Holding Power through Mastery of Self

Take responsibility for it, dear ones; hold that energy in your heart. Find the love, find the caring and find the passion that you came with. Dare to take responsibility for your own happiness to begin with, and pass it on. Dare to find those things that come in from high. Dare to trust your own inner guidance and speak it. Share it with others, not as the ultimate guidance from Heaven, but as offerings for empowerment for each to discern for themselves. We have said it many times and we repeat it this day: please do not listen to every word we say, for that would only serve to take your power from you.

You are the magicians; you are the masters of the Game Board. We think that you can take this energy now completely and step forward. Your own relationship to the Central Sun is changing your relationship to what you call Heaven. You know that the relationship with your Angels has changed. You know that your relationship with your own guides has changed. You have set that into motion by raising your own vibration and we tell you now, especially in the days ahead, that you will have opportunities to open up enhanced states of creation. Be careful what you ask for. For everything you hold in your head will now become reality very quickly.

## Personal Drama

Choose first to become masters of your own thoughts. Examine each thought from a higher perspective. Examine everything that you do. We tell you also that there is one series of events that humans repeat over and over and over again that can become very destructive at this time and that is something we will simply call personal dramas. Oh, personal dramas are quite interesting, for humans are attracted to drama. It is a way for them to recreate a scenario of their own choosing. It is part of what you call your imagination, and many times people channel through dramas. Yes, we know that the word drama has a negative connotation. We tell you, that it is not seen from our side of the veil. We think it very interesting that many times you play things out, for if you watch a television show, if you watch a movie you walk out of there many times with your own heart expanded.

There is nothing wrong with that kind of drama. All we ask you to do at this point with your own personal dramas—that is, scripts that are playing within your field that are making you repeat things over and over and over again—all we ask is that you not judge them as good or bad, but simply pull yourself out to your higher self and take a look at the larger perspective of your own personal dramas. Choose carefully which dramas you allow to play out in your life, for now you have much more control at this than you have ever known before.

And now you will see that you have opportunities to create your reality with every step that you take. You are the masters of the Gameboard. You are the ones who set this into motion yourselves. You are the ones who have created the ability to walk past the first and to actually have a second checkpoint.

Dear ones, we are more proud of you than you could ever know. The love we have for you is not describable in terms that fit into any of your languages. The love from Home is all that we can express for you. The love and the energy of Home is all that we can give you and we wrap you in our wings regularly. We ask you to take this, amplify it and create it in your own worlds. Find ways of passing it on to others. Touch another heart. We have given the Keeper a phrase that he likes to use now. We wish to share it with you. On any day that you can touch another heart or be touched by another heart . . . "This is a good day." Today is a good day. Claim it as your own. Dare to step into your own magnificence, into your own divinity and walk in it clearly, for now those opportunities will be supported like never before.

You will find the opportunities to bring through your own information. The only challenge that you have run across time and time again as you bring in information in what you call channeling is that many times you wrap it up in your own personal dramas. And when you do this you judge it. You call something good; you call something bad, and you create an energy around it that does not exist. It is part of your own personal drama at that point. We ask you to simply balance the energy with your own discernment. Make space on the planet for all the channels. For each of you has a piece of the pie. Every one of you has a connection that has something of value.

You have considered the earth to be a very dark place and that is why we call you Lightworkers. A Lightworker is simply a soul who has made a conscious choice to spread light on the planet earth. Now you have opportunities beyond your wildest dreams to do that, but it demands that you take responsibility for yourself and step into your own passion. Dare to trust that information coming through you. Dare to lean into it and dare to be happy. Dare to take a step out and look at your own personal dramas and evaluate those parts you wish to keep and then release those parts that you are done with. Bless them all, for they have served you well, especially now. Now that these alignments are taking place and you have passed this second checkpoint, you have opportunities to step into higher-vibrational status immediately.

Even that which was originally set for your year 2012 has begun this day. You are Home. Now what are you going to do? Now, where is your passion? Here you go, dear ones; the torch has been handed to you. We tell you, you have changed everything, even your own relationship with Home, even your own relationship with the Angelic realm, those Angels who used to jump into your world and help you at critical times, those Angels who used to sit on your shoulder and tell you to turn left, turn left, turn left will no longer do that. For you are reaching a stage in your own development where it can only hamper you instead of enhance you. So now it moves forward. Now you are beginning a process where you will determine your reality at every step.

Even the last five years there have been huge changes on your planet. Many of you have noticed that the time lag has become very quick. And there used to be a time lag in your own creations that gave you a safeguard that was very healthy for you, for you were not yet masters of your thoughts. As you created a thought you had days and sometimes months that you could say, "Oh, never mind, I do not think I really want that," and it would not happen. And now every thought you hold in your head before you reach your next step in your own pace becomes a reality.

## Emotional Re-wiring

Choose your thoughts carefully. More importantly, choose what you hold in your heart. For that blending of the emotional energies will now become more important. That is the reason that many of you have felt this through your emotional body. These changes of the sun erupting and the Crystal Energy coming in to the earth itself have brought about a whole series of things that have created emotional disturbances for you. It is because your emotional body is being rewired. It is becoming the spirit-body. The emotional body spanned the connection between spiritual body and physical body. Now they are becoming one. For as you step into the next vibrational state, it is a simplistic energy that is combining to make things easier than they were. That is part of your evolutionary process. That is what is happening now.

So you are being rewired as we speak. So what do you do about it, how do you work with it, what does that mean? Does that mean I have to be emotional for me to step into the next state? No, it does not. But many of you will be. Now what we ask you to do more than anything else is to reach out and touch another Angel. Reach out and let them know it is okay. Find ways of gathering, find ways of touching each other, and find ways of sharing your own channeling and your own information with other people. Not as a divine source of everything, to listen to every word that you speak, but as a possible solution to find happiness. Take that energy, empower the others around you and you will create Home very quickly on your planet. The time is now. You will see it happening every day. Things will get easier, but not in the way you think. For you will learn to acclimate to this energy. You will learn to use this energy.

Many of you will begin having memories of the Central Sun. That veil has been very thick for most of you. You do not see books in your marketplace about the Central Sun, but you will soon. Yes, it will be called many different things, but it is the first place of origin as you come from Home to a place of finiteness. That is what is taking place today. Your connection is being revitalized. Take it, move with it, and hold the energy of Home. Hold the love that you have, for it will create anew, every day that you walk, every day that you create the energy. Dare to be happy. Dare to hold your power as creators and step to the next level.

## Creating Home

The magic has begun. The second checkpoint is here. Five more remain. Do not wait for the next one. Know that this trigger has changed things for you. So it is not about how many years down the road or how many months or anything else; it is about how do I be happy? How do I acclimate to this new energy? How can I make the most of what I have today? That is what we charge you with this day.

Take the ball and run with it. It is all yours. Create the highest reality that you can create. Release your attachments to the past and you will understand your own personal dramas, for you are reborn this day. Welcome Home. Dear ones, we know you have been challenged, we know you feel alone. We know the veil is thick sometimes and we wish we could just pull it aside, but that would not work. So, instead, we tap you on the shoulder. We give you hugs. We ask you to reach out and hold the energy for one another and teach each other any way you can. For human attributes will change from this day forward. You will see much of what is ahead as you create it every step of every day. It has begun and it will now go forward faster than you imagined it would.

Dear ones, the energy of Home is all around you. Memories of the Central Sun…you will begin hearing things that you have not heard before in a very long time. Your own physical attributes will start allowing you to see things beyond the veil. Connection with your parental races will begin soon. For they have been around you for a very long time. Many of you will activate those energies in the very near future. That is part of this, your own connection to the Central Sun. For that is where it took place.

We also tell you that as time goes forward the attributes of your own solar sun will now change. It is nothing to be afraid of. You will see it slowly over a period of time. For humans need time to acclimate to new energies and that is what you have set into motion. Be patient, reach out and hold each other's hands, let each one know that they are here with reason. You would not be here if you did not have something important to do. Just wait for that guidance, wait for that energy on the shoulder and even if it feels like you are making it up, if you step in that direction, you will know. Dare to take those steps. Dare to move forward, for that is what will so quickly change All That Is.

The energy of Home is behind you. You will see it now. You will feel the support as you reach out and touch each other. You are in a magical time. You are magical beings and we love you so much. Feel that love, accept it and then pass it on. For you are the magicians of the Game Board. You are changing All That Is. We tell you that your tolerance levels will now change. You will not have the opportunity to misdirect energies in the ways you have before. As you raise your vibration you will become more like the Indigo children. For you will have less patience with energy mismatches. Take your time with these changes. Allow yourselves to acclimate to this energy and allow others the opportunity to make mistakes. For you are human and those mistakes are what define you.

## The Human Angels

Dear ones, you are the Angels of the new planet of free choice. You are Angels-in-training at this moment, but we tell you we could not have picked better candidates. Hold it proudly. Take it with you every step of the way. Walk with a spiritual confidence on earth that you are here on purpose. That is why you came. And even though you may not be able to define that exact purpose at this moment, even though you may not be able to define that exact passion, know that it is there. And when the collective vibration of humanity reaches a level that can trigger it, it will surface very quickly. You will understand. There are no beings on this earth who do not have a specific purpose to be here. You, however, have total free choice so you can choose to step into that purpose or you can choose to hide from it from yourself. We have no judgment on what you choose, for all choice is honored. But if you find yourself frustrated, if you find yourself in a situation where you are not feeling usefull, if you find yourself in a situation where you cannot think you can touch your passion, all we ask you to do is to have the courage to choose again. Pull yourself back and look at the higher perspective. Look at your personal dramas that have repeated themselves in your life and mak a choice.

It has begun. The magic is here this day. Step out into the sunlight, soak that magic in, for that is how it is coming through. You are the Lightworkers on Planet Earth, but more importantly, you are the Lightworkers of the cosmos. It has begun. It is with the greatest honor that we ask you to treat each other with respect, nurture one another, and play well together.

Espavo!

the Group

# Lightening the Load

## Ready for Cosmic DSL?

November 2003

Greetings from Home.

Dear ones, you have made an important move as you have stepped into your personal realities and gone through some very difficult situations, but you are still here. Here you are, looking around, trying to figure out where the next step is going to be, trying to figure out what is happening, what your energy is going to do next. We tell you, you cannot imagine the applause on this side of the veil that you are still there on Earth. Many times, you have had opportunities to go Home. Many times, you have had opportunities to call it quits. And we tell you, if you had done that, you would have been welcomed with open arms. But here you are asking, "What can I do next? How can I help? How can I find my passion?" Many of you still think it is selfish to think about your passion, yet we tell you this is when you become the highest use to the Universe you can be. Find that passion. Find any way you can to move into that and create that passion even this day.

Dear ones, a polarity integration is happening every day from this point forward, for it will lead to the next step in your own evolution. It is important beyond your understanding, so that is what we wish to speak of this day: how you can integrate the polarity. Polarity is the illusion in which you have lived your lives. You have always understood there is black and white, up and down, love and fear, right and wrong. Yet we tell you, that is simply an illusion of polarity, for it is not real. The only thing that is real is the integration of all of it. There is neither black nor white. It is all shades of gray. There is neither love nor fear. There is only the energy, the base energy that you call love.

## The Roller Coaster of Personal Dramas

As you balance your own male and female parts of yourselves, you can adapt to this energy much more quickly. But, in the meantime, there is emotional strife, for many of you have felt emotional stress over the past four to six weeks. It has been very intense. You feel as if you are on a roller coaster ride. We tell you, yes, you are. But there is a secret about the roller coaster ride, for it is not grasping the bar a little harder so you can hang on even tighter; it is that you can learn to enjoy the ride. It is that you can learn to be thrilled when you go over the next bump, that you can learn to accept all the opportunities. More than anything else, in the time you have here in the next weeks and months that lie ahead, the easiest way for you to acclimate to this roller coaster ride is to lighten the load.

We spoke of it the last time we spoke here, and asked you to please carefully watch your personal dramas, for they hold keys to this load you carry with you. Your own personal dramas are the part of you that you love playing. Now, we use the word drama differently from how most of you understand it. Most of you think dramas are a horrible thing, saying, "We do not need dramas in our life." But we tell you, humans are greatly attracted to drama. And why should you not be attracted to drama, for after all you are playing the Game of Hide-and-Seek? You are on the grand stage. All we ask you to do is understand that dramas can be changed and you can change the drama to one of your own choosing, for that is the more important part. And in this time, there are opportunities for you to lighten your load. For you will understand, as you are going around a corner on this roller coaster you call life, as you are going over the ups and the downs, it is actually the physical mass that creates the thrill that pulls at your emotions. If there is a way to lighten that mass, the ride can be more comfortable. So now we ask you to please look unwaveringly at all your dramas. Look at all the things that play over and over again in your life, and see what serves you and what actually takes away from you. For now is an opportunity to lighten the load like never before. This can be a time when you take charge as creators, for not only are you in charge of your own reality, but you also set the energy around you that helps to create the reality of others. You are not alone. You are part of a greater whole. You are part of Unity Consciousness and, as everyone connects to everyone else, every thought you have ever had is felt by everyone else on the planet at some point, for it falls into the Universal Subconscious Mind and works its way throughout the Universal Energy. So when you experience emotional stress, it is because you are tapped into this energy too tightly sometimes. You are hanging onto the bar of the roller coaster so tightly that it gets difficult. It does not need to be difficult, dear ones.

## Higher Truths to Support Higher Vibrations

We tell you many times, as you move from one level to the other, there are times when you will experience pain. You are aware of that. But please know, dear ones, that misery is an optional experience. You do not need to get stuck in a drama that supports the repetition of that pain over and over and over again. Releasing that part of your dramas becomes one of the most important things you can do as you integrate polarity. That is the balance of the male and female energies that are so helpful as you walk into the next stage of life. That is the one thing you can do above all else that can make life more comfortable and allow you to move into your passion more freely. You know there are belief systems that will keep you from moving into new creations, but you are getting very good at re-evaluating the belief systems. As you raise your vibration, several things happen and one of them is that you start reaching for higher truths to support your higher vibration. As you do, you make choices. You create your reality just before your foot hits the pavement and just before your foot hits that next step, you create the pavement in front of you. It is magical to watch from this side of the veil. If only you knew how much you were in charge, you would change everything about the way you do things. But in order for you to play the

Game comfortably, it is necessary for there to be a time lag. It is necessary that you do not see your own creations in each moment. So in order for that to happen, it is very common for you to get wrapped up in the personal dramas. That is when it becomes your creation over and over and over again. The challenge about the whole thing is that you do not believe it is your creation. You do not see you are the ones creating your own reality. You do not understand and therefore you think something is happening *to* you, and you ask: "Why are the energies so difficult right now?" Ah, but are they? Is the fact that you wish to create drama actually creating reality? Ah, yes. Not creating drama is the easy part to say and the hard part to do. But what we offer you here is not to try and pick everything apart so that you understand every little piece, for that is not important. The important part is to know you are in charge and that, at any moment, if you are not happy with your reality, you can choose again. It is the integration of spirit within each one of you that helps polarity integrate within you, and that is what is happening now. It is changing very quickly.

## Right Turns of the Phantom Death

It is a human nature for you to look at your own patterns in your lives and to try to figure out ways to change as you look for the 180-degree shifts. You ask: "How can I change this? How can I shift the energy? How can I turn around and change everything in my life?" It is here many of you have gone through the Phantom Death experience. These are opportunities when you had the chance to leave the planet. These were exit points for you. And as you look back on those experiences, you will see they offered you very ample opportunity to turn 90 degrees and change your reality very quickly. Yes, dear ones, you have that opportunity. And you look back and see how easy it was and how comfortable it was, but at the time it seemed so difficult. At the time, it seemed so stressful. Everybody thought you were going crazy. All of your friends wondered what was happening to the person they knew and loved. The funny part is, after you made the right turns, many of those people are not your friends anymore. They have simply drifted into another reality very close to yours, but a reality that no longer intersects with yours on a regular basis. You are a changed person. You are different.

Your entire energy has shifted as you have jumped from one vibrational level to the next. Ah, but it is not just that, for you do not jump one vibrational level at a time, you jump eight at a time and that is exactly what you have just done. You have created an opportunity to jump eight levels in one fell swoop. It has happened. And now you are trying to look around and stand up and function in the same world you did before. But you are not the same, and that is why you can no longer see yourself, why you cannot feel it and why it is so intense emotionally.

Please remember, you have asked to be here at this time. Many of you are Aboriginal healers who insist on sitting in the front of the class. You are the ones who insist on being the first ones through the door so that you can hold the door open for everyone else. You are the grandest healers, for you have created the opportunity for Planet Earth to take this step through your own dedication, and focused intent. And you are to be applauded, dear ones. You have no idea what you have done. But, by creating that opportunity for you to be the first ones through, holding the door for everyone else, you also create more of a roller coaster ride for yourself. So know that the whole key to the entire process is learning to enjoy the ride. That is what we will call: "grounding the miracle."

## Touch of an Angel

We have talked about grounding many times before but let us speak of it this day. A tube runs through your body from the very top of your head, right in front of your spinal cord and ends up in the Earth itself. Your greatest use of this tube, your overall purpose on Earth, is to take things from the ethers and run them through that tube, bringing them into the Earth. That is the process of creation from a human perspective. Now imagine that things that exist in the ethereal realm have no substance. When you bring things into the Earth through this tube, you give them substance. So perhaps you can understand that grounding the miracle is actually taking things that have no substance and giving them substance.

You are infinite beings in a finite physical form. Your spirit is infinite and you know that, but please understand, your real gift and your real beauty are that your bodies are finite. They are physical and they have a beginning and an end, and they have substance. Even though many of you are lightening the load in the area of the physical body as well, we tell you that the physical body is beautiful beyond description. It is a manifestation of spirit in physical form that can do things that spirit by itself cannot. So please understand that you have gifts that even we, in the angelic realm, do not. All we ask you to do is to use those gifts to the highest of your purpose, to find your passion and to figure out ways of working with that energy.

Polarity integration is how you will move higher into the angelic realm. That is how you ascend. No, it is not about leaving the body behind. It is not about abandoning the physical form and moving straight into what you call Lightbody. You are aware that this is the direction in which you are moving, but if you jumped in there tomorrow, the Game would cease. You would not be able to achieve the next levels of definition you are now working on. So you have gifts, humans. You have the most beautiful ability to touch one another, not only through your words, not only through your love, but through physical touch. Being able to reach out and take someone's hand is an important part of human communication. To touch someone on the back of the heart chakra with the Touch of an Angel is very magical and you have that ability. We do not.

## The Energy Tube is the Seat of Your Emotions

Understand that the ethers are up here. They have no mass, they have neither substance nor physical form. To bring things from the ethereal realm through this tube and give them form is how you create. Bringing ethereal items through the energy tube integrates substance into them. Now the tube has an interesting job, for it has to span the gap between the infinite spiritual self and the finite physical self. It has to span the gap and exist both in the ethereal realm and the physical realm simultaneously. The only way to do that is through energy. It holds an energetic place in your being, for that is where the connection is. So let us just say for a moment that this ethereal part is your higher self and that this lower part is your lower, or your physical self. It is easy to see there has to be a connection point between your higher self and your lower self. There must be something that spans the gap between both of them. That is the energy tube itself and that tube is also the seat of your emotions. The reality is, the tube is your emotional expression in humanity. Therefore, any changes in your own vibration of either your lower self or your higher self will trigger emotional release. In the last few months, you have changed that entire structure. It has been important for you to do. But now we tell you, these recent changes go far beyond your understanding. Many of you have known you bring things from the ethereal realm through this tube and create them into your reality. An easy way to describe this is to simply understand that everything man-made started first as a thought form. A thought form is in the ethereal realm, and has no substance. When you bring it through the tube, you create something that has substance and mass.

Now we ask you to understand that energy stamps are human experiences that stamp energy upon you. Those experiences are actually stamped and carried through life on the outside of the energy tube. So, many times, when you have life experiences that help you facilitate primary life lessons, they are stamped on the outside of the energy tube. When you have an important contract play out that is put in place by you in the first stage of life, or the planning stage, it helps you to facilitate your primary life lesson. It is sometimes acted out through an actual experience and – especially if that experience happens to be negative in nature – you carry it throughout life as an energy stamp on the outside of that tube. Please know that you move energy through this tube every second of every day. Now imagine that all of a sudden, you have an energy stamp that is stamped on the outside of your tube. It is almost like stepping on a garden hose as it restricts the flow of energy through the tube. And every time you push the energy through, it hurts a little bit. And, of course, with the energy tube being the seat of the emotional body, you feel it in your emotions.

Ah, there are many ways you have dealt with this in the past. Many of you simply deny it and look the other way. You may choose not to run energy through that tube, or even create little magical tubes on the outside to re-route the energy so you do not have to deal with it. Then some of you bravely step in there and do whatever work is necessary to heal. That is the gift. That is the act of the grandest creators. It is here that you have done so well. Do you understand who you are and what you have done? When you find yourself crying alone in your room thinking you are all by yourself and that nobody cares, do you understand the entire angelic realm is looking upon you, flapping their wings in applause? Do you know they are all touching the back of your heart chakra with the Touch of an Angel? Generally, you do not see it in that fashion. It is much more difficult for you to look beyond the veil when it comes to your personal experiences. But if you understand that the process of the tube itself is going to trigger an emotional release, you welcome it. You look for opportunities to do it safely. You share with others how you got through so they can get through more comfortably. That is where the magic is. That is when you find your passion. That is when you find the things that you came and love to do. That is your charge, now.

## Grounding the Miracle

There is a time directly ahead that will create an opportunity for you to integrate polarity in your own life. Things will then pop up for you and you will wonder why they are happening. If you will simply look at both sides and ask, "Where am I into duality? Where am I into polarity consciousness? And where can I integrate both sides into one?" then this time will be very powerful. The energy has been set into motion, for the changes with the Earth and the cosmos have already started. Now you are integrating all of these changes within yourselves. All of these things are grounding the miracle that is happening. If the miracle happened in the cosmos and you would go through the entire Harmonic Concordance all over again and no one bothered to ground the energy, it would not take. You are the magicians, dear ones. You are the ones creating Home where you now are. Now each one of you has the opportunity to take this and ground this information yourself and bring all of this wonderful energy through that tube into your own life.

Oh yes, it is going to upset your emotions — we will tell you right now. Some of you are going to get very scared. Some of you are going to get very concerned. Some of you are going to feel unsupported. Some of you are going to feel completely alone. And we simply tell you, do what you can to look honestly at all the dramas going on in your life. Look honestly and figure out ways to lighten your load emotionally and physically, for those opportunities will move much faster now. What has happened is that as you have gone through your life you have figured out ways to move the energy through this tube without pain and emotional difficulties. Here you have healed your energy stamps. The interesting thing about an energy stamp is when you do that, the healing goes forward and backward in the timeline. You not only heal yourself, you heal your father and his father; you heal your sons and daughters as well. But the nice part about the process is, after you bring energy through the tube at that point, it does not hurt. There is no longer a restriction at that point. There will always be a little bit of a trigger there because, even when you heal something on yourself, there is always a little bit of scar tissue left. Please do not look at that scar tissue as a difficulty. Understand that the scar tissue itself is the re-minder of the experience and the gift that is given to you to keep.

## Vibrational Leapfrog Stretching the Energy Tube

But now, something magical is happening, for you are jumping many vibrational levels at once. And as you leapfrog these vibrational levels, as you move through many levels simultaneously, the energy tube begins carrying a whole lot more energy than it ever carried before. Here it is necessary for that tube to actually stretch and, as it does, you begin feeling the scar tissue because it does not stretch at the same rate as your normal structure. Many of your old issues start coming up at times when you thought you had dealt with all of this. "Yes, I made a commitment to be a Lightworker. Yes, I have exploded into this energy … so why is all my old junk coming up? How come I have to deal with that again?" Oh, dear ones, do you know who you are? Do you know the magic that is happening?

## Opening to Channel

We tell you, it will not take years of therapy to do this any more. It will not take the same energy it once took to run energy smoothly through your own being. Now it is different.

Now you are the ones who have the opportunity to create it and to integrate this polarity consciousness, for that is what will change the energy tube itself. The connection between higher and lower self is quickening. Many more of you are beginning to channel, to connect to your own higher self, to bring information through your own intuition. And that will continue to happen because of the stretching of this energy tube. So when you have these old issues come up, when you have this stuff you thought was well dealt with and you have an opportunity to go back and re-work the scar tissue, please welcome it with open arms. Please look at it as an opportunity to move all of you to the next level. You are here in physical form. You are the most beautiful beings able to dance in density as spiritual family. Hold each other's hands. Help each other, one unto the other. Figure out ways to make it easier for the next person, and help yourself by putting yourself first and you will begin integrating polarity very quickly.

During the time ahead, many of you will find opportunities to change your lifestyles. Some of you will change physical lifestyles. Some of you will change your relationship to the Earth herself by changing your relationship to the magnetic structure of the Earth and even to gravity. Please understand, dear ones, as you experience these things, they may seem very mundane at first. But they will trigger a whole set of emotions and, if you will welcome these emotions with open arms and understand they are not a setback, it will be easier to move forward. It is an opportunity to move even more forward than you were before. Embrace it. Ah, yes, we know there are difficulties with this process. If being human were easy, everyone would do it. Know that many of these emotions will surface only to be aimed at those who are safe around you, even though it is not your intention. Make it clear through increased communication what is happening. Understand and listen to your own self, for you will see much of the opportunity that lies ahead.

## Cosmic DSL

The magic of being able to connect through your own higher self is stronger today than it has ever been. Now you will see a triggering of events that will open the door for even more than before. Now the connection between higher and lower self will put you into a direct connection with the Universal Energy. A way you can imagine this is your own computers – since the Keeper thinks in that manner we will put it in a similar analogy – for many of you have computers and you have a lot of fun there. Then comes the day you realize you can get a faster connection. Well, you have just moved from a 14.4 modem to high-speed DSL, for that is your connection to your own higher self. The new connection is there. How you use it at this point is up to you.

You have the cosmic connection through your own higher self, and the first thing that is going to happen is the emotional energies are going to stretch as that energy tube opens. You will feel it over the weeks and months ahead, even more than you have previously. You are right in the middle and the good part is, you are still here. Ah, yes, dear ones, you are at the top of the roller coaster. Do not grip the bar harder, but just sit back and enjoy the ride, because we have got you. You could not fall if you tried. Yes, some of you still try pretty hard. But know that what is happening here is not happening to you alone; it is not going only through you. You are opening the door for all who are to follow, and as each one of you works consciously to integrate the higher self, to integrate that part into yourself and to integrate your male and female presence, you will let the energy flow. You will see the connection of all things very quickly, for that tube is getting wider. It is getting shorter and the connection distance between your higher self and your lower self is now diminishing. It is happening very fast. So figure out ways to use it. Ground the miracle, for even if the miracle is up here in the ethereal realm, if you do not intentionally bring it through that grounding tube to give it substance, it will remain in the ethereal realm.

Oh, yes. Many of you listen to channels, as the Keeper calls them, and many of you read the books and say, "I wish I had the Group on my shoulder. I wish I could talk to my guides like that." And you have no idea how close you really are. You have no idea that we are standing right next to you. All of you have connections and even though most of you will not channel the Group, as the Keeper calls us, each and every one of you has connections to the Universal Energy. This is the matrix which runs throughout all things and, when you tap into that, you come out with your special blend of magic. Each one of you will bring out a different flavor of the truth as you tap into that energy. Yet, if you do not tap into that energy, even though it sits there waiting for you, eventually it will fade away. Know that you are the magicians, dear ones. You are the ones who have the capability of reaching up and grasping that energy and creating it in your own life. But if you do not reach up and grasp it, it will eventually go away. Figure out a way to bring that through the tube. Figure out a way, even though it may cause restriction for you, even though it may cause some emotional changes or alterations for you, do so willingly. Do so bravely. And allow yourself to step to the next level because we are here, waiting for you with the grandest of hugs that you can only imagine.

The magic lies within you. The miracle is here, waiting in the ethereal realm, just above your reach. And now you find you have a ladder right in front of you. Reach up. Pull it down from the ethereal realm. Bring it through. Dare to create your highest reality and lean into it. Dare to create the things in your life that give you a better reality and a higher existence on your planet, for only when you place yourself first will you have full integration of polarity. Putting yourself in that energy will allow all things to balance comfortably and magically. The weeks ahead will be key, dear ones. Yes, it may be stressful, but it also may be joyous beyond your greatest imagination. You are entering a time of celebration. We ask you to pull yourself out of your dramas, to look at a higher perspective of your own lives, to choose carefully which dramas you allow to play out and which ones you allow to release. Lighten the load as you get started on this downhill slope of the roller coaster. Instead of grasping and preparing for the most difficult ride of your life, figure out how you are going to enjoy it; how you are going to tell your friends and neighbors, and your children, about the most joyous ride you have ever experienced. You are the magicians of the Game board. You are the greatest angels who have ever lived, and you are moving at the speed of love right now. Let it happen. Share it with yourself and others. Open the door, but go through first and then hold the door for the others, for that is where the magic is.

Dear ones, if it were possible for us to pull the veil aside for even a short time to show you the magic of who you are, we would. The challenge is, if we did that, you would all go Home and that is not what you have designed for yourselves. So instead, we will touch you on the heart chakra with the Touch of an Angel, we will touch you from time to time to re-mind you, and we will give you these re-minders from Home. Not for you to follow each word implicitly but only to re-mind you from whence you came and where you are going. You are creating Home on your side of the veil. That is only possible through the magic of who you are and the tubes you carry, so welcome it. Bring it on. We charge you to find passion, even if it is only for a brief moment, for that is where your easiest transitions will begin. You are magic beyond your understanding and when we get you Home, we will hug you for the longest time and bring you back into the family.

It is with the greatest honor that we speak to you this day. You gather before us to listen to words to help re-member the energy of Home and to help re-member who you are, but you do not understand that we also gather. For we gather to watch the magicians of the Game board. You are not just changing your reality; you are changing realities in all dimensional levels at one time. Take your power and use it. Fear not making mistakes. Make lots of mistakes and make good ones, for only then will you understand there are no mistakes. Step forward. Take your power and create this day. It is with the greatest of honor that we ask you only to treat each other with respect, nurture one another and play well together.

Espavo.

the Group

# Death of a Star

## Akarru and the Third Earth

## April 2004

Greetings from Home.

As each one now reaches into the very depths of your soul, you create a reality with each breathe out, for the in-breath of God has begun. You have set it into motion yourself, and will now see the reality you have created this day. The beauty that surrounds you is more than you will ever know for, even with your new vision and sight, the veil is still firmly in place. But, dear ones, when you look into each other's eyes, and into the hearts of one another, that is when you can see God. From this day forward, you will see such a reflection, for the energy has been building since August of 2003. The grand changes have begun. The energy has been shifting in order for you to see the new reality that you have created for yourself. And now it is set into motion in such a way that you will be able to actually use this energy – to set it into motion to create your reality every step of every day. It has begun today!

## Parallel Light from a Parallel Universe

We have told you many times of the portals of energy that have opened. We have illustrated how the inter-dimensional realities work. We have planted seeds to help you understand that you are not alone, and that there are many concurrent realities existing side by side in parallel universes. Today we talk about parallel light, for the energy has shifted and now is an opportunity for you to see how this works. The connection you make to the Universal Energy is stronger than it has ever been before. That connection to the Universal Energy is what runs between each person, but also connects you to each blade of grass. It connects you to the stones. It connects you to the hills. It connects you to the sun. That energy is the Universal Energy which runs between and ties together all things. Whenever you send a creation into the Universal Energy, it is felt as a ripple in that fabric and returned to you in that exact form. That is the process of creation.

But you have come in to play this Game behind a veil with the intent of forgetting your magnificence. You have done well, as the veil you created has worked as you planned it. We are here to help you re-member your magnificence. We are here to help you understand you can take your powers again, even with the veil in place. We are here to help you work with your own energy as creators, for the time is right for you to set into motion the next grand creation. That is the purpose of telling you how life really works. For when you have the larger overview, you can understand and grasp what is right in front of you this day.

## Emotional Roller Coaster

Ah, but many say, "I have been so emotional lately. I don't understand what's wrong with the energy." When you find you are actually a part of the Universal Energy, you then understand you share that energy with everything, everywhere. And as you strengthen that connection to the Universal Energy, you will feel it in your emotional bodies. Understand that the energy is going to change as your connection to the Universal Energy changes. Thus, emotions may be at an all-time high for a while. But it is not the stronger connection to the Universal Energy alone causing this influx of strong emotions. There are other things unfolding in other dimensions of time and space that also place ripples into the Universal Energy, which you then feel as emotional upheaval. Even as you read the energy reports, or try to equate what you are feeling with external events. such as the Crystal Energy entering through solar flares, a few days later you may feel emotional or excited. Understand that the emotional infusions not only happen because of the things taking place in your reality, but they are also because of events happening in parallel realities. Much the way you have had global tragic events that have shifted the emotions of the greater part of humanity, these same tragedies have also been felt in parallel realities where they seem to have no obvious cause. Likewise, you have been feeling much of that yourself. We wish to share with you this process, for you are currently receiving a tremendous amount of energy from parallel universes. Within each of these 'multiverses' is a phenomenon we call parallel light. That light connects all emotions in all realities. When you understand what it is, and understand the process, then you can make adjustments in your own life to incorporate it fully. Take those things that have caused you negative challenges and find positive uses for them, for that is the process of mastery. That is why you are here.

Dear ones, you look at yourself in the mirror and ask, "What did I come here to do? Why am I here and what is my purpose?" Our answer is that it has been there in front of you all along, and now is the time for you to step into it with full intent. There are opportunities now for you to both send and receive these ripples of Universal Energy that cross between the parallel universes. To help explain the current situation, let us tell you a story.

## Death of a Star ~ Leilu, Amarah and Trudge

Leilu was a young man in his early thirties. He had started a family, had a good job and basically loved his life. He even liked what he did for a living. Leilu would go to work every day and enjoy the people he worked with, for he got to work with people on a one-to-one basis. Although he was not in a traditional healing modality, Leilu was a healer. Leilu now had opportunities to stretch into new areas and begin teaching. He would come home and talk with his wife, Amarah, who would greet him at the door. Amarah had the very rewarding but difficult job of keeping the home for the family. Amarah would greet him every day, "Honey, how was your day?" And they would share what happened during the day and would share where their high spots and low spots were. Leilu and Amarah were very good together, and they worked to raise a family in the shadow of their own love.

Then Leilu found himself going to work and not enjoying it as much as he once had, for many things started to happen at work that changed his perspective. He noticed, over a period of time, people were starting to get very strange. They seemed to be very stressed for no apparent reason. Even though he did not consider himself a counselor, he found himself in that position quite often. People would come into his office at odd hours and simply burst into tears. He could not figure out what was going on. He did not understand what was happening, so he would do the best he could to make people feel comfortable, to make them feel empowered, to help them see life from a higher perspective and to live in the now. In a very short time, Leilu had become a leader at work, even though it was not his official job title. He worked very hard, for it seemed as though everyone was under stress lately. He could not figure out whether he was drawing this into his life, or if in reality, everyone was under more stress than usual. Whatever it was, tensions were high, and everyone was feeling emotions being triggered.

As he returned home each day, he was greeted by Amarah and their son with the greatest of unconditional love. She felt his stress and his pain, but would act as a sounding board for him without taking on his stress. They worked well together as she relieved much of the pressure that allowed him to make a difference with the people he reached each day. She would say, "Honey, it is going to be okay. You are making a difference." And he would say: "I hope so, because I do not know if I can continually take this kind of stress. It is so difficult and I am feeling so emotional myself. I am able to keep my balance because I'm so busy helping others. I just do not understand what is happening."

After several months of this increasing tension, Amarah finally told Leilu that she was feeling very emotional herself. She, too, was having thoughts that included ending her own life, that she had never had before. It seemed that everyone was suddenly searching for a higher purpose in life, almost as if they were nearing an end to a game they were playing. Amarah was wondering if she was in the right place, doing the right things?

Then there was their son. He was a big boy, for he had a large physical body that was needed to hold the immense energy he carried. And although he was a gentle being inside, his physical being was big, and his name matched his energy well. His name was Trudge. During these last few months when the tensions were high, Trudge would come to his mother to comfort her. He would give her a big, bear hug and you could almost hear her bones cracking in her body when he did. He knew that he could take the tensions away and make her feel better, even if only for a short time. More than anything else, Trudge wanted to make her realize that she had purpose and meaning in her life.

The extreme emotions continued and it seemed as if this energy were moving from one to the other, being passed from person to person in a strange way. People continued to have more challenges in all areas of their lives and Leilu felt this at his place of work. He would go home and work with Amarah, and she would carry the energy so tightly in her own body that she did not even know what was happening until Trudge finally came over and gave her a big hug. Trudge, even at age eight, had his challenges as well. He became very distressed, and ultimately depressed, which was not common for Trudge as he was normally a jovial being.

Although Trudge had been big all of his life, he also found that now people were threatened by his size and he had never experienced that before. As much as he simply wanted to get along with other people, it seemed as though he was having a more difficult time doing that. Trudge found that smaller children would come up to him and pick fights for no apparent reason, as if to prove themselves to the largest child in the class. He found himself the target of many and they seemed to focus their fears on him. He found himself in fear, which he was not accustomed to.

The energies of Leilu's family became very tense over the next months. One evening, they were all having dinner, sharing the events of the day and trying to make sense of it all. Trudge would say, "Mommy, it's going to be okay. Do not worry." And Amarah would say, "Leilu, do not worry. Some day you are going to start your own business and you will not have the problems that you now have."

Leilu would go to work and tell the people who came to him for encouragement, "Do not worry." In reality, it was not getting better. It was as if a heavy layer of fog hung quietly over everyone. Amarah told her best friend one day that she knew she could make it through this difficult time if only she knew what was happening and why. This energy was not normal. It triggered emotions, making everyone doubt themselves and lose hope. The crime rate had risen drastically but not in violent crimes. It was as if people were asking, "What's the use?" An interesting side note was that creativity flourished during this time. Some of the most beautiful songs were written, and the most wondrous art surfaced. It seemed as if this heaviness stirred the creative juices in everyone.

One evening, the family was called to the Great Hall. The Great Hall was a meeting place where many in the neighborhood would gather when there was something to discuss. Someone came to the door and called everyone to the Great Hall for an emergency meeting. Amarah thought it strange that they came to the door. As they arrived, they found thousands gathered in the hall, many more than the hall would hold, many more than was usual for a meeting of this sort. The mayor of the city stood on the stage and began talking, began telling a story. It was a story about planets and solar systems and stars. He told it in story form, as he thought it would be easier for people to understand. As everyone listened to the story, they did so with great patience. They could tell from the mayor's demeanor that this story was important to all. Their planet was named Akarru and it had been on somewhat of an elliptical orbit around their own sun. The seasons were extreme as a result of this orbit and much of their technology had been used to adapt to the changes in their season. Recently, those who studied such events had become aware that the elliptical orbit had changed recently. As the mayor finished his story, it became obvious that there was a very good chance that Akarru's sun was in the process of dying.

In the moments of silence that followed, everyone felt the energy throughout the room go into fear. The mayor encouraged everyone to keep up their daily tasks and continue their work, but at this moment, his words fell on stunned ears. Many people were scared and many people were relieved, because they knew what they were feeling from everyone around them was the fact that Akarru was ending. The death of a star was about to happen and it was their star.

Leilu, Amarah and Trudge went home in silence. That night Leilu and Amarah connected and made love like never before. Upon awakening the next morning, Trudge jumped in bed and hugged them both good morning. A new day had begun and for that day, they celebrated.

## Tugging the Universal Energy

The story we have just told is true and it is happening at this time. However, it is not your sun we are speaking of. There are many alternate realities that exist simultaneously. These multiverses are connected with the Universal Energy that ties all things together. The change throughout the universe begins in the Universal Energy, for when one thing dies, another is born. When one ripple happens on one side of the Universal Energy, it puts a bulge in the other side.

The Universal Energy is the substance and engine of cause and effect in which all things exist. Although the solar sun of Earth has been in sympathetic vibration with the sun of Akarru, the ultimate outcomes of each are quite different. The sun of Akarru is completing its cycle of life. Because the Universal Energy connects all things in all dimensions, the sun of Earth is using the same dying energy of Akarru's sun to infuse extra life force energy to Earth. This is the Crystal Energy that has been entering through the solar flares of your sun for the last three years and will help you to move into higher vibrational status. The energy from Akarru – including the energy from Leilu, Amarah and Trudge – are creating a tug in the Universal Energy that is triggering emotions on Earth at this time. It is also the greatest gift that can be given. Before they knew what was causing their tension, everyone on Akarru was looking for purpose in their life. The interesting thing was, once the facts were known that their time was limited, everyone became spiritual. The nice part about that is, at this point, the entire planet began to change. At first, many people went into fear, and went crazy doing all the things they had hoped to do someday, since they were going to die anyway. But shortly after, the first ripple in the Universal Energy settled down and people realized it was time to return to spirit. The people of Akarru now have recently begun a new focus. Every breath they now take has new meaning.

Now, dear ones, please understand that we have told you this story for a reason. For Akarru is ending and with that energy of the death of a star comes a ripple in the Universal Energy which will affect every one of you. It has already been doing that over the last eight months. You are feeling the energy of Akarru leaving. You do not feel the grief over the loss of a planet; instead, you feel the other side of the Universal Energy. You feel life-force energy. Many of you will actually interpret this and feel it as sexual energy. Many of you will feel it because it will stimulate the Kundalini running up and down your spine. Depending on how you are accustomed to dealing with that, will make the difference on how you assimilate this energy. If you are accustomed to hiding and denying life-force, or sexual energy, you will have more to hide. If you are accustomed to expressing it, you will simply have more to express. If you are accustomed to transmuting it into other forms of energy, you will find there is much potential there including increased creativity. Please understand that, over the months and years ahead, you will be feeling this ripple of extra life-force energy that will come into your planet. It will come into your existence through parallel light, for a huge ripple in the Universal Energy is happening and it will affect each and every one of you. For it is as if someone took the rug, shook it, and you are just now starting to really feel this ripple. You have felt the beginning of this shift in energy and in the months ahead you will feel it more intensely.

## Lightworkers Call to Light

It will affect you in many different ways. Some will feel fear. Some will feel love. Some will feel a great need to move into whatever it is that you came here to do. That is why we tell you there will be no more closet Lightworkers. The truth is, you are needed now. In the midst of these heightened emotions, if you can only re-member this is much larger than you. This is the gift of a dying planet and what you know to be a solar system. Take that gift and move forward with it and it will not be in vain. Move yourself to find your own energy of greatest desire and your greatest work. What pulls at your own heartstrings will allow you to become the highest use to the universe that you will be. The next level of creation is at your door today. It has begun and you will set it into motion. The door of creation is open as a result of the death of Akarru. The energies are entering your reality now. We also ask you to please practice discernment. Discernment is the art of making life choices without judgment. It is used in the higher vibrations of the New Planet Earth and it replaces judgment. Judgment requires you to label something as good or bad, and apply polarity consciousness to it, and that is no longer appropriate in the higher vibrations of the New Planet Earth. So we ask you to begin replacing judgment with discernment, now more than ever. Because as these possibilities enter through the Universal Energy, and as these huge ripples that are placed into that energy, you will see that all things are achievable. You will begin to feel emotions on many levels. Watch those around you, as this energy can easily overwhelm people. This is a time to take a step back and practice your discernment of energy, then teach it to others. Choose what feeds you. Choose only those things that add to you and leave the rest without judgment. Do not take responsibility for all things everywhere. If you only take in the energies that add to you, you will very quickly find yourself very magically in your creations, and in your passion.

## Mastery of Light

The time is here and we tell you that the increase in energy will be great, indeed. Share with one another how you work with this. Share with each other the magic of what works for you. The Universal Energy binds all things to all people, and to all beings everywhere on all dimensional levels. Share with someone else where your successes are, where your failures are, where your perceived weaknesses are and those attributes will then become your greatest strengths. That is when you become the highest use to the universe you can be. That is the process of mastery. Create well, dear ones. Know that much of what you are feeling at this time and in the days ahead will be intensified by the Universal Energy and, even though you feel it as personal, some of it is not even about you, so apply your discernment well. Take those things that add to you at every opportunity and love it all unconditionally. Reach out and touch the hands of those next to you, for that will bring heaven to Earth this day, riding on the wave of the ripples in the Universal Energy.

Dear ones, when you signed up for this, you placed a veil on your head that kept you from seeing your magnificence and your true origin. You have spent much of your lives in search of the higher knowledge of your spirit. Many of you have gone in circles. Many of you have searched and have become professional seekers. We know and we honor you for that role, for it is only through that role of placing that veil that God can see himself/herself.

## Smells and Sounds Piercing the Veil

The intensity of the Universal Energy has increased in recent months. Additionally, your connection to it has also grown stronger. Many of you know you have been having connections with portals through inter-dimensional time and space, and sometimes that activates smells within your nose. Many times your own sense of smell can identify a portal between dimensions. We tell you also, become aware that your hearing will now change, and even as you start hearing buzzing, it simply means that sometimes those buzzes are the precursors to shifts that are about to happen as a result of the ripples in Universal Energy. At times, you will hear a rumbling or buzzing in your ears just prior to feeling these energy infusions. We offer this to you only as a key, only as a potential to help you understand that, even though sometimes you will feel like you are going crazy, you are not. You are here. You are a spirit playing the role of a human being and you are doing it well. All eyes are upon you, for you are making a difference by assimilating the death of a star. By experiencing the energy that flows through you, you are opening the door, now, for new events and the creations of a higher, greater, planet Earth. Thank you for setting it into motion.

We only offer you three suggestions. Nurture one another at every opportunity. Treat each other with the greatest and highest of respect, for you are God and understand that you are playing a wonderful Game and do not forget to play well together.

Espavo.

the Group

# The Third Earth

## A New Hologram for Earth

### May 2004

This month's message is a climax to the last several months' messages. The Group's messages are rarely presented to be read in any specific order. However, if you look at the last seven monthly Beacons of Light Re-minders from Home, you will see a definite order building to the creation of the Third Earth. The past messages have planted the seeds of understanding for Vortexes and Portals, the Crystal Energy, our changing relationship to time, and the Universal Energy. All of these messages are about us standing in the doorway to a new reality. Last month, the Group told us about the death of a star, and told the story of a family on the planet of Akarru. The story they told was about how this family dealt with learning that their sun and planet were dying. It was a beautiful but sad story about what life would be like if you had just learned that you, everyone around you, and your planet were about to die. One of the interesting points was that after the initial shock and reaction, the people of Akarru became very spiritual and focused only on the really important things in their lives.

With an understanding of the Crystal Energy, we know that energy never dies. Since we are energy, even in our own death, we simply change form, from one energy form to another. It is the Universal Energy that facilitates these transformations. Therefore the death of Akarru and Leilu, Amarah and Trudge is a gift to us, as the other side of their death is the opportunity for a wondrous birth. For this reason, the Group said we would be feeling an increase of life force energy entering through our sun. Most humans feel this as Kundalini or sexual energy.

Our own solar sun has been charging our planet with the Universal Energy for more than three years now. Recently, in November 2003, we had the largest Coronal Mass Ejection or solar flare ever on our sun. In fact, our scientists are really wondering if our own sun is in the process of dying. The Group says that our own sun is a portal for the Crystal Energy that will help us to step into higher dimensions. They say that the gift of the people of Akarru, including Leilu, Amarah, and Trudge, is being channeled to us through our own sun. Now we will use that energy to birth the Third Earth.

Recently in Belgium, we presented the 8 Sacred Rooms seminar. Our seminars always include a lot of hugs. As I was hugging a special lady, she looked up at me and told me, "You just gave me a Trudge hug." In that moment I came to understand that Trudge had given us all a wonderful gift, and he was probably looking just over my shoulder as I hugged her. Since the Third Earth will begin as a hologram and a collector for our highest thoughts about what we want in the fifth dimension, my first contribution to the Third Earth is a big Trudge hug to everyone I meet!

Greetings from Home.

Ah, here we sit at Home and watch with amazement as you create Home right in front of us. You are magical beings. You carry the energy of everything we have done in heaven, but you now carry it on Earth. Do you know how magical you are? Do you understand the essence of the true beings that you really are? We tell you, from this day forward, you are taking on a new role here and it is incredibly important for you to understand. That is why we have been here to help you remember. Now you have enacted a whole new level of creation that was not possible any other way. You have set into motion the possibility of creating something higher than was ever dreamt of, even as you play the Game. And now you sit at the precipice of the entire valley, looking across from the highest cliff, deciding where to go from here.

### New Abilities to Re-Create Heaven on Earth

Each one of you has gifts not fully understood, and yet you are starting to understand them now. Yes, you know that each and every one of you holds an important piece of the puzzle which is totally unique. That is why we call you the magicians of the Game board. That is why you are creating new energy this day. Now that magic goes to all new levels. The Harmonic Convergence and the Harmonic Concordance have given you capabilities that were not even dreamt of in the beginning. That is what we wish to speak to you of this day.

Dear ones, we cannot tell you of the excitement here in Heaven as we tell you this. We cannot fully explain the possibilities you now hold before you as you step into the power of your own individual creations. What you did not know is that in order to create your next step in the evolution of a soul, you will now re-create Earth. We will offer you a different perspective. We do not offer you the ultimate view of anything, but our purpose as angels is simply to help you see yourselves from a different view, the view of the angels. We will offer you that view this day.

## The Second Planet of Free Choice: Human – Human Angel – Angel

You are aware that until recently you have been the Only Planet of Free Choice. Now there is a Second Planet of Free Choice in motion on a separate timeline, evolving rapidly. Your own evolution is moving from that of human to Human Angel, and eventually into the angelic realm. And when you finally assimilate all the energy we are trying to gift you, you will step into the role we have been playing, for you will become the angels of the Second Planet of Free Choice in much the way we have been the angels of the First Planet of Free Choice. That is why you are here. In the meantime, you are becoming the Human Angels, for each of you is finding ways you can touch another human. We love it when you open your hearts and touch each other, for that is exactly what we have done for you, over and over again. Now you have the capability of angelic acts, we ask that you claim and use that ability. We ask you, as angels-in-training, to use it for each other. A Human Angel is one who makes a commitment to be placed at the exact junction of time and space to help another human. Then eventually you will use those gifts to be an angel to the inhabitants of the Second Planet of Free Choice. That is the purpose of the portals that have been opening on Planet

Earth. Not only will they open up other dimensional realities for you, but also they will eventually provide you with access to the beings on the Second Planet of Free Choice.

In the very beginning, we spoke of different boiling points, or hot spots, on Earth, all over the globe, that would connect to each other as you connected to your higher selves. It is happening this day. You are creating it yourselves. It is not the land. It is not the portal. It is you. You are the ones who have set this into motion through your own intent for your own opportunities to connect to other souls. The centers of light you all have created have already made a difference on Earth. That is why so many of you have had the dream of a healing center. Only by holding that dream within your hearts were you able to create the centers of light you will now use for the next creation.

In the near future, you will see movement though these portals as contact from what you call 'space beings.' We think that is quite humorous, as that is what the beings on the Second Planet of Free Choice will call you at one point. We love your conceptions of other life in the universe, although they are rarely accurate. There are inter-dimensional realities that live within your own time and space, and this is where many of the beings that you call 'visitors from outer space' have been all along. They have been waiting for the appropriate time. Oh yes, some of them are far advanced of you technologically. And some of them have been waiting a long time, with the full knowledge that they are not alone in the universe. Some of these beings are your own parental races. Some of them you will recognize, some of them you will not. We tell you that when the time is right, they will come through the portals and start showing up in your reality more than ever before. But it goes much farther than that. That is only the first part of the process. On the First Planet of Free Choice, you decided to put on the veil in a very unique way so you would completely forget your abilities of creation. You would be pushed into a survival mode, where you would not be able to re-member or use your power. You have done well at re-membering Home and taking your power while still in physical form. That is why we say you have already won the game. That is why a Second Planet of Free Choice has begun. But it does not stop there for, as advanced beings, you will start re-creating Earth itself to take your next step.

## The Third Earth: A New Hologram for the Fifth Dimension

This is why we show you how we have interacted with you as angels; for you will be using these tools exclusively in the future as you become angels yourselves. It will be important for you to interact and find effectiveness in your world first as a Human Angel, for that is how you will spread your joy. That is how you will know your own passion and what you have come to do. For even though you may find small pieces of it at this moment, it will become more important as time goes on, for there is something happening here that we speak of this day. In the beginning there was the Only Planet of Free Choice. Now there is the Second Planet of Free Choice ... and now we speak of the creation of the Third Earth.

As you move vibrationally from one level to another to another, it is important to understand that you have been playing a Game on what originally began as a hologram. Even your ancient human writings speak of the creation of the Earth as a thought-form of God that was created in six days. These ethereal thought-forms are actually holograms of light. Therefore it should be known that, even as the Earth is a living, loving and sentient being, she began her incarnation as a thought of God, as a hologram. Earth is the stage where you play out the dramas of your lives. You get up in the morning, brush your teeth, comb your hair, get into the car and go to work. You are playing a wonderful Game pretending to be human, when, in fact, you are spirits playing a game in human form. Many times you are creating the dirt below your feet as you step forward. You create every second of every day as your expectations and beliefs allow. Earth has been the most generous host for the game you play when you put on the veil. She is a part of you and you are a part of her. But even as a living, sentient being, there is much evolution that the Earth must undergo to fully support the dimensional shift to make space for fully empowered humans. Your evolution from the third dimension into the fifth dimension has already begun, yet there must still be adjustments to fully assimilate the attributes of the fifth dimension.

To facilitate those adjustments, you will now create a new hologram for the new Earth. Once again, it will begin in the ethers as a thought-form of God, only this creation will manifest from the God within each of you.

You will build the hologram of the Third Earth with the highest intent that you wish to carry forward into your next evolutionary step. Then, when the image is complete, the Third Earth hologram will imprint itself over the top of the First Earth. At that stage, a unique thing will happen, for all vibrational levels will move as one. That is what you have known as ascension. It is in progress now. Yes, we know this whole hologram thing is hard to fathom for some of you. Let us put it very simply. Imagine a sacred space where you retreat and rejuvenate. It is your special room. You may have a favorite space beneath a walnut tree that sits on the edge of a lake. You may have a room with a golden chair right in the middle of it where you claim your power. Whatever it is, all of you have used such places to reset your energy from time to time. Then, when you have incorporated the serenity within your heart that this sacred space offered, you will walk from that special space carrying the energy within you. That is the space that you are creating in the Third Earth. That is the uniqueness of what you create in the mental image that you will now project to create this hologram. It is not that you will go and live on the Third Earth at some point, but rather it will come to you and lie over the imprint that is now Earth. This will effectively reprogram the original hologram and make space for fully empowered humans to begin a new game.

So you have the First Planet of Free Choice, you have the Second Planet of Free Choice and you now have the Third Earth. Yes, your minds will want to know much: "Where is it? In what part of which quadrant of the Universe does it exist? What dimensional reality is it in?" We love the questions and yet we laugh hysterically when you ask them, for how can we tell you the exact location of a thought pattern? How can we explain to you the coordinates in the galaxy of your dreams? That is what you are creating this with, dear ones. Now is the time to become masters of your thoughts, for all of Earth is in the process of a grand creation.

## Reconnecting to the Parental Races

The energetic machinery that has helped to create the veil has been in place for a very long time, and now you are starting to perceive it as the veil thins. Your own ears are advancing to a level where many of you will begin hearing more and more of that machinery that has existed behind the veil to help support it. Many of you will hear mechanical sounds that you have never heard before. Many of you will hear things that are not of your own biology, but instead are hearing the actual machinery that breathes life through All That Is. You will be hearing the Universal Energy as it pulses through you and connects you to the Earth.

As this activates, it will call in many of your parental races, who will begin showing up en masse. They love you dearly and will go to any extent to stay out of your way to allow your

Game to move gently and naturally to the next level. There may be some, however, who will approach with great audacity and say, "We are here. We are back. We are here to help you move forward." Hold your power, dear ones. Although your natural curiosity will want contact with them, you do not *need* help. You hold much more power than you can possibly imagine. Are they the bad guys? Of course not. They are your parents in much the same way that some of your countries were first started by other countries. Hold them in respect and learn what they have to offer, yet remember that their highest hope in creating a race of humans was for that race to hold their own power in human form.

They will come to you with advanced technology and intellect. They will come to you with knowledge of the universe that will help you tremendously. Some may tell you that they are here to save the day and to move humanity to the next level. Please understand, they are simply here to watch, because you have already saved the day. You have even altered *their* reality. And although most will sit in the background and wait quietly to be called upon, some of them will come right to the forefront and claim an illusive victory. You are the ones who created victory. Do not ever lose sight of that. Please do not give your power to anyone, for you will use that power to create the hologram of the Third Earth.

## The Crystal Energy Will Be Used to Create the Hologram

The portals that are opening on Planet Earth now will connect you with realities instantly, and you may never know what quadrant of the universe they are in, nor will it matter, for you will create the image of the Central Sun in this space.

The Central Sun is the first place of origin of physicality. It is the first place of the infinite energy becoming finite. You have been imprinted with the crystal energy which has been coming in from the sun in what you know to be solar flares. This energy has been storing in the Earth for several years. It has been building and will now provide you with the material to manifest this new hologram for the intentional creation of the new earth. This will help you and the Earth herself to form crystalline bodies. The Crystal Children will soon inhabit the Earth. They carry the imprints already, contained within their own DNA. Yours are advancing toward that now. Every time you see the master numbers* on a clock, every time you see certain imprints, every time you see the figure eight or the infinity sign, it is an imprint and trigger for your own DNA to begin the reconnection process. That is exciting beyond belief, for you are advancing into the crystalline form. The crystalline form will allow you to move to the next level and create your own imprints. The hologram you now create in your own thoughts is the Third Earth that will create the new stage for the new you. The interesting part is that some of you will see it and some of you will not. For it will be of such a vibrational level that those of high enough vibration to see it will incorporate it readily. The rest will not fully see it at this time. It will take time, but you begin first by creating it. You begin first by understanding the process and helping others to adjust to it. These are the acts of a Human Angel.

As time goes forward, there will be another breath of God. And at that point, the Earth will take on its original form and once again become the library of the Universe. It was halfway there. It was well underway in the beginning, but the Planet of Free Choice meant free choice for all, and the game took a turn. Now you have an opportunity to re-create that same library again. All it takes is to hold that pure thought in your own heart and intentionally send it to the hologram of the Third Earth.

---

* In numerology, the master numbers are 11, 22, 33 and 44.

## The Magic of Three

You will see much about the number three in the very near future. Yes, there will be many who talk about different aspects of the Third Earth. Please know that all you see before you is made up of threes. It is the base number for creation, as all things are based on the triad. We are not the first to speak of this. All we wish to do is to offer you a different perspective of what this looks like, to share with you our excitement, our love, our energy, and to hold our wings out in front of you so that you can see yourselves the way you can only be seen from heaven. You are the masters of the Game board, dear ones. You have created your wildest dreams and now you are starting all over again. It took six days to create the Earth and now you will begin counting backward in time to create the Third Earth. It has begun. You are doing it and you are doing it in a more grandiose fashion than you ever dreamt of, for the hand of God is at work here. Dream your highest dream. Dare to step into that room with that golden chair. Dare to put yourself under that tree and overlook that lake. Dare to find yourself happy. Dare to accept your full abundance of all energy on all levels you can. Turn around and share that, and project it out and create the most beautiful place that you can create and you will have the Third Earth. It has begun. It can either be created as an intentional creation or it can be handed to you by default. The decision is yours now. It is moving faster than you can possibly know, for we tell you, many of the opportunities that were to happen in 2012 are already given to you. You have surpassed the days of Lemuria and Atlantis. You are now a higher vibration than ever dreamt of by your parental races. The possibilities are endless, dear ones. Claim your power. Step forward in every moment. Know that even what you see in front of you as turmoil on your planet can be healed by the smile on your face, for you are responsible for your reality and none other. Create that reality first and create it in your heart, which will create it all around you and on the Third Earth.

## Lemuria Did Not Sink – Create in Unity

We tell you, the tales of Lemuria are confusing for most of you. The writings talk about Lemuria sinking into the sea itself and ending. It did not, dear ones. It ascended. It was such a simple, advanced society that the beings went forward to step into the next vibrational level to hold the door open for others to follow. It was a wonderful, beautiful experiment. It did not work the way they wished it to work, for the door closed very abruptly in the sinking of Atlantis. And even though it was done with great heart desire and great energy, there was a misdirection of energy, for some went ahead and some stayed behind, and we tell you, that will never happen again. Even as it was offered from the heart, that act of selflessness added to separation and not unity. When you move into the next stage, all of you must move into the stage. That is why you have turmoil on your planet at this moment. There is energy that must be distributed in order for all of you to find a base on which you can build a base of love. Please do not put yourself down or ridicule yourself because there is war upon your planet. Things are playing out now. There will come a time when you will look back on these things and say: "Thank God that happened. We are so glad we do not have to go through that again." Step forward with it. Stand in your truth. Create the Third Earth in love and unity and from what you have learned as a result of all the negative energy that you have gone through. Take that negative energy which has dropped below the line of normal and use it in a positive form to create the Third Earth. Then you will have created a sacred space for the Children of Crystal Vibration to enter. They will then help you move into that crystalline energy yourself, comfortably and quickly.

Dear ones, the task is at hand. You are up to it. Your beauty is beyond description, for you stand tall as the creators, the Masters of the Game board. We can spread our wings to show you who you really are. Take the energy you have this day. Take it from your sacred space and allow others to see it. When your space includes the beautiful Third Earth, you are inviting them into your sacred room. Share the dream.

It is with the greatest of honor that we touch your heart with only three re-minders. Treat each other with respect. Nurture one another other at every opportunity. Re-member that it is a Game, and you are supposed to be having fun. Play well together.

Espavo.

the Group

# Lemurian Energy Reservoir

## Web of Love Activation

### September 18 2004

From Steve:

This message from the Group was originally presented the day of the Web of Love experiment on September 18, 2004. The Web of Love activation had well over 200,000 participants representing many parts of the globe. It was a true heart connection to open a new grid of love for all of us to use.

The data collected will be used as the basis for a scientific study and subsequent published paper among the scientific community. To accommodate different time zones, this experiment was conducted on two separate occasions at 11:00 a.m. (1100) and 4 p.m. (1600) US Pacific Time on 18 September 2004 for 25 minutes duration. See all the Web of Love information at

www.Lightworker.com/WebofLove.

Under the auspices of Measurements Research Inc., an independent laboratory in Providence, Rhode Island, and in conjunction with our partner hosts, we presented a global experiment called the Web of Love to scientifically monitor the effects of human emotion on specified target objects.

The lead scientist, Edward Chouniard, oversaw all of the experiments and measurements personally. I got to know Ed very well during this time. He was a true scientist at heart but had come to search for higher answers. We met at one of our seminars in Attleboro, Massachusetts. This was a life long dream of his, as it was of mine, and after talking, I offered to organize this event if his laboratory would take the measurements.

We had done this several times during our seminars before, so we knew we were on to something. In Oostmalle, Belgium, we stopped the seminar for a 20-minute experiment, with the laboratory measuring the results. We repeated these experiments at different seminars in Baltimore, Maryland, Kona, Hawaii and Elspeet, Holland. Then the global experiment took place just preceding this channel on September 18, 2004.

It took Measurements Research Inc. about 30 days to publish the first findings of the experiment and they all led to positive results. Ed cautioned that there was a lot of data still to be studied but he was now without a doubt that this worked. His goal now was to publish a scientific paper in the scientific community to show other scientists the results. Those papers are published on the Lightworker web site at: www.lightworker.com/WebofLove (click on "Results").

We will warn the reader these papers are very technical and high level science. A synopsis of the paper's conclusion follows:

Conclusions

Though this is just a beginning and lots of data needs yet to be unraveled, nevertheless, but there can be no doubt that the worldwide mental protocols presented herein have dramatically affected the response of physical scientific apparatus. Man appears to be directly coupled to the geomagnetic fields, and mental influences from great distances can and do affect the targeted geomagnetic environment and consequently mankind itself via the coupling of these fields to the cellular structure. Such telepathic type phenomena can no longer be considered a figment of misdirected emotions and/or of an overactive metaphysical imagination. This is the physical reality of a new world order.

Edward Chouniard, lead scientist of Measurements Research Inc. never published these papers in the scientific community as far as we know. He died only days after sending them to me to put on the web site. A cancer he believed to be in full remission returned suddenly to take his life very quickly. In talking to his wife, she said that this experiment was a life long journey for Ed and now that it was done, Ed was complete.

Our heartfelt thanks to Ed for being in his passion. He made a difference on Earth, even if no scientist ever sees those papers. More than 200,000 of us know and felt what happened that day. We owe that you Ed, but then I am quite sure that you know that.

What follows is the message from the Group that showed some of the practical uses of this new connection. It also marked the first in a new series of messages they have called "The Practical Magic Series."

Happy creating!

Steve

Greetings from Home.

Ah, yes. You have created Home this day. You are now connecting to each and every one of you. You are beginning to see things you have not seen before. It is a new time. It is a new age. The energy of love now connects each and every one of you. You have created a miracle in the space that is now before you.

What we will offer you this day are only a few new games to play within that new miracle you have created. We offer you some ideas of how you can activate it further and use it on a practical basis. All the information we have given over the years is nothing more than words on paper. The truth of the matter is, none of it has any magic whatsoever until you use it in your life in a practical manner. We offer you this day a view of how to use the Web of Love and the connections you have made for practical magic. These are practical applications of how you use this new connection.

Much of our focus from this day forward will be speaking to a higher form of humanity. You will notice it, as have we. We will make adjustments to reach you on a higher level from this day forward because of your actions, your willingness, and your intention to set about your own connections of your hearts. You are the new humanity. You are the chosen ones, for you have chosen to be here at exactly this moment in time. You are the ones who did everything you could to make sure that you came at exactly this moment so that you could be here to help the miracle happen. And here you are. The miracle is unfolding now.

## Practical Magic

So the practical magic we will show you this day has to do with strengthening that energy that forms the Web of Love, for it has begun. But like any creation, any great painting, any music you play or books you write, if the creation loses the connection to other people, at that point it dissipates and fades away. It goes into the annals of time as "the big flash that was not." Although we make very few predictions, we predict that this new connection will grow and not fade. Now it is up to each and every one of you to use it in some practical way, for that is the only way to ground this new energy on planet Earth. By the very nature of the Web of Love, using this new energy in your lives will ensure that the connection is strengthened. Thus, we will share with you some of the opportunities to utilize that energy on a practical basis. This will begin a new series of messages we will call 'The Practical Magic Series.'

## The Distribution of Water-Energy

In order to see this from a different perspective, let us take you back to a time when many of your communities on Earth were beginning. There were times when you would gather in high-energy spots. These were the early settlers of planet Earth, being drawn to these energy hot spots. In fact, by doing this, they determined the location of most of the big cities that exist even today. Many people would come together living in the same area, sometimes because the hunting was good or the terrain provided security or shielded you from the elements. You inhabited caves in some locations, and in others you formed small cities simply on the flat land. All of these settlements began because they were energy hot spots that connected people together. In fact, they were the first origins of what you know today to be the Web of Love.

Still, there has always been a challenge when groups settle in this fashion. The distribution of energy that you call 'water' is critical for a group of people to bond and grow. It is necessary for water to circulate evenly throughout the entire community. If that was achieved, then the foundation was in place for a city to grow. The same is true with the Web of Love, although it is a different type of energy. Water is a base energy that must circulate for humans to flourish. We will show this in comparison to what you have done this day. The Web of Love is an aqueduct that will allow the water to circulate.

Man no longer searches for a central location to gain strength in numbers. It is now about finding ways to connect wherever you are. That is the advancement you have accomplished in your evolutionary cycle to place you here at this time. That is what is happening. So as you do this, it all becomes magic. It all becomes 'practical magic.'

You learned something in the early days of humanity in your early existence as infinite beings in finite form, for you ended up doing some very magical things. One of the things you learned to do with water was to create a reservoir to ensure constant supply to all. Here you created great reservoirs to collect the water for the community so it could be distributed equally to all of you. This helped your cities grow. This helped the foundation of communities, connecting hearts together on a very practical level, to grow to the next level and to evolve into human form.

## The Lemurian Ascension

Now we ask you to consider applying this same concept to the Web of Love. In reality it is a concept that has been used since the days of Lemuria. Lemuria was an advanced civilization. It was so far advanced that the Lemurians did not need many of the things you believe you need even today. Many of you are here from the days of Lemuria and from Atlantis. Many of you have concepts about what that was like and remembrances of why you are here and what you are here doing. We wish to correct some of the concepts because it is widely written that Lemuria sank into the ocean. We tell you that did not happen in quite that fashion, for the souls of Lemuria were so far advanced in understanding that they became childlike.

When humans become so advanced that they become childlike, the Earth becomes a very difficult place to inhabit. The continent of Lemuria did not sink. Instead, Lemuria ascended into a higher state of vibration. Even today, Lemuria exists in the same physical location as it has always been. It is simply in a higher vibrational state that places it into an altered dimension of time and space which supports the advanced beings of Lemuria. It was done so by the intent of all, by the connection of each one, for it was understood that all of humanity at that point was reaching a level where it was possible to move to the next vibrational state.

Those of you who were there in those magical days of Lemuria decided to go ahead and hold the door open. You went ahead and created the space, but what you did not understand was that the Universal Energy will never support segregation. Even though you did so from the heart, a segregation was set into motion that eventually led to the sinking of Atlantis.

In those days, there were some magical things you used, as advanced souls working from the heart energy. We will share these tools with you over time, for you are now ready to listen. You are now ready to put these tools back into practical use.

## Secret of the Lemurian Energy Reservoir

One of these tools we will share with you this day. It is now possible, since you have activated the Web of Love. It is the Lemurian Energy Reservoir. It has been in use for a very long time. Much the way you have found ways to collect and distribute the energy of water in your cities, you will now use that same concept to collect and distribute life force energy.

We think it is very interesting that the Keeper and the Keeper's keeper now are living in Las Vegas, where there is a five-year drought in progress. The residents here are being motivated to find ways to distribute the water more efficiently.

It is that distribution which will determine the future growth of this area. And as you move into this, you now have the same choices with the Web of Love. Creating and re-creating the Lemurian Reservoir of Energy is now available to each and every one of you because of the Web of Love. That connection – that heart energy that allows each and every one of you to connect to the other hearts – is now strengthened 177 times over what it was just a few hours ago.

With that increase, allowing the energy to move through you without being overwhelming is your next task at hand. That is the energy you are to incorporate as you move forward, for it is the practical use of this energy that will determine its relevance in your own evolutionary cycle and your place in universal history. We tell you this: the Lemurians, those who ascended, are with you this day. They are watching every move you make, for you now have the opportunity to take that energy – that love, that heart connection – and put it into practical use in your daily life. This was their intent in the beginning. Perhaps you can now see the magnitude of the cycle that is completing this day. All eyes are upon you.

For those of you who have incarnated lifetime after lifetime in order to bring that Lemurian energy back, what we will say next will be something you already know deep within your being. There is a place of storage that exists and crosses into all dimensions of reality. This is the Lemurian Energy Reservoir. Like any reservoir, the more energy you place into this storage facility, the more there is for all. Increasing the distribution capabilities of this energy leads to faster advancement of the whole. This one factor will help the collective vibration of humanity rise more than you may know.

## Energy Knows No Lack

Please know that lack is only an illusion of duality. Energy is the expression of abundance; therefore, it is not possible to have a lack of energy. It is only possible to have a restriction of the distribution of energy. So now we ask you to consider strengthening your distribution of the Web of Love energy. Use those hearts to connect with everyone else on that Web of Love. Know that there is a special place called the Lemurian Energy Reservoir and your job, if you so choose, is to add to that reservoir.

Take time every day, when you feel good, when you feel energetic, when you feel the love pulsing through you, and send energy toward that reservoir. You will find the true meaning of "energy knows no lack," for even as you give energy, you will find yourself filling at the same time. In those times when you are feeling the love energy from whatever source, for whatever reason, take just a moment and store a piece of that beautiful energy intentionally. No, you do not have to do three hours of meditation to get there. You can simply close your eyes and make it so. You are magical beyond belief!

Being human, there may come days when you are tired and do not feel like adding to the reservoir. There may come the times when you are not feeling well, when you fall into reversed polarity and try the things you have done successfully time and again and you just miss. Those are the days when we ask you to tap into that same reservoir, allowing yourself to fill from it completely. Know that it is not possible to deplete the reservoir, for energy knows no lack. It is the movement of energy that makes it grow stronger. Practice this, and soon you will find your energy can be re-set in a heartbeat. Your energy can change, and you have new capabilities of working with your energetic structure inside a physical bubble of biology that you have not had before. That is practical magic, and it is available for you on levels that you have never seen before because of the miracle you have set into motion this day.

## Humans Have a Problem with Reality

Humans have a problem with reality. You think it is real. It is not. You are not separate from each other. You are part of each other. The veil of forgetfulness you wear allows you to play the Game in a human bubble of biology. It is what keeps you from seeing you all share a stream of consciousness which connects all of you as a whole. That stream is now more accessible because of your intent in activating the Web of Love. Understanding the concept of the Lemurian Energy Reservoir will allow you to put it into practical use on a daily basis.

As in all things, there are no rules as to how to access the Lemurian Energy Reservoir. We do not tell you: take three steps forward, touch one knee to the floor, move to your right, turn the doorknob, and walk in, for that is not the way to get there. You have to determine the path for yourself. That is the second wave of empowerment. What works for you? Your intent and your practical application of these useful tools will depend entirely on your own choosing. Play with it. Dare to make mistakes as the children of Lemuria would. Make lots of good mistakes, and find what works for you.

Just knowing the concept of the Lemurian Energy Reservoir – that there is a place in the midst of the entire Web of Love where you can store energy for your own personal use and to share with other people over the world – is your first step toward being a Human Angel. That is the step in your own evolutionary process, which allows you to put something out there for everyone else. In so doing, you feed yourself beyond your understanding. That is what makes you shine. That is what makes you glow. That is what makes you Lightworkers.

## Scripting the Grand Plan

It is in motion this day. We are so very excited at your movement. We are so very thrilled and so very proud of you.

You have no idea, for you think you are sitting somewhere in a small group of people or in a room alone. You are not. All eyes of the Universe are upon you as you connect your hearts together. Your intent to do so has elevated you. Know there is no grand plan in place but you have dipped the quill in the ink and you hold it over the parchment, and we cannot wait to see what you write. Your game is in overtime. Now there is no limit as to what you can do, for you are moving from one step of becoming the humans to becoming the Human Angels. It will not be long after that you move into the angelic realm, and you will become the angels to the Second Planet of Free Choice. That is what is happening. You are in training, and we cannot wait to see the frustrations you will experience that we experience now. And when you hear enigmatic laughter over your shoulder, know that it is we, for we will be there with the greatest of love.

## Do You Believe?

We have offered you the practical magic of the Lemurian Energy Reservoir. It is up to you, as all things are. It is simply one of the tools you may use that we consider to be practical magic. We will use those words a lot in the days ahead, for recently we asked you, "Do you believe?" And then we asked you, "Do you believe in magic?" And then we asked you the important question, "Do you believe in the magic in you?" And you all nodded your heads "Yes." You have set the stage for the practical magic that now lies ahead. Our highest intent is to be here as the angels, spreading our wings so we may reflect your magnificence.

It is with the greatest of honor that we have joined you this day and watched the miracle you created. You have done something beyond the understanding of your own level of vibration. All eyes in all levels of vibration have watched what you have done this day. Be proud. Stand proudly in the love of Home. Stand in your own truth. Hold the energy of who you are, and share it openly, lovingly, with all who will take it. Set that energy on the Web of Love, and when you have more than your heart can hold, send it to the Lemurian Energy Reservoir and know that it will be safe there and well-distributed.

It is with the greatest love that we ask you to treat each other with respect, re-member the E-factor, and nurture one another at every opportunity. Keep in mind that it is a game you are playing and you are supposed to be having fun. Play well together.

Espavo.

the Group

# The Fifth Stage of Life

## Practical Magic Series

## May 2005

All of the OverLight modalities we teach at Lightworker are based on the material in Spiritual Psychology. There, you will find the Group's explanation of why we are here and how we venture through seven stages of life. At the close of the Spiritual Psychology book from Lightworker Publications, the Group told us that, as we advance, these stages will change very little. What will change is that we will start going through these stages all over again without having to die and leave Earth. Here they give us an opportunity to experience just that, as they walk us through the last three stages of life.

Since the publication of these three channels, we have heard from many therapists, teachers and healers that they have successfully used these techniques with their clients. This is an astounding way to clear your energy for a now life without having to leave the body. That is what the Group calls ascension and it is available to each of us today.

This was broadcast as a VirtualLight Broadcast and can be seen as it was presented live at www.Lightworker.com/VirtualLight

Enjoy the journey.

Steve

Greetings from Home.

## From Destination to Journey Consciousness

We join you this day at your request, not to tell you which way to turn or to tell you what you are doing right or wrong, but to hold the mirror in front of you so you may see who you truly are. Do you re-member who you are? We do. We have come for the specific purpose of helping you see what you came to do, and to show you where you are on that journey. Now you are asking, "How can I step forward into higher vibrations and how can I be 'on purpose' as an intentional creator?" Ah, but it does not end there, for many of you have found your purpose. Many of you have found your passion – or at least part of it. Keep in mind that it is not about moving into your passion; it is about moving in the *direction* of your passion, for moving from destination consciousness and into journey consciousness is your natural evolution and why we are here. In that way, we can even say that all of life is about learning to enjoy the ride.

It might interest you to know that you are all going to the same place. You are coming Home again ... but not before you create Home on Earth. That is why you came here in the first place. We have been doing our best to give you suggestions to let you see yourself from a different perspective so you can re-member pieces you forgot. Today, we will take that a step further. Practical magic is our passion. All the information the Keeper puts out, all the books, all the seminars, all the DVDs he loves to play with, are simply ideas in the ethers. The ideas have no meaning whatsoever until someone takes something and uses it in a practical application to make their life a little better. That is practical magic.

## A New Perspective on the Seven Stages of Life

This day we offer you one more piece of practical magic, yet what we offer you today will go on beyond our message for you at this moment. It will stretch over a period of three months. First let us share with you a vision of yourself from the perspective of the spirit looking at the human. We have given much of the information the Keeper calls Spiritual Psychology, but let us share with you the next step in that evolution. There are seven stages of life. You go through each one incrementally, on purpose, to pick up specific mastery opportunities. These stages are not defined by years, but by your vibrational evolution.

Humans are evolving. You are no longer the lower vibrational people you used to be only a short time ago. You are now reaching for higher truth to support higher vibrations. As you evolve from one level to the next, you start grasping new ideas; you start seeing yourself in a different way. We wish to offer you a suggestion this day about how to see yourself over the next three months. It is a game, but then all of life is a game, so we offer you a new game and a new way to view the last three stages of your life. The fifth, sixth and seventh stages of life can now be viewed in a new timeline. As you evolve, there will not be any new stages added. Instead, you will start over again in the same physicality. You will be re-birthed within the same physiology; the connection to spirit will have a new ignition and you will be able to move through another lifetime in the same physical body.

## Enlightened Seeker to Enlightened Knower

The process of re-birthing and moving into the next level can begin today. Let us share with you how you can look at the next three stages of your lives. In the fifth stage of maturity, things start changing for you. You stop looking for your truth outside of yourself and start accepting it inside of yourself for the first time. Instead of being the seeker, you become the *"know-er."* The evolution of that fifth stage of life is the opportunity for you to understand that you are God, that you are a creator, and that you have a responsibility to All That Is to use those powers of creation.

Yes, we know. It is difficult for you to comprehend that. We know that your egos get in the way and you try to hold them off, and it becomes difficult for you to see who you are. We also know there is a difficulty for you in understanding the difference between when to create and when to allow. We will offer you a very simple solution for the question, although it is all semantics anyway, for even a state of being is actually a creation. Let us offer you a simple suggestion. When to create and when to allow is answered by a single question: are you happy where you are? If you are, then be. If you are not, then dare to choose again and create a different reality. We tell you simply that all change leads to something better. Yes, we know. Humans do not like change. They resist it with great effort; however, all change will lead you into evolution.

## The Fifth Stage Question: What Is Really Important?

At a point in your evolution, you begin to grasp truth on a soul level. It is then that you start to direct your own change and to activate your own changes and creations. What we offer now is an opportunity to put that into practice. It is then that you become creators, taking responsibility for your own happiness and passion. It is then that you become of the highest use to the Universe you can be. That is where the magic lies. The fifth stage of life becomes about finding that truth within yourselves. The question asked of everyone in the fifth stage of life is: "What is really important?"

The seekers begin seeking in the third stage of life. Finding the truth within and becoming an enlightened knower does not generally happen until the fifth stage of life. Finding that connection point, that ability to create, that opportunity for you to take responsibility for your own creations and holding that little sense of peace, is what is before you this day. We ask you to consider setting your intentions to step into that stage of life with us now, no matter where you are. The seven stages of life are the general course each soul takes in a journey of evolution within each lifetime. What we are suggesting now is to intentionally step through the last three stages together with us over the next three months. This exercise will offer advanced souls possibilities to experience intentional creation.

## Starting Over Without Dying

We will offer some very simple suggestions, but before we do, let us take you down the road, for you love walking backward in time. Let us share what we will speak about for the next three months. Each stage of life has a specific purpose for the evolution of the soul. It is not always done in the order we have specified, nor are all the stages always completed in each lifetime. They are simply the general life guideline your spirit has laid out for your evolution within each lifetime. As we take you through the last three stages of life, one every month, it may be helpful to know what will happen after that journey. How is this going to evolve and where does it end? It is very simple. It does not end; you simply start over at the beginning. Stage one is the planning stage where most contracts are made before the incarnation. Can you imagine what it would be like to plan your next incarnation while still remaining in physical form?

We are going to offer you opportunities to see how this can apply in your daily lives now, no matter what stage of life you are in currently. As we lead you through the applications of incorporating those pieces, it will lead you to re-write your game – to start over, to re-birth, and to blossom with a new bloom. It will allow you opportunities to move through the process of evolution and what you have been calling ascension. This day we talk to you about the level of maturity, about reaching an opportunity where you can find the essence of your being and what is really important.

## Determining What Is Important

One of the suggestions we will offer you is to pretend that everything has been taken from you. If your family is important, move it away for just a moment. If your job is important and helps define you, move it away for just a moment. If your possessions are what you have clung to so desperately, move them away for just a moment. What is left? That is the question we ask you to bring yourself to during the next 30 days, for moving through the fifth stage of life will open the door for all the remainder to go forward, and for you to step into your own evolutionary process this day. So that it is not necessary to physically remove these items, we ask that you energetically remove your attachment to all the things you have deemed as important and release them with love. Then and only then, can you really determine what is really important from a soul level.

We love games. We have been watching yours with great intensity and playing whenever possible. We love to enter your game when you invite us in. We are doing so now, but it is your game. We are here as the mirror to keep you from forgetting who you really are. We are here to pick you up off the ground every once in a while and re-mind you of your magnificence. We are here to blow the dust away so you may see your own light and understand the effect you have on others and your responsibility to create. That is the role of the angels – to reflect the magnificence of humans. We ask you this day to send yourself forward into the fifth stage of life, to bring yourself forward and pretend that you are here in a situation in your life where everything must be re-evaluated. Everything you have must be looked at for its true importance in your life.

## When the Stuff You Own Owns You

It was not long ago that the Keeper and the Keeper's Keeper moved. They had been in one place for twenty-seven years. He called himself a collector and she called him a packrat. He collected everything that meant something for, "Someday I might use that item." We tell you, there comes a time when your stuff owns you, and we ask you to look at that now. We ask you to look not only at possessions but also at relationships and all things you believe are important to you. When you release the need for all the things outside of you, then you may enjoy even more than what you had in the first place, for only then do you understand its true place in your life. That is the process which opens the door, and it is usually defined in the fifth stage of life.

That sets up the opportunity for you to move into the sixth stage of life, where you may experience a true Lemurian existence. Each one of you goes through it as you become childlike. We will speak of that next month, for it is an important part of your process as human beings evolving back into the soul and releasing the body. The evolutionary path is that you come in as a Spirit, jump into a body, and go through all this time on Earth in a process to lose that same body. In the fifth stage, we are trying only to help you remember what is really important and who you really are.

## For Thirty Days ... Evaluate Everything

During the next thirty days, with everything that you encounter, we ask you to look at its true relevance to your Spirit and find out what is really important. It does not mean you need to release it. It does not mean you need to give everything away. It does not mean you need to fill two dumpsters like the Keeper did. What it does mean is that you are changing your reality by shifting your own perception. Find out what is important to you by releasing all attachment, and you will begin to understand what is important to your spirit as spoken through your higher self.

The connection to your higher self is much closer than you think. Many of your own life decisions are not made by the lower conscious mind but are made in conjunction with the higher self. The death process is not a conscious decision in most instances. This and many other important decisions are made from a junction of the higher and lower selves. When that connection is in place, your own higher self relieves you of the need to carry the body. The fifth stage of life is the first step in that direction. That is usually the conclusion of life. Now, it is not about leaving. It is returning to spirit. It is not about re-membering Home or going there. It is about creating Home where you now are. It is about learning how to live, learning how to be in your passion now. That is the expression of God you have the capacity for, that no one else has.

Even we, the angels in heaven, cannot do some of the most wondrous things you can accomplished behind the veil. We cannot hug another person; that is reserved for you. We cannot touch another life. We cannot ignite another soul through looking into their eyes and helping them re-member. by way of a physical glance. who they are. You can, and that is why you are here – to work with yourself and ignite your own light and turn around and look into the eyes of another person. To do that, we ask you to look at your life and experience everything that comes into your life over the next thirty days and see what is really important to you. The interesting part is, it doesn't make any difference what you decide. It is not the outcome of the decision your soul is looking for. It is simply the experience of reviewing. It is not the destination; it is the journey.

## Merlin's Path

Step backward in time and shift your reality, for as you do, you become like Merlin and walk backward in time. Your vision is faced toward your past. If you are very present, your consciousness will see where you are, but you do not see your future. So, in fact, you are always walking backward in time. When we tell you to walk backward in time intentionally, it means turning around and walking into your future. That is what you are doing now in the next thirty days. More capabilities are available now than ever before on the planet because of your collective rise in vibration, because of the energy that you share. Set that into motion this day and watch the magic unfold. Dare to look around you at everything that happens and everything that enters your life – at every person you meet, at every thing that you grasp that has had importance in your life – and simply evaluate its true meaning and its true usefulness to your soul. We will walk you through these last three stages of life very effectively and very quickly, so you may begin a new planning session – the first stage of life. Purposely write your script for what you have called the ascension.

Dear ones, you are there for each other. Reach out often. Hold your power. Do not give it to us. Do not look to us for all your answers. Do not listen to every word we speak. Take only the pieces that resonate with your heart, for you are the ones who must hold the power. Discern what is right for you and create magic. Pull it from everywhere you can find, and watch as your world begins to change for the better. If you find that this means nothing more than walking with peace of mind and a smile on your face, we ask you to consider that perhaps this may be what you had in mind when you came into this planet.

It is with the greatest of honor that we sit with you and offer reminders from Home. We have waited for eons for the opportunity to do it. If we can hold the mirror, if we can brush the dust away so you can get a glimpse of yourself, then we have done our job and are in our passion. We leave you with these simple reminders: treat each other with the greatest of respect. Nurture one another every opportunity you can, for you are actually nurturing yourself. And re-member that it is a game; play well together.

Espavo.

the Group

# The Sixth Stage of Life

## Practical Magic Series

### June 2005

This Beacons was presented in Zeist, Netherlands before a family gathering of 300 lightworkers. This channel was originally presented as a VirtualLight Broadcast and can be seen as a video as it was presented live at www.Lightworker.com/VirtualLight

Greetings from Home.

We visit you this day with the greatest joy, for we now sit in the presence of masters – those of you who have played on this Game board, daring to forget your mastery, your heritage and own royal lineage. Your willingness to do this has set into motion a whole process of evolution never before reached. We sit at your feet and honor you. Do you know who you are? We do. We only wish to spread our wings for you this day so you may get a small feeling of what it is like to hold this energy from Home. Every time any one of you holds your own passion in your own heart and steps further into your own development, every one of you comes a little bit closer. You are doing that even now for as your own evolution continues, you will find changes happening in your own process of the seven stages of life.

## The Final Stage of Life

It was only last month that we asked you to envision yourself going through the fifth stage of life and to experience the process of mastery as experienced in the stage of life known as maturity. Instead of being the grand seeker, you became the enlightened seeker. As each one of you began doing that, you began to understand what was truly important in your lives for there comes a time when your stuff owns you. What happens is that it diverts you from your primary purpose, your own passion and your own joy. Having the courage to intentionally go through change opens the door for you to receive all the gifts of the fifth stage of life. Having experienced that during the last thirty days, let us now lead you into the sixth stage of life, for it is why you are here today.

In the series we call *Practical Magic*, we wish to offer you insight of what it is like to go through the final three stages of life, but not to stop there. It is no secret to tell you that we will leave you on the third and final month with the challenge of re-scripting your next life, to step into the next newness of yourself that you will create intentionally. Every moment your foot hits the ground, you are creating the grass beneath your feet. The road is only created in front of you because you are moving in that direction expecting a road to be there. Life is a self-fulfilling prophecy. Is that not an interesting equation? Now you will move even further into that and further into the potentials and possibilities that you have before you right now. Let us speak of the sixth stage of life. Let us show you what this process can be because it is beautiful beyond description.

## Simplicity of Universal Truth

In the first stage of life as an infant comes in, it holds the memories and vibrations of Home. As a young child, you attempt to adjust to the vibrations and cellular memories of Planet Earth. It is like having one foot in both worlds. The sixth stage of life is similar, for this is a time to prepare for the transition and to become simplified. The fifth stage of life was to determine what was truly important in your life, thus to prepare for the simplification process in the sixth stage. In the days of Lemuria, you advanced as a society so much that all of you were childlike. It is only possible to do that when you simplify everything. Likewise, it is only possible to simplify when you are aware of what is truly important. In the days of Lemuria, the collective vibration of all Lemurians had reached a stage of evolution where you existed in simplicity. The complications of life are a byproduct of the veil you wear. Please know that all truth in its purest form is simple. Imagine there are many different levels of understanding and therefore different levels of what you know to be truth. The key to moving to a higher level of understanding is always finding the simplicity in truth.

In order to access the next stage of your understanding and truth shared throughout the universe, the collective vibration of humanity will naturally simplify as it evolves.

## God is Simple

There was a time the Keeper was asking us for answers. He used to do that a lot. At one point, he asked us, "What is it all about? Show me how everything works." He thought it was an interesting challenge he put to us, so we did. At that moment, he found himself sitting on a cloud, looking down at planet Earth, watching the Game board of Earth. As he watched it, he began understanding everything he saw. He comprehended everything he was able to perceive, and understood how all the connections were made. At that moment, he looked up at us and said, "You are not going to let me re-member this, are you?" And we said, "Not in the normal way."

Then he began to bargain with us, which we think is so imaginative. He said, "Let me take back one piece that will re-mind me of all the others and how everything comes all together. I just want to re-member how simple it all is." Even to this day, all he can remember is that it is all so simple. Life is so simple, it would bore most humans so we try to complicate it just enough to engage you. It is often that we share with you the embellishments around the truth we share with you, rather than sometimes just giving you the truth. On the Planet of Free Choice, it is only possible for you to find your own truth, and that is accomplished through the illusion of complexity. Complexity is the veil you wear to play the game. As you advance, everything becomes simple.

Simplify and you become childlike. Simplify further and you become godlike.

Because of your recent advancement as a collective, you no longer need the complications of the veil in the way that you once did.

## Sixth Stage Exercise: Thirty Days of Simplicity.

During the next thirty days, we challenge you. If you wish to play the Game we offer, find ways of seeking simplicity in everything you experience. For thirty days, find ways of becoming simple and you will understand that all the life experiences you have had up to this point come down to just a very few things. For the next 30 days, look at the energy.

Follow the energy, for that will tell you where to find simplicity. Energy in all forms is simple. All energy forms seek the path of least resistance. We have spoken of the divine water. We have spoken of the divine flow, for water is an energy form. It never dies. It is never created. It only transmutes from one form to another. Like energy, all energy forms always find the path of least resistance. If you can follow that path of least resistance in your own choices, in your own life, in your own evaluation of your own relationships, in everything that you do, you will find the simplicity in your life. Watch where the energy flows in your own life, and you will uncover the motivations of what is behind the energy. If you understand that, everything becomes simple. For the next thirty days, we ask you to follow a similar search for the path of least resistance in all things. This will help you to develop a habit of simplicity. In the human experience, the sixth stage of life is important for the seventh stage of life to have its greatest effect.

## Simplicity equals True Beauty

When you find the simplicity, the next time you see anything complicated, it becomes easier to bring it to its true essence. Finding the true essence in anything allows you to see the true beauty in all things. Smile a lot during the thirty days, for it will help you simplify everything. It will help the energy around you to bring only the core essence. Enjoy the ride.

Dear ones, we thank you for calling us in this day, for we are only with you because you have created the space for us to join you. You have created a space by asking to re-member Home. It is our honor to greet that call and to be here to reflect your magnificence. Do you know who you are? We do. You are the greatest angels who have ever lived. It is our honor to offer you only three reminders. Treat each other with respect of the highest degree. Nurture one another at every opportunity for you are helping All That Is. Re-member that it is a wonderful Game and play well together.

Espavo.

the Group

# The Seventh and Final Stage of Life

## Practical Magic Series

### July 2005

This channel was originally presented as a VirtualLight Broadcast and can be seen as it was presented live at www.Lightworker.com/VirtualLight.

Greetings from Home.

## Pulling Aside the Veil

Dear ones, the energy is astounding, for you have created magic this day. We come to enter your magic space you have created, for in that opportunity, we will help you see yourselves. You come here to put on the veil, to pretend not to know who you are, and to bump into each other and play the wonderful Game of God hiding from Himself looking for Herself. There are the times when you want so desperately to see the other side of the veil and re-member Home again. That energy is a validation of all you know in your heart, for you have an understanding of the energy of Home; you just have not felt it for a very long time. For those of you who find the veil thinning, many times there is a sadness that pervades everything you do, for the sadness is all about the fact that you are here and not there. So this day, we wish to remove some of the veil for you enough to show you the opportunities that await. We are going to take you through the seventh stage of life.

## Experience the Final Stage of Life

During the last two months, we have led you through the fifth and sixth stages of life, so you can see how the energy builds to create an opportunity for you to experience this final movement. Over the next thirty days, we ask you to experience exactly what each soul experiences as it transitions and returns Home. We tell you that the evolutionary process will not change the seven stages of life. There will not be an eighth, or a ninth, or a tenth stage added. Eventually, what will happen is that you will be going through the seven stages of life but instead of dying, you will go through the seventh stage of life while you are still alive. At some point, as you evolve even further, you will then re-do the first stage of life and begin a whole new life cycle while you are still here in the physical body. This is what we call 'ascension.' This is the process that is underway as humans raise their vibration through the evolutionary process. Today we ask you to take a deep breath and pretend for just a moment that as you exhale, it is your last human breath.

## The Greeters

There is a natural struggle that goes on, for you are imprinted with a survival mechanism which makes you fervently cling to life even though it is an unnatural state for your spirit. A survival instinct kicks in as you near death and that is why transition team members are so helpful in saying, "It's okay, Dad. You can let go. We're going to be okay." In fact, many of you have contracts with people around you to let them go at the appropriate time, so re-turning Home becomes very important. Then there is another entire process that begins, for even though you step out of the body, you are not yet Home. There is a gate you must enter and it must be done of your own free will. To get there, you travel through a tube, a tunnel, a valley or whatever you choose to call it, but it is a course that must be traveled and can only be traveled by a single soul. But before you start that journey to the gate, you begin to see the greeters who have come to coax you out of the physical. Your greeter may be Uncle Harry who you knew very well as a child, or it may be your grandfather or your grandmother. Sometimes it will be someone you do not even re-member, for you never met them, yet they made a contract with you during the first stage of life to greet you when the time came. Your greeters are the ones who are there encouraging you, "It is okay. You can let go of that last breath. You can release it. We are here to take your hand. You are safe." And then you step out of the body and feel free, but you are not Home. You are simply on the other side of being human. You are simply in another vibrational state that is not human, but you are not yet Home.

## Entering the Gate

When you arrive at the gate, you are free to go through it right away. It is not possible for anyone to coax you through the gate. Instead, you must go through of your own free will. It is here some souls become stuck or confused. Sometimes they are in a car accident or a bicycle accident and they step out of their physical body, not knowing they are dead. Since they are on the other side of humanity, they step into that same natural state of creation you all have when you are no longer hampered by the illusion of being human or by the physical body, so your creative abilities are vastly increased.

The challenge comes when you become confused and step out of the body, not realizing you are dead. You do not wish to go Home through the gate, for it is possible for you to create a reality that makes you think you are still alive. Please understand, dear ones, even in this state nothing is wrong. There is actually nothing people are stuck with, for even in this state, all is free choice. Although many times in great tragedies, people get confused and they follow the vast hoard of souls that are literally going nowhere rather than think about going Home. Most of the time, this is caused by a mere lack of knowledge. After all, this simple truth is not taught in your schools, is it? Many times, education and concepts such as these can make more of a difference in the evolution of humankind than most will ever know. That is why we honor the Transition Team Members so, for they are some of the greatest healers who move humanity forward in quantum leaps.

## Meeting Your Tutor

What happens next? When you move out of survival mode, let go of the physical body and enter the gate. You are Home. Then you meet your tutor. This is a soul whose contract with you is simply to remind you of your own magnificence and help you to stretch out in Heaven. Your tutor reminds you how simple everything is and takes you through the entire process of how things work in Heaven and helps re-acquaint you with Home. This tutor shows you the different processes that comprise reality, and helps to clear the cobwebs from the memory of your human experience.

## The Seventh Stage of Life: Assimilation

Then there comes a very important part which we call the seventh stage of life. After you become comfortable at Home, there is a process you go through called *assimilation*. It is a soul integration of all you experienced in your lifetime. Every event you experienced is evaluated for its highest use to your soul. What remains useful to your soul on its evolutionary path is integrated into the soul's core personality, and what is no longer needed is gently released.

There was a time when you were nine years old and the class bully took your lunch, gave you a black eye and told you that if you told anyone, he would come back and not only beat you up, but beat up your sister. You did not say a word and you hid that within yourself all your life, always fearing the person who had abrupt and abusive energy. The funny thing is, you called them into your life over and over again. In fact, you married two of them. The interesting part is that we create these things over and over as humans playing the Game, as spirits pretending to be human. As you create this process, when you go Home, the first thing you do is go through all of these experiences one by one. No, this is not the flash of memories that occurs as you are leaving your physical body.

That is quite different. This is an elongated process and you must be comfortable in the energy of Home for the assimilation to be effective. This is the seventh and final stage of any life.

In your ancient scriptures, it has been misinterpreted as Judgment Day. Nobody judges you. After all, who would judge God? Only God could judge God. In your early development as souls pretending to be human, the polarity of judgment was useful. We tell you that in your evolutionary path, you no longer need the illusion of polarity. Now we ask you to consider replacing judgment with discernment. It is the first tool for living in the higher vibrations of the New Planet Earth. Rather than calling one thing bad and one thing good, the use of discernment allows you to make choices without judgment. The seventh stage of life uses only discernment. Your soul goes through each one of these experiences, discerning its future usefulness to your soul path. In this stage of life, you not only call up each one of these individual experiences, but you also call the essence of a soul who may have been involved in the experience to sit beside you, even though they may still be on Earth at the time. You have them sit right beside you as the two of you go through this and objectively revisit the experience. You say, "Was that not fun? Boy, I didn't remember you at all then. And here you are beating me up. Do you remember that? Thanks for playing that difficult role." And they say, "Yes. Next time, can I play the role of a friend instead? I didn't like playing the bad guy for you, but I loved you enough to do that."

## Core Personality

The essence of your own soul is called the core personality, for the essence of who you are as a soul is the culmination of all the experiences your soul has incorporated up to this point. When you are on the Game board of life, you carry all experiences as part of who you are. The good, the bad, and the ugly are all part of what you carry around each day of your life. If you carry negative experiences as energy stamps, they affect every thought and every relationship you have. If you choose to work toward evolution, you use these experiences to master your primary life lesson. Once mastered, you may release the negative stamp of the experience and, in effect, re-write your own history. You never fully erase the experience, for it will always be a part of you, but instead, you release the energy stamp that makes you overly sensitive and overly reactive. This is the greatest healing achieved on Earth, and it is always accomplished from within. Even though humanity is evolving at a rate never before seen throughout All That Is, most of these energy stamps are never used. It is in this seventh and final stage of life that the soul resets its own energy stamps in preparation of the next lifetime, keeping the energy stamps (experiences) that maybe useful in future lifetimes and releasing those no longer needed. When the soul keeps an energy stamp, it is stored as a cellular memory, ready to be triggered the next time it may be used for mastery of a life lesson.

## Accepting the Gift

Please understand that you live in a field of polarity. You have the illusions of up/down, good/bad, right/wrong, and fear/love. This polarity does not exist at Home, so there are times when these experiences humans would call negative are actually chosen for keeping because they will be useful in future lifetimes. This is why many of you have past life experiences or patterns that can actually be traced back many, many lifetimes. You, as a soul, have chosen to keep that energy stamp and bring it forward for your own evolution. When this happens you store the energy stamp in your cellular memory. It is not good and it is not bad. It simply is. In fact, it is quite an effective way to do things.

There are times when you will release positive as well as negative experiences you have had, because they no longer serve you. But in releasing any experience, there is one point you will wish to consider. We tell you that you have hidden a gift in every experience of life. If you are to release anything, you must first find the gift of that experience. All events contain a gift. Finding and accepting that gift allows you to assimilate the highest energy in all experiences. Once the gift has been received, the energy stamp that can control your life may be released easily.

## Thirty Days in the Seventh Stage of Life

During the next thirty days, you have a chance to experience the seventh and final stage of life without dying. This will represent the evolutionary process that all of humanity will experience as the collective vibration moves into higher vibrational status. During these next thirty days, you have the opportunity to assimilate and discern the new you. We will ask you to find a time to sit and go through different portions of your life and intentionally bring up the memories and the experiences that have made you who you are. In examining each one of them, you decide which experiences you wish to keep and which you are finished with. Keep in mind that an experience never leaves you, only the energy stamp that controls your life will leave you. And, if you wish to release the stamp, it can be done at that time if you have found the gift and no longer need the stamp to help you master a life lesson. It is the reason you scripted that role for this to happen. The moment you find the gift in the experience – whether you call it positive or negative – is the moment you incorporate that gift into who you are. You may then choose to release the energy stamp of that experience, for it no longer needs to be controlling your life. You have a choice. Because of your advancement, you no longer need to wait until the seventh stage of life after death to do that. That is why we have led you through this experience over the last three months. It is an opportunity for you, today, to take charge of your life and move your soul forward intentionally.

## The Big Question: Why Am I Here?

You have come here to find your passion. We wish only to reflect your magnificence, for part of the veil keeps you from re-membering who you really are. That is the way you scripted it. As beautiful and as unique as each one of you are, you look in the mirror and say, "Why am I here? I know there is a reason, but what am I doing here? I know there is a meaning of life, but what is it?" And if you listen very carefully, you will hear a thunderous laughter on the other side of the veil when you ask that question, for it simply means that the veil is working. You are here having this experience because of the veil. We have just given you one of the tools to temporarily remove the veil.

Spend time and go through each segment of your life during the next thirty days. Pull in the spirit of each person you had these interactions with. Have them sit next to you as you watch and catalog each experience of this lifetime. Ask the question of your own higher self and it will show you everything you need to ask. It is all written in the Akashic records. It is a part of your being. It is stored in your own cellular memories until you decide to release them. Keep your review to this lifetime because, even if you bring something forward into the next lifetime, we tell you, you will always have an experience in each lifetime that will reactivate that same energy stamp. And, although it is wonderful to go back and have the understanding of why you have tried to accomplish something in many previous lifetimes, you have everything you need here, today, for you to evolve as a soul. When you go through that life and bring the essence of those people who played a part in your life in some fashion into your experience, and sit them down next to you, the two of you will look at the wonderful series of events playing out in front of you. You will cry, you will joke and you will laugh. You will remember the joy of the time when you originally scripted this together. For the first time, you will probably see the true connection to that person that you had in order for them to play a very important part of your life. From that point forward, you find the gift. Once you find the gift, you decide whether that experience becomes part of your core personality or whether you wish to release the energy stamps around it. That is your choice today. You do not have to go Home to accomplish this any longer. That is the reason we have shown you this entire series of practical magic, for we tell you the practical magic series is complete this day.

## The Magic Wand

We now hand you the magic wand. It is no longer for us to show you. It is yours. It always has been. Take it. Use it in your life in some fashion. Find a practical application to bring a little bit more of a smile to your face. What did you come here to do? What was your highest intent as a soul to come in and put on this veil and play this Game? What if we told you that your highest intent was to walk around with a smile on your face? Yes, we know, some of you are not able to comprehend that. Humans must complicate things just enough to understand, but the truth is simple. When you are smiling, when you are happy, when you are in your passion, when you are experiencing your joy, you are reflecting God. You shine the Light of Home and all who see you experience the unique part of God that is yours alone. That is what you came to find. That is why you are here. That is when you become the highest use to the Universe you can be. Step forward, take the magic wand in your own hand and use it now.

## Making Space for Grief

During this time we have together, we wish to pause for a moment for there is so much excitement here. We tell you there are three of you here specifically in this room who have lost people in the last six months to the other side of the veil and they are standing right over your shoulder now, touching you, waiting to hear how you accept this information. There are those of you watching this broadcast, watching this light beam, who understand that they are here and around you when you think of them, for that is what happens after the seventh stage of life. You do not get into a huge queue or stand in line so you can turn around and come back in. You come back in when you decide to come back in, but please understand that time on the other side of the veil is quite different from the linear time you pretend to play your Game in here. For past, present and future are all together as one, and you do not need to go from Step A to Step B all in one moment.

Your evolution as a soul continues even at Home, for the Game is still going on, and the moment someone thinks about you on Earth, your spirit is called in. Of course, you have choice whether you go or not, but your energy is called and, as many of you have been thinking about those who have passed recently, they are right over your shoulder hugging you. They are right there embracing you, holding your energy for you.

We will tell you one other secret you will learn in the seventh stage of life, for it is helpful for humans playing the Game on a daily basis to know this: As an evolution of a soul, when you cross over and go Home, one of the things you as a soul may be interested in doing is going to visit those people whom you loved so much. You do not miss them, for you are a part of them more than you know. The separation and the illusion of separation are gone at that point, but you are there. You are sitting sometimes in their bedroom, watching them sleep at night, but you cannot interact with them in any way, shape or form if they are still grieving. During the grief process, if a soul interacts with you, it is only possible to make the grief process more difficult rather than easier. So humans, your task with all who return Home and cross over is to find the gift of their lives in your own and release them in love. Much like the seventh stage of life, find the gift and the ways in which they live on in you. Then and only then will they dance with you in your dreams. They will be over your shoulder every second of every day, smiling. They will sit in your room at night and watch you sleep, with a big smile on your face. They will come up within an inch of your face and smile real big and in your dreams, you will smile real big back. In that way, they interact with you. Grieving is one of the most difficult processes humanity goes through, but it is one of the great essences of spirit, for it means you trust in the spirit of who you are. Releasing those souls allows them to go on their own evolutionary path from that point forward.

You have come here to be the perpetrators of the Light. You have put on the veil and come pretending to be human. You do not re-member that you are the greatest angels who has ever lived, but you will. It is our job to help re-mind you of the memories of Home, of your true purpose and of your highest vibrational state here. If you can practice that seventh stage of life here today, your life will be reborn again and you will find less restriction in your life and more joy. You will take very real strides toward living in the higher vibrations of the New Planet Earth. Take those steps, each one of you. Allow yourself to step forward and to be the Human Angel you truly are and Home will begin here today. That is what you came here to do. That is what your smile creates. Find the gift in everything ... and Home will be here around you now.

As each one of you moves and walks from this space, know you carry a special energy. There is a family re-union going on, not just on this side of the veil, but all Games everywhere. We must tell you, in the short time you have gathered this day, these rooms have gotten very crowded. In fact, there was a little bit of a parking problem but we dealt with it. The over-dimensional levels, the overtone levels which are all around you, have filled, for we tell you that this is not about you. It is about All That Is. If you are quiet in yourselves, you will hear the most thunderous applause. Dear ones, you have already won the Game. Now you are sitting around asking, "What can I do next? How can I be of service?" Step into the seventh stage of life and during the next thirty days, try it on. Play with it. Please remember that everything you do is a grand Game. It is not possible to fall, even if you try. You are the masters of the Game board.

We ask you instead to re-member only three things. Treat each other with the greatest respect, for you are looking in the mirror. Nurture one another as you would nurture your own. Re-member that it is a grand Game you are playing and play well together.

Espavo.

the Group

## Connecting the Heart
## Core Personality
## By Barbara Rother

There is a part of the message that Steve and the Group wrote about that especially resonates with me. When core personality was discussed, it really made me think. What core personality have I carried on lifetime to lifetime? I know it all connects with life lessons and learning from the experiences I have had. I have always felt the love of music and of singing, the love of fashion and I have enjoyed being female. I like to be around people, but have insisted on my alone time, as well. I have always felt financial abundance was my right. I feel I have dealt with trust issues many times around. I have had to define my boundaries time and time again. I feel in this lifetime, I uncovered my true self learning from past and present experiences. It has taken lifetimes to reveal my true self but isn't that what life is, discovering who you are from past experiences? My veil of forgetfulness was very thick in the past. Now I am discovering all that I am.

Many years ago, Steve did a past life regression with me. I am what is called a 'somnambulist.' It is quite easy for me to be hypnotized or go back into my past. I found it amazing in that, the last two lifetimes, I discovered I was a very strong female, putting myself first, almost to the point of being selfish. This was my protection, my wall to allow myself not to be emotionally hurt. I feel I am a fairly new soul, but the lifetimes I have experienced have been eventful and full of lessons in life that prepared me for my current time here on earth.

My first lifetime I recalled was living in the Victorian Age. I lived in a royal setting in the most beautiful, Victorian, upper-class area. I recall being a young girl in my preteen years, with blond spiral curls, dressed in the finest fashions. Even to this day, I feel the financial abundance that was mine. I secretly want to scream now, "Where is all my money?" My catalyst then was my sexually abusive father. I would speak my mind to everyone around me, except him. I know my every material need was met then, with almost all that I demanded. I had a grand piano I played and sang to entertain family and friends. Although I enjoyed the music, I felt I was not doing it for my enjoyment, but as a showpiece for my family. The world was mine to all who would view me from the outside. My secret world held a life of desiring unconditional love from my family, not of conditional financial abundance.

I remember having a distant mother and a father who would show me love in very inappropriate ways. I know in my heart, this was a confusing time for me. I so wanted love from my father but not in this manner. I recall stepping into my power one night after my father had behaved inappropriately. We had been sitting on our Victorian porch swing on a warm summer night. After he left me to go inside, I felt a surge of anger and power come within my young body. I kicked the ground lantern that had lit the porch, causing it to overturn and quickly set the entire home and family, including me, on fire. Still to this day, I have a respect for fire. I also have a memory of my power. It scares me how I misused it. It was a lesson in standing in my own power. I know how strong a person I was then, even at an early age. I just did not have the voice to speak my power then. It was the custom in those times.

My next life time was when I again came in again as a very strong woman. My memories brought me into the 1940s. I strongly felt then that I would never have anyone abuse me in any way. As a child, I recall a distant relationship to my mother and father. It was like this time I would not let anyone be too close to me. My core personality of love of music found expression as a nightclub singer. I would sing my heart out much to the delight of those who came in for a drink and a good time. My main purpose was to have all the fun in life I could obtain. I was always dressed in high fashion, flaunting my style. I remember deciding that family would not be a part of my life this time around. I somehow seem to recall the hurt from my past, desiring unconditional love and not receiving it. This time, I would receive love on my terms. I had a wall around my heart protecting me from everything. In this wild lifetime, I could find all the love I ever wanted, but once again, not the true love I was searching for. I did have a voice this time around. I spoke and everyone listened, whether it was with my words or with my singing. I have to admit this was a fun life. Yet, even though I seem to have it all from money to adoring people, I still was searching. I feel I died in this lifetime from a jealous wife.

This takes me up to my current life. I remember these last two times so well so I would learn from them and that is what we do with our core personality. I came this time as a very shy child. I outgrew that, as I learned it was safe to speak my truth. In this time, the most important things I wished to create were a loving husband and children. Ever since I have been a little girl, this was my main focus on life until now. Although this has always been an important part of my life, I know it is only a part of my life now. I found my true love at the age of sixteen and have been with him ever since. Children came into my life at an early time of our relationship. My whole focus surrounded around family. This time, I was ready to accept all the love I could receive and give in return. The love of singing came strongly into this life but in a safe way. I was in a singing group with girlfriends in high school, and the girl singer in a band the same time period. I was in church choirs at different times, have sung for weddings but somehow have always not allowed my singing to come into full potential. I feel that I remembered the past lifetimes where singing was an important part of my life but I associated it with pain in some way. It is a block in this lifetime that I am determined to overcome.

My mother died early in this life. It is interesting that this has been a pattern with all life times with the distance with a mother, female figures. This contributes with my trust issues, especially with women. I still deal with this, although I am well on my way of mastering this. The love of fashion continues this time around, although I was not able to explore this till later in life. My loving father did not know how important such a thing was to a girl. Now that I am an adult, I have discovered my own love for such fun details.

I have learned to stand in my truth and state my boundaries. At times, I feel I overstate them. I am learning the balance as I go along this path. Abundance is mine in all areas of my life. I said before that I used to feel the great abundance that was mine in the past, and wonder where it was in this lifetime. I know I have now found the true meaning of abundance. I have learned that I have abundance in all areas of my life. Money is only one part of true abundance. As I accept this, financial abundance flows. I have learned to stand in my truth with my definition and I am singing again. Even if it is just in the shower, my voice will be heard.

I like this lifetime as I discover who I am and who I have been in the past. It's fun putting all the pieces of the puzzle together, although I'm sure I will save a few pieces for the next lifetime. I choose to believe I will carry on my core optimistic viewpoint that will see me through any experience that I encounter. I feel the very core of my soul in my heart. Now I put myself first. It is not like in the past where I felt as if I had to be selfish, watching out only for me as a self-protection. Yes, there are times I need to take a step back to regroup and remember who I am now. But with all the unconditional love I have allowed in my life, now I can do this and move forward. I have a love for people around me that I enjoy sharing with our biological and Lightworker family. I am learning as I experience each new day.

Remember your core personality. Learn to like yourself wherever it has taken you on this journey called life. It's all about being comfortable with who you are. The adventure continues. Enjoy!

With Love and Light,

Barbara

# The New Spiritual Family

## Forming the New First Family of Light

### August 2005

This channel was originally presented as a VirtualLight Broadcast and can be seen as it was presented live at www. Lightworker.com/VirtualLight

Greetings from Home.

# Why?

Dear ones, you sit this day in a room of energy you have created that expands far beyond the room. It expands on the Web of Love. This love energy expands on the web you call the Internet. It expands throughout all beings and all dimensions of time and space. It is a web of love. It is a connection of hearts you have created through which you set about to find yourselves. God searching for Himself, looking for Herself, has caused you to look into the mirror and ask the questions "Why? Why am I here? What am I doing? What does this all mean?" And when you finally get an inkling of what it is you came here to do, and you step in that direction, you take two steps forward and one step back. You doubt yourself and wonder what you did wrong. It is a human attribute that is wondrous on this side of the veil to watch. You do not understand; you chastise yourselves for taking that one step back. Yet we applaud you for only taking that one step back. Sometimes taking this one step back actually allows you to gain the momentum to move forward in your own courage, even if you don't yet know everything you wish to know.

You say, "If only I could have validation. If only I could see it clearly." Yet that, too, is not possible. For you are the creators. You see, even if we were to enter your world with irrefutable proof, you would find a way to negate that which was not meant to fit into your Game. You would find a way to make it go away, or to make it fly into the ethers or you would ignore it. Do you understand that you not only write your future, but also your history? You re-write history all the time. If there is ever a point at which you have something in the past you do not care for, that does not support you in your forward movement, you re-write it. If you doubt that, simply ask those who publish history books. It is a constant, evolutionary process to publish a history book, for history is constantly changing. Not only do you change what you teach, but you change what you know in your heart. Why? That is the question we ask *you* today. Of course, we would not ask you the question if we did not have an answer waiting. This leads us to what it is you are looking for when you look into the mirror and ask, "Who am I? What am I doing here? What did I have in mind when I came here as a soul? What was I thinking? I want to see the dotted line I signed because I do not re-member getting myself into this. I do not re-member this pain clause in here. I agreed to come down and play this Game, but I don't think this is it."

## In the Beginning

But you did come to play this game and there is a reason. You are discovering that reason every day. What is happening is that you are here in your search not only to find answers for yourself, but as you step forward in your own search, you are actually helping others to progress in their own searches. You are connecting the dots of the original spiritual family, which is part of what you came here to do. We have spoken of original spiritual family before, but we will fill you in on the details as a refresher.

In the very beginning, planet Earth was a hot, gaseous ball because She was born in a state of very high vibration of which you call heat. The atoms in Her were vibrating at a very high rate and you began your incarnations in this Game of Free Choice at that stage as ethereal beings without physical bodies. You literally incarnated for eons of time, working through your own life lessons and working with the essence of the Earth, Herself, through your ethereal bodies. You were spirit. Then, as the Earth cooled, you began to lose your connection to Her for She began to lower Her vibrations and become more dense. Your high vibrational status made it difficult for you to stay in touch with Her at that time. It was here that six parental races came together to help you form the dense bodies you inhabit today. There was a lot of concern about that. "Is this going to work? Is it possible for one of these grand, spiritual beings to try and fit into one of these tiny little bubbles of biology?" No, the spirit never completely fit, so part of you stayed behind to bridge the gap between Home and what you call planet Earth. Today, you call that part of you that was left behind your higher self. When you tap into that, it has a higher vibration and bridges the gap between you and Home. That is your connection to Home, and your connection to the other hearts connected to yours.

## The Original 500 Human Prototypes - The Family of Light

However, that first time the experiment of putting spirit beings into physical bodies and going into Earth was tried, there were no more than 500 souls who came to Earth in the first incarnation. These five hundred souls were known to all as "The Family of Light." Over a short period of time during a few hundred years, Earth began to evolve and then evolve further so that souls were able to start coming in on a very regular basis. But just imagine, it began with 500 of what we call *seed souls* that were the original prototypes of humanity. The interesting part is that each one of you is asking, "Was I one of those souls?" We love the way humans think. It is so joyous. Yes, of course you were. You all were one of those souls. You all have memories that can be traced back to one of the original 500 Family of Light, for you are all descendants of one of those 500. Literally, you have a soul family that goes back to one, and then goes even further than that. Even as ethereal beings you played the Game in unified consciousness, rather than as the separate players you became in the physical body.

You remembrance as one of the first 500 souls is what you experience as a result of a spiritual awakening. As one of the first 500 beings, you were considered royalty and are often referred to in the cosmos as the First Family of Light.

## The Seven Great Clans

The Game then evolved very quickly. Of course, at the start there were two souls of the 500 who got together and found they had a very similar purpose. For souls do have a purpose, do they not? They formed a group of two and said, "This is going to be our purpose for it is easier to be two than it is to be one. And so we begin playing the Game of separation. We believe we are either male or female. We each believe that we are only half of a person so we will join with another person and together pretend to be a whole person." What fun! You humans think of the most imaginative games. As you did, you formed what we call 'clans.' There are seven great clans – two of which we have spoken about – that came together out of the original 500. It was not long before 30 or 40 people were included in this group, all focusing in the same direction. We will not speak of all seven clans this day, for it is too much information at once, but we will speak of the two we have laid out already. We wish to give you the overview of this entire process and unfold it for you, so you can realize that when you look in the mirror, you are searching for something. You are seeking from whence you came, so you may answer the question: "Why?" You are searching for that connection of the original clan and your original spiritual family. That is why you search. That is why you come to groups like these. You have not necessarily come to hear the wisdom we offer through the Keeper, but to feel the heart connection you have with all – not just with us – the people hearing and reading this message. For as you share in this message, you are actually connecting with spiritual family. As you do this, you understand there are certain groups that have come together with a specific purpose.

## Clan of the Bright Eyes

One group got together and said, "We have certain attributes in our physicality and we have all great spirits within us, for the Spirit shone a little bit brighter in the early days than they do now. There were many reasons for that. It is not right, it is not wrong, but there were much brighter eyes at that time in the history of the Game. We tell you that one of the clans in the early days was the Clan of the Bright Eyes. As you looked in the eyes of these beings, you felt the energy of Home. They decided to get together as a group of beings and actually carry the energy of Home through their eyes intentionally. Any time you looked at them for any reason, they would flash their eyes and a smile, and you would re-member Home. The brightness in their eyes carried the re-minder of the energy of Home. This is the Clan of the Bright Eyes. It is a beautiful story. Many of you reading this still belong to this clan, although it may have escaped your conscious memory.

## Clan of the Reflectors of the Light

As time went on, there were other focus groups that came together. There were many who tried to be incarnations of the light, different expressions of the light in various ways. For you created an imaginary place you had called 'darkness' so you could give yourself the chance to be the Light. Even to this day, there are two ways you can work with Light: you can either be the Light or you can reflect the Light. That is the second clan. The Reflectors of the Light decided that their purpose was to help other beings. They did not feel the need to stand front and center and be the Light all the time. Instead, they would be the ones who would work quietly behind the scenes and then appear just at the right time to make sure this little light beam did not go unnoticed. They were there with a mirror to catch Light at just the right point to reflect it back to someone who needed it. With their help, the Light would hit someone's heart and help them see the Light of Home. They did this not only to reflect the Light from other beings, but so that they could see their own Light as well. They would hold the mirror in front of you so you could see yourselves and the essence of who you were. And then they would reflect that Light on to others. In every meaning of the word, these are Lightworkers. They did so very quietly, for their intent was to be a perfect mirror and not have their own Light interfere with other reflections. It is a great art and takes tremendously stable souls to play that role in the Clan of the Reflectors of the Light. The ego must be in constant balance to do this important work. These groups of souls would go through daily life looking for ways to reflect Light; it helped humanity make major transitions more than you will ever know. Even today, these wonderful beings seem to emerge from nowhere when a great transition is at hand. Today, this clan is reuniting and reactivating itself to make the next steps ahead for humanity much smoother.

## Extended Spiritual Families

These are the clans we wish to tell you of this day, the first two. There are five more clans we will bring to you in time. But during this session, we wish to give you more of an overview of what this all means to you. It is not just about the clans and which clan you might resonate with. We think it is wonderful to see the energy you have given the archangels. You believe they are certain families, in essence, they are families of angelic purpose, but it is also possible to be part of many families at once as far as the archangels and angelic purpose are concerned. We also tell you that you are part of a family. We see that many of you have set up lessons of *Trust* and set up opportunities to run into brick walls so you could learn to trust yourself. You had the rug completely pulled out from under you so you could better learn to stand on your own two feet. Because of many of those experiences, you have difficulty trusting yourselves. You also see everything from a limited perspective, for you still believe that one vibration is better than another. They are not. They are simply different. The fourth grade is not better than the third grade. They are just for different purposes. We ask you to release the whole concept of good and bad, of right and wrong and of the direction you are going. We tell you, you are part of many of these families, and you may resonate with many of these clans as your extended family. Even so, you have a spark of God that is like none other. You are a part of the Creator carrying a unique part of that energy. When you find your unique beauty, it allows you to share it with all of those families. You are then able not only to stand up and say who you are, but also to help others do the same. It is not about the destination; it is about the journey. It is about movement forward but, as you are moving forward, allow yourselves to take two steps forward and one step back and say, "Gee, was that not a wonderful step back?" That is when you become the Human Angels. That is when you carry a light in your own eyes, in your smile, in your being and in your voice that awakens others in your own spiritual families. That is what you are here doing. That is what you are looking for when you look into the mirror and ask, "Why?" You are simply trying to find others in your spiritual family.

The moment you find others in your original clans, does not mean you all need to go off together and start a commune. Those days are over. You tried that once and drove each other absolutely crazy. It did not work as well as you thought it would, for to concentrate the energy of a family restricts the usefulness of that family. The reality is, when beings of light vibration come together, they reinforce each other. That is great for rejuvenation and finding direction, yet in the long term, beings of light must be exposed to those of differing vibrations so they may do their work. So literally, a clan was originally intended to be located in different parts of the world and to come together once in a while to support one another and validate each other. That is what you are doing when you look for these other members of your spiritual family. That is why most of you are reading this message now.

Since humans often set up negative experiences having to do with family, many are repelled at the idea that they belong to a wonderful group of souls who share their original imprints. We tell you that spiritual family is different. Spiritual family holds your original vibration and can help to redirect your life when you find yourself off course. Spiritual family gives you an accurate reflection of your unique beauty, which is the God energy within you. That is what you are looking for. And you find it when you look in someone's eyes and make a heartfelt connection that changes both of you. When you meet these people, you may have lunch and make a friend for the rest of your life, or maybe you will never see each other again. It does not really matter where or how long your relationship goes from there, as the instant it happens, you have activated them and they have activated you. That is what you are here doing and the answer to the question "Why am I here?"

## A Call to Lightworkers

Those of you who have stepped forward to be workers of the Light, or what you call Lightworkers, are here to spread the Light on this planet. You often do this by activating your own spiritual family. You find them in all walks of life. Some are reading the books you have read, and understanding the concepts you carry, and some do not. Some do not have a clue as to where they are going. Some say, "Ah, I believe exactly what

I can see and that is all I can see." Yet, if you see that spark in their eyes, you will know there is something there that both of you can benefit from. Be patient and plant the seeds of light. Love them when they take that one step back and quietly hold the energy for them. Share your truth with them when asked, yet hold it quietly inside, letting it only be seen through the smile of spiritual confidence. That alone will not only give them the confidence to walk in their beauty, but will also give you the confidence to walk in yours. That is the purpose you look for in humanity. That is the purpose of your incarnation in this lifetime as a Lightworker.

Yes, many of you came down with difficult lessons to work with, yet all of it can come down to the fact that you are here to connect yourselves to others. Very simple, is it not? Some of you say, "I am only going to work with animals because animals are pure and humans drive me crazy." We love it when that happens, for then others speak to you through your animals. The reality is, you are here awakening hearts and whether that is animal, spirit, rock, plant, insect, human or spirit makes no difference, for you are part of the whole. When you find those for whom you came, when you find the beauty of you in other people, that is when you have a soul confidence that lets you take three steps forward before you take one back. That makes you feel more confident as a soul pretending to be human, as an infinite being pretending to be finite, as a Spirit playing a game of separation in a bubble of biology. You are here, connected to each another. Find those parts and you will be Home. We tell you one attribute to watch for, and it is more important than you could possibly know now. All of you go back to the original 500 souls. No matter how or when you came to Earth the first time, your physical origins can be traced back to the original 500. That simply means, in all of your life, no matter how difficult things appear on the news, no matter how difficult you think your world is, there are only 499 people you have to get along with.

## The New Spiritual Family

There will also come a time when you see not only that you're awakening other spiritual beings and part of your original spiritual family, but also there will be new ones who wish to join your family. You will begin to see those who wish to discover why you have that light in your eyes. That is really special. You have laid out contracts throughout your life. Some are even to connect with family, yet you also have very special chances to create new extended families each day. When you have those golden opportunities to have others join your spiritual family, you will hear the wonderful laughter over your shoulder. The New Family of Light is forming right now. You are creating new families every day, and you do so to thunderous applause from this side of the veil. Keep in mind that you are not the only one on this planet asking the question, "Why?" Making space in your life for new members of your family can advance you and the collective of humanity more than ever before.

Just re-member, the next time someone looks at you – maybe even suddenly doing a double take in the middle of a crowded store – you have but an instant to decide whether or not to look away, to look down, or smile and invite them in. Re-member who you are and re-member the soul confidence you have. Re-member, even in that brief moment, you have much to give, for it is planting the seeds of creating the NEW spiritual families. As you reach this level of your own evolution and step to the next level, you are creating new possibilities, new realities, and new energies every day. As you do that, you will form the nucleus of NEW families that will grow into the next level of human expression. Those are the energy families you are creating here this day. Reconnecting with original family will give you the soul confidence to begin the NEW spiritual families. The joy it will bring you is beyond description. Expect a miracle and we will help you create it.

We tell you, it is beyond your imagination to see the support you have on this side of the veil. You have not only won
the Game, but now you are also looking for new games to play.
You are creating new realities as you step forward every day
with every breath you take, and we honor you. You await with
great expectation the time when you will return Home again.
Yet, we tell you, it is not possible to do certain things even
with all the might in heaven. When you come Home, we will
greet you with open arms. We will welcome you as the heroes
who played and won the Game. We will welcome you as the
heroes who had the courage to leave behind your memories
and place a veil in front of your face and not even remember
your magnificence. We will ask you what a hug feels like. With
all the might in heaven, we cannot hug each other here the
way you can touch one another on Earth. Please remember,
you have gifts we do not, so share them often. Re-member
Home. Reflect each other's light whenever you can, and smile
with the smile of spiritual confidence. Come be an active part
of the New First Family of Light. That is who you are. That
is why you came.

It is with the greatest of honor that we ask you to treat
each other with respect. Nurture one another at every opportunity and play well together.

Espavo.

the Group

# The Gift
# of Tragedy

October 2005

This channel was originally presented as a VirtualLight Broadcast and can be seen as it was presented live at www. Lightworker.com/VirtualLight

Greetings from Home.

You have traveled a very long way as souls so that each one of you could be here at this perfect juncture of time and space. Your greatest purpose as souls before coming into this lifetime was to find an opportunity to be here, reading this at this time. Your greatest dream was to come in and place a veil on your face so you could not remember that you scripted it yourself. Your greatest hope was to come in at this time and pretend to be totally confused. You have been wildly successful.

## Why Do We Have So Much Tragedy on Earth?

So now you ask: "What is happening to the Earth? Why are all these changes taking place? And how can I help?" We wish to share with you this day some of the answers to those questions, for change is taking place on such a global scale that literally the entire world is being affected by these beautiful events that are unfolding.

Yes, you see these events as tragedies. You see many things as a tragedy, but we also tell you, your reality is created by the perception from which you view it. If you wish to find and release the difficulties of any tragedy, the first thing that we ask you to do is to find the gift in that event. The moment you find the gift, your perception changes and you have no longer have need for the difficulties. You have no need for the loss of life or suffering. You have no need for the difficulties you experience in your heart when you see this on your television sets. We tell you, there is a greater purpose in these events. The illusion you attempt to keep from yourselves is that you are one. You have been one from the very beginning. You have come in to play the Game of pretending to be separate individuals inhabiting bubbles of biology, but you are one heart. You are connected in ways you will never see. Many of the seemingly tragic events that happen serve to shake that carpet beneath your feet. As you watch the ripple that then spreads throughout the carpet, and into your world, it serves to send everything on the carpet flying into the air. This you see as tragedy, for you do not believe you had a hand in the creation of these events, yet you did. But it is during these times that you easily remember you are one heart. This is one of the gifts that these tragedies offer. Every time you look at the news and see the once healthy cities now filled with water and places that are reduced to piles of rubble, your heart opens along with all the other hearts watching these events unfold. In that instant, the one heart re-unites.

## Accepting the Gift

In those times when you feel great sadness watching the trauma taking place throughout the world, when you see the people who seem to have lost everything and cannot even find their own children, take a moment and send them thanks. Send them thanks for connecting hearts all over the world. Find that little bit of a gift, no matter how small and insignificant it may seem at the time, and you will shift the reality along with your own perception. You know, being human is not easy. You are on one of the most difficult Game boards that exists throughout All That Is. The challenge of pretending to be separate is that you cannot even remember your own heritage. You cannot remember what you had in mind by coming here. You cannot even remember that you have been here before.

## The Third Perspective

We love to observe the way you play within the field of duality. You always look for either good news or bad news. Today we have both for you. The bad news is that you are dying. The good news is that for most of you, it will not be today. This is an important truth every one of you shares. All of you will experience death as finite beings. Due to the very nature of your Game, no one gets out of Earth alive. Now we ask you an important question. With that knowledge, what would happen if each of you spent every day of your life as if you were dying? What would happen if each one of you had to examine your every choice as if it may be your last choice? We tell you, there is no tragedy in death. The only tragedy is living a life unfulfilled. Many of you think of yourselves as being in a body that you must preserve so it lasts your entire lifetime. When you finally do leave that body, we hope you leave it well used, carrying the marks and scars of an exciting life. Ask yourself, "How much passion can I experience today?" And bring that passion forward into today, into each and every moment. How would the world change if everyone did exactly that? We tell you, you would have no need for the traumas and events you call tragedies now.

You are in a field of polarity. You are moving from the unity consciousness of being one as God, into a Game of separatism played in a field of polarity. Here you have been for a very long time, in this field of polarity duality that exists. You live in a land of light and shadow, but you believe in either the light or the shadow. It makes no difference. The reality is, they are both part of the same. Your cycles of light and shadow have created your reality, but you see things as up/down, good/bad, right/wrong, and love/fear because you live in the reality of duality. That is changing, for you are now moving into a field of 'triality.' Now not only will you have both the light and dark sides, but you will also balance that with the third perspective of your own higher self. As you make further connections with that spirit part of yourself, you will have a different view of the light and the dark. You see, they are both part of each other, part of a big circle. It is not that one is good and the other is bad, because each is actually part of the whole and one cannot exist without the other. Light does not exist unless there is a stage of darkness for it to play upon. So what you have examined in your world of calling one good and the other bad is starting to fade, and creating the balance of the third perspective. The third perspective of your spirit and what you call the higher self will now walk you into living within a field of triality. Here you can watch these events and be part of the collective as a conscious creator, instead of stepping back and becoming a victim. Now your scope of vision becomes much larger and you no longer see success as having 3.2 children, a white picket fence, a cat and a dog. All of your game is made up of threes, and now your own perspective will be widened to include vision from the full field of triality.

From this perspective, you will easily see how important passion is in your life. Where is the dance of life you know has always been within you? Where is the spark that has been hiding? What do you see in other people that you would love to see in yourself? Begin that search today using the vision of triality. From this new perspective you, *within each time of darkness upon Earth lies a unique opportunity for Light to shine.*

Every time you see tragedy, difficulty, or suffering of any kind all around, you receive the gift of that opportunity for the spirit to shine Light. As you watch tragic events on your televisions, you know this could easily be you. And even though those people sometimes have lost everything, their spirit is always intact. As long as the spirit is intact, they will rebuild. You watch and say to yourself, "Thank God, it did not happen to me." We tell you that it *did* happen to you. The moment you watched the events on television, it happened to you. Even as they stand in the rubble of what used to be their homes and speak into the microphone, they are telling of what they are thankful for and not what they have lost. In those special times, the spirit and the Light of Home can be seen clearly.

That is the gift they give to each of you who watch. They will rebuild with a new, fresh, unique perspective because of the clearing that has gone on and because of the connection they have with all the other humans who watched this event. As long as you receive the gift, everyone wins and there is purpose in tragedy. That is the piece of sadness in the back of your heart you have not been able to bring forward.

## Earth Changes the Relationship to Man

There is no secret in being able to understand the higher meanings of tragic events. It is no secret to tell you there is more to come in the days ahead. With this knowledge, you try to figure out why Mother Earth is changing and becoming so seemingly drastic in Her changes. What if we told you She is not changing that much? It is really your relationship to Her that is changing. If you can imagine there are 40-year cycles to these things you call hurricanes and that 40 years ago, the land masses were not covered with nearly as many people as they are now. Even though there were huge hurricanes in those cycles 40 years ago, there was less impact on humanity because of the lower population. The fact that it is a new relationship to the way you use the Earth is creating much of what you see as an increase in tragic events. In many ways, She is creating her normal cycles and you are becoming adjusted to them. What we tell you is, there is an evolution in process and your connection to this has to do with your own evolution that is going on every day. For you are not the same humans who came here to inhabit Planet Earth. You are not the same beings who found expression in physical bubbles of biology by pretending to be human for a few decades. You have evolved well past that point. You are now incorporating part of your own higher self and creating a new reality, moving from unity to duality to triality. As you evolve in this way, we watch you from this side of the veil with the greatest of awe and with the greatest applause, because you have stepped together as one.

You hold the heart energy of planet Earth in your heart, and you also have an effect on Her the same way She has an effect on you. So even though the first hurricane (Katrina) came and filled some of your cities with water, devastating and killing and creating challenges throughout all of your systems of dealing with Earth, the second one (Rita) was diffused by your heart energy. You have changed much of that already, and you have the capacity to change it every day by shifting your expectations. Remember, life is a self-fulfilling prophecy. You are God wearing a blindfold, and we love it when you bump into each other trying to figure out who you are, asking, "What you are doing here? What is the meaning to life?" That last one is our favorite question. And now we ask you the same question you often ask of us. What is *your* meaning to life? How are *you* going to perceive the gift of these tragedies? How are *you* going to live your life in a way you can utilize your connection and bless yourself every time you see something happen? For remember, it happens to all of you, not to just a few.

You will be assimilating this energy over the months to come. Not only will it affect your economics on a global scale, but it will also affect your hearts the same way. It was just a few days ago that the Keeper was in the gym and someone was watching the news standing next to him. The news talked about Hurricane Rita coming. This man turned to him and said, "Wow! If ever there was going to be a time for China to attack, it would be now." What is he creating, dear ones? What fear can you manifest in these places?

In these times of evolution, your creative abilities have increased as well. So, in those times, you have the opportunity to create love or to create fear. Balance what you create with the perspective of your higher self. Balance it with that part of you. Before you speak words of that nature, understand that this is happening to China and nobody is an enemy to any of you, for you are all one. You are part of each other and that connection will go forward more now more than ever before.

You may choose to view events through the perspective of duality and separation, or you may now decide to view them in terms of triality and how you are all alike. How well you connect the ways you are alike, rather than focusing on the ways you are different, will tell you how much of the gift you can receive from all the events that lie before you.

Some of you will feel a strange disconnection to these events. Even as you watch these events on television, you will feel distant and not reactive, as if everything was really all right. Those around you may even see you as cold and heartless for not feeling badly for these people. Let us put this into perspective for you. Your new perspective from the higher self in triality will help you to see the course unfolding. Watch for the gifts in these events and the times that the human spirit rises above the circumstances. That is the gift.

## What Lies Ahead?

More is coming. There is at least one more difficult hurricane that you will have the opportunity to diffuse in the near future. The truth of the matter is, it is up to you, because you are creating these opportunities. If you have received ample gifts from the other events, this one will pass you by. For a very long time, it was the global wars you created that gave you opportunities to see difficulties, trauma and harshness in the form of darkness. You wondered, "Will there ever be life on Earth without war?" We tell you, in much that way, war has provided the opportunity for you to shake up your world to gain a higher perspective. War is a man-made creation that does not exist in heaven. Much like your man-made creation called economics, it is based on perception of perception of perception. If there is any point where you do not like your reality, have the courage to change your perception, to find a way to look at it differently. If even only for a moment, shift your perspective for a second and to look at yourself from a different angle, even if you come back in and try to figure out if it fits into your perception of 3.2 children, a white picket fence, a dog and a cat. That time will provide you with the opportunity to look beyond what appears to be, and to find that little spark of passion that makes a difference in your life. That is the unique beauty which is you, individually. That is your spark of God for which you are responsible. Do not let it die. Feed it. Find that passion. Find that way of giving the gift of everything that has happened to any human on Planet Earth. When you see suffering, when you see tragedy, know it is *you* who it is happening to. It is *you* waiting in that bus, waiting to be stuck on the highway, waiting to get out of town. Know is *you* whose house has just been flooded. But also look for the possibilities, for there will be a rebuilding of energy in a higher vibration which will include more of your own spark of passion. Find the gift up front and you will release the need for the tragedy.

## The New Family of Light

Finding the gift and releasing the need for tragedy is what has begun even this day. You are coming together to form new families of Light. You are finding new connections. You are reaching for higher truth as humanity evolves. Each one of you, individually, is raising your vibration. You are becoming new people and new expressions of who you really are, seeing new possibilities, realizing new passions, and evolving into new ways of expressing yourself. But as a collective – as one – your vibration is also rising. Even though you see people who are in need, and you see people of lower economic stance who do not have the same privileges and opportunities that you do, why does that make it okay for you to move forward into rebuilding your abundance when all of this suffering is going on, on this planet? Understand that that is a part of you as well and that yours is a chosen position, so when you honor that, you make it an opportunity to be part of you. Not that you are going out to physically rebuild the city yourself, but in the tragedy, you may find a calling, a need to fill, or a place where you can discover your purpose and your passion. You may find, in those tremendous times of stress and trauma, there lies an opportunity for you to be of service as a Human Angel on this planet. If that is the case, then the suffering has been successful because it has pulled you into your passion. It has created a darkness for you to shine your Light upon, and it has created an opportunity for you to be a spirit in a physical bubble of biology and to express your gift. Do so now with great pride.

These are exciting times. The evolution of humankind and the evolution of Earth are proceeding faster than you may know. You have created it. You have stepped forward to allow this to take place. Watch carefully for those sparks of Light. Look for that part that connects your heart to the hearts of others. For dear ones, you have opportunities this time – today – to be the healers of Planet Earth. Master healers, awaken now. There will be no more closet Lightworkers. You are being called into action. We thank you for listening. You are not only changing planet Earth and your own physical beings, but your inter-dimensional beings are opening doors in heaven and through all dimensional levels for a depth of evolution that has never been accessible before now. Dare to ask, "What can I do? How can I hold the energy of peace? How can I find my passion even in all this tragedy?" and you will find the gift of tragedy. And you will find you are creating Home, here, right now.

Dear ones, you have come together to see your own reflection. You have come together to be in a room where there is the energy of Home. You have come together to help connect your hearts and to feel good about who you are and where you are going. Hug each other. Know that even as you leave here this day, there is a part of us that leaves with you and travels with you always, for you are our reflection of Home on Earth. Each of you carries a piece of the God energy you have agreed to hold and express in some fashion. You have our power at your back every moment of every day, for you are part of a wondrous family. The new Family of Light is gathering now. You are creating it. You have set it into motion through your own desires and we applaud you.

Reach out to everyone at every opportunity. Share your heart energy, for you are not many, you are one. It is with the greatest of honor that we ask you to simply treat each other with respect. Nurture one another every chance you get. Remember that it is a Game and play well together.

Espavo.

the Group

# The Second Moon of Atlantis

## Re-activating the Power Crystals

November 2005

This channel was originally presented as a VirtualLight Broadcast and can be seen as it was presented live at www.Lightworker.com/VirtualLight

Greetings from Home.

## The Second Planet of Free Choice and the Third Earth

This day, you have gathered to bring the energies through you, to make Home on Earth and to create your highest vision of where you wish to live. We wish to re-mind you that you have created something unique by having the courage to put on the veil and forget who you are, to come here to bump into each other and play the *Game of Spirit Pretending to be Human.* You have opened the door for all things everywhere to move to the next level of evolution. Even in the beginning as the Game of Free Choice took its first form, there were many skeptics. There were many who said, "Oh, that will never work. You have to give some sort of predetermination, some light at the end of the tunnel for guidance, otherwise all will be hopelessly lost." But here you are, finding your way through the dark, opening the door farther than ever before and letting in the Light for all. As a result of your success in this Game of free choice, a second Game has begun as you have literally opened the door for the Second Planet of Free Choice and something we call the Third Earth. The Second Planet is simply another Game of Free Choice that has now begun, and the Third Earth is where you – as creators pretending to be human – are focusing your thoughts on what you wish to create in this new world as you continue to evolve. There will come a time when the hologram of the Third Earth over-lays the original hologram of what you now call Earth. That hologram is strengthening even now, for many of you are con-sciously sending Light there.

The Second Planet of Free Choice is now well underway with the same lack of restrictions as for the first planet of Earth. You have opened the door for this event to unfold. The Second Planet is on a different timeline than yours in the evolutionary cycle, and is not in the same part of the universe as your Game. Yet it exists within your own time and space, simply on a slightly different vibrational level and a different timeframe. In other words, a year of yours does not equal a year on the Second Planet of Free Choice. Only a short while ago, the Second Planet consisted of a few amoebas playing in a pond of water, but it is currently in a rapid state of evolution, guided by the same lack of restrictions that have brought you both joy and frustration. The Second Planet will have the lack of restrictions that you have enjoyed and many times been frustrated with.

## The Story of Amor: Tyberonn's Dream

We will re-visit Amor today as we share with you another chapter of the story of Amor.

Amor was a young man who was raised in the days of Lemuria and later traveled to Atlantis to fulfill six primary contracts. There was a time when Amor left Lemuria on a grand ship on which he was the only passenger. Many days passed as he traveled on the waters of time upon the very large ship with no one else on board. The ship was actually an inter-dimensional time portal, for he had to move through many dimensions of time and space to place himself in the final days of Atlantis, where he was to fulfill his contracts. Today we will speak of one of these contracts.

Amor had a true heart connection in Atlantis. He was a collector of thoughts and was accepted among Atlanteans as a grand ambassador. He was greeted warmly, respected and welcomed everywhere, even in the most secret of places. Amor was known as an Ambassador of Light; he loved that title and the freedom it gave him. Amor rarely spoke of his six sacred contracts, for most would not understand. He was not even sure he understood really, as he only knew that there were six important connections to be made and that, if he followed his heart, he would be led to them. He was not in Atlantis with an agenda, nor did he want anything in return. He was simply there to make connections and follow his guidance. Doors opened for him everywhere as people welcomed him. He was magical in that fashion, for he allowed people to see into his heart, which made others instantly feel comfortable with who he was and his purpose for being there.

During his travels, he found himself being drawn to the power grids of Atlantis. The Crystal power used in those days was an energy source very few really understood. To the layman, it had magical properties and most simply took it for granted. Amor began working with the power grids in his search for knowledge. It was this search that brought Amor into a connection with a man named Tyberonn who was in charge of all the power grids of Atlantis. Amor made an immediate heart connection with this gentle giant. He connected with him in such a grand way, and, for some time, the two of them went about trying to figure out the next step and what they were intended to do together. Amor and Tyberonn became the closest of friends. Tyberonn's greatest dream was to combine the heart energy with the technology with which he worked; it was his dream to put the energy of the heart on the grid.

## The Emerald City

Now Amor knew how to time travel, for his vision across that great expanse called the ocean in that time portal allowed him to move forward and backward in time. At this point, Amor decided to share with Tyberonn his vision of the future, for he had already seen Tyberonn's dream immaculately unfold. Amor described the most beautiful vision of a city of green crystals known as the emerald city. He said, "Tyberonn, imagine the clouds hovering over the city of green heart energy. The green reflection from the heart crystals glowing softly on the underside of the clouds gives the emerald city a magical look even during the daytime."

Amor told Tyberonn that this vision of the emerald city was the manifestation of a dream that Tyberonn had held for a very long time. With that Tyberonn, shed a tear and shared with Amor the idea that had been haunting him for years. Tyberonn then told Amor the most wonderful story of the technology that made up the power grid having consciousness. Tyberonn said that his greatest dream was to blend this heart energy into the power grids of Atlantis. Tyberonn knew in his soul that this could balance the technology with heart energy and change the direction of a technologically unbalanced Atlantis to a very bright future.

"Your dream has already manifested Tyberonn, for I have seen it in the future," said Amor. "This is the emerald city of which I speak. The heart energy of Earth is held deep within rich green crystals. This vision is the manifestation of your dream and will allow you to set your heart energy, and the heart energy of all of Atlantis into the grid, my friend. Your next step will be to collect and connect that heart energy from the people of Atlantis and from the Earth herself. For this, you will travel throughout Atlantis to find out how the heart energy is being used and how it functions. You will then find the energy spots of planet Earth where these green crystals are held. These are magical spaces to which you will be drawn. This will fulfill your destiny as the Earth Keeper and will set your direction for eons of time and many future lifetimes. You will, in fact, carry this dream and this energy from one lifetime to the next as you return to blend the heart energy to the technology." Amor smiled at the gentle, weeping giant who sat before him, devouring his every word. For the first time in a long while, Tyberonn felt complete, as he took a deep breath and smiled back. Amor somehow knew that he had just completed another of the six sacred contracts and for just a moment, he had a glimpse of how important this contract could be for all of humanity.

## Balance Between Heart Energy and Technology

We pause the story here for a moment to cover an important connection between technology and heart energy. As we have said before, technology is a reflection of the vibrational state of the race it serves. Therefore, it is the heart energy that must balance the technology in any race of beings. If the technology goes too far past the heart energy, it causes an imbalance. As the heart energy rises, it will pull the technology up to match it. That is the reason you, in your times, have had such huge technological advances in the past 50 years. It has been incredible for us to watch. It is because your heart energy has evolved to support technology and to cause it to rise. In the days of Atlantis, the technological energy actually preceded the heart energy and the heart energy was lagging in an effort to catch up. Tyberonn's dream and destiny were to find ways to bring those into balance. So he tried to connect with the Earth to ground it and to put this heart energy and to collect it from everyone through the Earth. This made him very in touch with the Earth energies, while his work as the chief technician to the main crystal power grids of Atlantis gave him the perfect opportunity to blend that heart energy onto the power grid itself. This was Amor's vision of the emerald city, where the heart energy came through the green crystals to find its way on to the largest power grids ever created.

## The Vacuum of FEAR

After that meeting with Amor, Tyberonn moved forward and began to travel the lands of Atlantis. He began forming the Family of Light to bring a collective of heart energy, with the intention of blending it onto the power grid. It was very disturbing to him when he felt the reaction of the people he approached. When he started trying to collect that heart energy, instead there came a ripple of fear from most of the people he met. Even though most of them agreed with his intention, they feared the unknown result of Tyberonn's dream. Soon word traveled of the gentle giant who was collecting heart energy and the news had a ripple effect throughout all of Atlantis. He was considered a mind of technological greatness who had gone off the deep end. Tyberonn soon found that most people believed technology was man-made and heart energy was divine, so the two were never to combine. This belief system was the basis of their fear. Yet, he knew in the very depths of his soul that these two must balance for Atlantis to be able to move forward. It was here that Tyberonn began to withdraw from collecting human heart energy and instead began his deep connection with the Earth herself. The Earth also carried the heart energy and it was identical to the heart energy shared by humans. Tyberonn soon discovered that the Earth stored the same heart energy he had been collecting in certain crystals. The Earth was much easier to deal with than humans, as she gave her heart willingly and never displayed fear. It was then that Tyberonn found that these heart energy crystals congregated in specific areas of the Earth that he called Hot Spots. Often these were the spiritual portals where people gathered to feel the connection with Earth. These became the spiritual places on Earth.

Over time, Tyberonn gathered the green heart crystals of Earth into one spot where he began the emerald city of Atlantis. Due to the fear that he experienced, he hid the city from public view and did not tell many of its existence, with the exception of those who worked there. Even so, it was not long before word got out of the so-called sinister doings in the emerald city. Tyberonn was very concerned as to how that would impact his overall plan. Many times when a new energy is put forward in that way, fear is one of the reactions, for humans are usually afraid of the unknown. Fear only exists when one does not understand. Soon it was evident that there was a tremendous amount of fear about collecting heart energy. A ripple of fear was felt everywhere and, because the technologies were advancing so quickly, the heart energy was having difficulty catching up. Everyone knew that something big was about to happen, but very few viewed it in a positive light. Instead of expecting a miracle, the fear took root and made Tyberonn draw further into seclusion with his work. One of the biggest concerns now was how his project would be perceived when the green heart energy began to flow onto the grid. There was even talk of secret societies that were infiltrating people with green energy. Tyberonn's heart was all but broken as the work he had been doing was now reaching a critical point. The green energy that Tyberonn had been collecting was now reaching a critical level and had to either be placed on the grid or released into the atmosphere where it would dissipate and return to the Earth. Tyberonn and his staff knew the great potential dangers of releasing that energy into the atmosphere, as it would interact with the ionosphere and cause great weather changes including earthquakes, volcanoes and hurricanes.

## The Second Moon

It was here that one of emerald city's chief technicians approached Tyberonn with the idea to divert the heart energy and store it on one of the two moons that encircled the planet. Back in the days of Lemuria and Atlantis, there were two moons for the Earth, not one. Both moons played a part in Lemurian and Atlantean culture and were revered as sacred places. The larger of the two was known as the second moon from an ancient Lemurian folk tale about how the Earth was out of balance in the early days and we were given another moon to keep us in balance. One of the moons was always visible, and that provided a sense of stability to everyone, as the stories were told that as long as one moon could be seen in the sky, all was well. The second moon was larger than the other, and that was the one Tyberonn decided to use to store the heart energy until it was appropriate to blend it onto the power grid. This was a wonderful alternative for the project and everyone knew it to be a safe plan.

Soon the idea was put into motion and a great beam of green light was sent from the green heart crystals of the emerald city toward the second moon. It was then that Tyberonn found himself on the outskirts of the city looking into the cloudy night sky. The clouds above the emerald city were glowing with green light giving a beautiful hue of heart energy and love to this special place. He thought of his dear friend Amor and realized that what he saw before him was the exact same vision that Amor had shared with him that fateful night when this journey began. A smile came to his face and he imagined Amor standing in front of him, telling him what a great job he was doing.

There was one event that was unexpected, however. The same clouds that gave the emerald city the beautiful green glow that night were also noticed by many of the people in surrounding villages. Tyberonn found that it was all right for people to feel the heart energy as he intended when it was mixed with the power and placed on the grid. Yet when they saw the green light being beamed into space toward the second moon, another wave of fear took form. It was this wave of fear that tainted the energy that was being transmitted. Rumors soon started about the green devils and energies, how evil they were, and how the government was doing something subversive. Because of that fear, the green heart energy carried with it fear that was not originally intended to be part of what the second moon received.

It was not long after that that the second moon began to wobble in its orbit. This wobble of the second moon was felt by all humans on Earth. At that point, your own emotions were drastically altered. You could feel the pull on the second moon as the elliptical orbit started to stretch even farther into space. The greatest fear at that point was that the wobble of the second moon would make the Earth wobble in her own orbit. Different locations on Earth began experiencing major weather patterns shifts, and fear was increasing every day. Tyberonn knew what had happened and was aware that the second moon would regain its natural orbit after it assimilated the energy. Yet, the Atlantean officials did not trust his assessment and gave the order to take the energy of the regular power grid and help pull the moon back into place out of its elliptical orbit in order to stabilize it. They believed that everything else could regain its own orbit and that the Earth would not wobble as a result. It was at this point that the technology of Atlantis preceded the heart energy so much that a critical imbalance was reached. Even though Tyberonn pleaded with the council, he was directed to force the second moon back into orbit. That was one of the final misdirections of Atlantis.

## Return of the Crystal Energy

Though it took many months for events to lead to the fall of Atlantis, this was the final blow. It began in earnest as the second moon of Earth blew apart one day for all in Atlantis to see. It was told to all that, "We shot down the moon." The pull of the heart energy was beyond description and is still felt this day. This is the sadness around the heart energy that is still felt as we tell this story. It is this sadness that has kept you from using the crystal energy in your current lives to advance your technology, even though it is far superior to anything you have at this time. In place of the crystal energy, you use electricity and fossil fuels to feed your technologies. That is now changing on Earth and it will not be long before the crystal energy of Atlantis returns. You are being motivated now to look for alternative energy sources. The crystal energy will soon return for the Atlanteans now reading and hearing this. You are back. All of you. The days of Lemuria and Atlantis are back, and you have surpassed that vibrational stage, for your heart energy has now preceded and is pulling the technology behind it, as it should be. The balance is working more together now than it did even in those magical days. You are seeing opportunities to use energy in new ways. We tell you, as long as there is a balance of heart energy and technology together, it will work well.

## The Seed Fear

As that green crystal energy was focused on the second moon, it only caused it to fall farther out of orbit. Eventually the moon destroyed itself. It was known throughout all Atlantis that the green heart energy shot down the moon. Fear had taken things so far out of balance that everyone went further into fear at that point. Largely it was fear that sank Atlantis, fueled by the imbalance of the heart energy. These events are imprinted in the cellular memories of human beings everywhere even to this day. This was the cause of some of the greatest Seed Fears that any human has ever carried. If you carry this Seed Fear then. as you step into your Lightwork, as you step into heart energy, there will be a fear that something is wrong, something is going on. There is an energy stamp deep within you that you have carried from lifetime to lifetime. Changing that energy stamp has become one of the most challenging things for all humans to do and to make peace with the Guardian at the Gate, to understand that it is part of you that should be pushing you forward instead of holding you back. In that time, as the second moon disappeared and you 'shot down the moon,' as it was known, it caused Earth to start wobbling. Earth created a different spin on its own axis and changes occurred to balance the energy with the continental divides. That is when the continents started shifting to form the new balance around the axis that had changed. It is not the first time Earth has changed its axis. It has happened five times thus far and was to happen a sixth and final time around the year 2000. You have altered that plan. You have changed what was originally written and here you are. Atlanteans awaken!

The days of Atlantis are back. You now have opportunities to blend that heart energy to the grid. You now have opportunities to work from the heart. You now have opportunities to see the blending of heart energy and technology together, for it is actually the blend of the mind and the heart that was out of balance in the days of Atlantis. The fear factor was the biggest piece. There will come a time on Earth when love will speak louder than fear. However, that is not the case today for, at this moment, fear is more clearly heard on planet Earth than love is. You are the ones who will change that energy. You are the precursors of the Light. You are the ones who are setting out the heart energy first to overcome the fear before any of it happens, and we are watching with the greatest anticipation, for you have already taken the Game past the highest outcome of what could have possibly been. Now you are picking up the pieces from the days of Atlantis and correcting them in your own heart.

## Re-Activating the Power Crystals onto the Web of Love

Amor was able to show that all to Tyberonn this day. He showed him what the possibilities were and he showed him as the Earth changed and the sadness as those final events unfolded. Many people, as they saw the waters recede into the land, headed for the mountains and the highest points.

Tyberonn stayed behind with Amor because a very important contract was about to take place, but that is another chapter. We will tell you that it was important to place those green and clear power crystals of Atlantis in a very sacred and safe place. That is what Tyberonn and Amor did. The crystals have remained covered to this day. They have been in parts of what you call the Atlantic Ocean and they have been reactivated already through your own anticipation and your own heart energy. This is what has been causing all the turbulence in that area and the weather pattern changes that Earth has been experiencing. The energy of itself, of those power crystals, has been there since day one. You do not deny energy, for it exists with or without you. We ask you to claim your birthright. We ask you to hold that energy and feel that energy as it passes through you, not that you will use it to light your rooms or heat your buildings or do your travel or technology, but that you will now use it to filter through your own heart and create Tyberonn's dream. This time, you have already created a vehicle that will energetically hold all the ambient energy that needs storing. It is stronger than any moon, for it has been designed specifically for the purpose of storing heart energy. Even fear will automatically be transmuted into love energy on this special vehicle. That was by done by your own design. It was also necessary for this vehicle to be feed, nurtured and strengthened over time and now that has also been completed as you have been doing that over the past year. This vehicle is a pure thought of God manifest. This vehicle is the Web of Love you have created and used to connect the hearts of humans. The Web of Love allows the continuation of Tyberonn's dream to re-activate the green heart energy through the crystals of Atlantis.

They will now become part of your energy once again. Although you will not move them for some time, you will feel the measurable energy coming from those areas, for it has already begun. You have measured them so far in hurricanes and weather changes. We ask you to grasp that energy – not of the hurricane and tornado – but the love energy. Blend it with your own. Find the connections of that heart energy. Re-create the new spiritual family. Blend that energy together and feel that energy on the grid of your daily life. And this time, you will not shoot down the moon, for we tell you something else. On the Second Planet of Free Choice, there are two moons. There will come a time when you will visit the Second Planet of Free Choice but not as humans, for you are in training as Human Angels. You are learning to be Human Angels to each other, and will eventually evolve into the angels of the Second Planet of Free Choice. In those days, you will experience the wonderful frustration that we sometimes experience with you and we cannot wait to watch. There will come a time when you look into the sky and see the second moon once again. When you do, feel the hearts of Atlantis coming together again. That is your evolutionary path you set into motion, and right now is the time to grasp that energy. Do not fear it. Let love speak louder than fear in your heart for it begins with you. It begins in the energy and you will carry the contract of Tyberonn and Amor to the next level, for you are going to create it yourselves right now, right here, and we get to watch.

It is our greatest honor to be here to reflect your light, to be with you in a simple way to hold up a mirror to you so you can see yourselves, not as the perfect person, but from a different view. When you have many views, you get a larger picture of who you really are. We ask you to re-member that, because the time is not very far away when you will be asked to hold that same mirror for others. Begin holding it to the people in your lives. Begin holding it and working with the people you see moving into fear. As you feel it within yourself, know that the seed fear is a part of you that is restricting your lives even today. Know that the fear can be transmuted into love energy. Work with it. Play with it. Enjoy it. We leave you with only three simple reminders:

Treat each other with the greatest respect for you are God. Nurture one another at every opportunity. Re-member that it is a Game and Play well together.

Espavo.

the Group

## Connecting the Heart
## Transformation from Hardships to Heartfelt
## By Barbara Rother

I have never felt that the times of Atlantis and Lemuria were part of my past. I hear other people telling sentimental remembrance stories where they knew they were there. I feel I missed out on a grand adventure from the wonderful heartfelt experiences to the hardships that these great lands endured. I feel I am a very young soul here for the first few times. But somehow in this current life and the few I recall in the past I have learned so much that it makes me feel like a very old soul. Perhaps I have learned to understand the stories of those who have come before me and appreciate their lessons and experiences. We all teach each other if we are open to listening, understanding and keeping an open mind and heart.

We share unity consciousness. Even if I did not experience these past times in human form, I know my spirit was absorbing what was going on at another level. So when I did finally decide to be human, at some level I knew what my predecessors had learned. It is a part of my cellular memory. We are all connected. Even if an experience is not individually happening to you, you feel it in some way and store it in your soul as something to learn from and adapt in your future way of thinking and feeling.

Steve and the Group have talked about the connection of the heart energy. This is exactly what I am feeling is going on with all of us. With the current earth changes, we move emotionally backwards and forward in our timeline. When a disaster happens, no matter what space in history it occurs, we are all affected. I have heard some people express concern when tragedies happen and they feel sorry for, yet distant from, the people involved. It seems so far away from their reality that it is almost like a story being told. When we read the newspapers or watch the news on the television, we all can have the same reaction. It is like a drama unfolding that seems surreal, not a part of our daily existence. Here again is what I feel about the days of Atlantis and Lemuria. It is a story that intrigues me but doesn't seem to be a real part of who I am. Oh, but it is. Everything that happens to one person becomes a part of what is happening to each and everyone of us. We can deny this or choose to open up our hearts to the emotions of humankind.

A beautiful part of life challenges that cause our human connections to endure hardships is that, with the right attitude, it can allow us to fully open our hearts to helping others. Yes, when we give to charities or help the less fortunate in some way, we are the ones who benefit by feeling better. We feel we have made a difference and we have, but it does more than that. By opening our hearts, we heal ourselves and others with past hardships and all those involved in current and future conditions. We as individuals can make a difference to those around us, and this then lifts our own life up to a new caring level of who we are.

A few years ago, Steve and I were in Belgium when the horrible fires swept away many homes in the San Diego area. Being so far away, there was nothing we could do to protect our home. We knew our family was safe and to us, that's all that mattered. We had the realization that even if we lost all material belongings, it was alright. We chose right then not to become victims but to know this was a clearing of our energy. We knew we would start over again. We were among the fortunate ones who did not lose anything. This was the beginning of a change within ourselves that led to us selling that home, opening up our hearts and trusting Spirit and ourselves to the direction that took us to Las Vegas, and to a totally new adventure in our lives. I realized then that I have the power to choose the perspectives of my world. I determine where I go from any experiences that I create.

In the past, I have written about how I was taking on the hardships of others as my own and allowing my heart to sink into a state of distress. Changes on this earth are always going to happen. They can lead to new adventures with the right attitude.

I have such gratitude for my life. I open my heart now to help others see the gift in hardships. These are lessons in life. I reflect on my own past now and see the greatest difficulties I faced are now my greatest triumphs. We can choose to go on and create a new wonderful life, or we can choose to live in regret of what happened in the past.

We are starting to feel the magic of the holiday season begin. What a perfect opportunity to open our hearts to those who been experiencing hardships. Individually, we can make a difference in someone's life. If you have been the one experiencing hard times, decide now to turn your life around and be open. Polarity of life is about being able to make the most of the negative and positive sides. When we open our hearts to another and to ourselves, hardships will lighten and in return we will be open to beautiful potentials.

In Love and Light.

Barbara

# 144 Points of Light

## Enlightening the Globe

December 2005

Greetings from Home.

## The Challenge of Igniting 144 Points of Light

You have come a very long way to be here at this moment. You have come through time and space for your soul to be sitting in this bubble of biology at exactly this point. You have a job to do. You have known that since you were born, yet you have never quite known what that job is. We tell you, you have activated something that has started a new path on planet Earth, for the Game of Free Choice is now expanding at an astounding rate. It is becoming exponential, for it does not go 1 to 2 to 3 to 4; it goes 1 to 2 to 4 to 8 and the advancement of humanity is moving as never seen in any game before. So this day, we will tell you about the 144 points of light and what that means, not only on a global and cosmic level, but on an individual level.

Recently, you have reactivated the Atlantean Power Crystals, yet that energy is stagnant until it has a path to travel to be of use. Therefore, we have challenged the Keeper to ignite 144 separate points of light on this planet in different places on the globe to energize the new grid. There is an opportunity to connect points of light on this planet which will ignite the Web of Love and take it from a thought form into a reality. Currently, you use the Web of Love as a tool, to draw energy from it or to send energy to it. Yet we tell you, there is so much more that the Web of Love will be used for. Originally it was a communication grid used to connect the hearts of planet Earth. In a game of pretending to be separate from each other, this grid could begin the process of living in unity with each other and reconnecting that which was separated in the early stages of the humanity. What would it be like for you if you took every step of your life in full connection with that unity as part of your being? That is what is ahead and is what happens when you ignite the144 points of light and actualize the Web of Love.

## Tending the Light

Igniting the lights can be very simple, although humans do enjoy complicating things.

One way to activate the grid is to travel to 144 different places and intentionally set your energy to create a vortex, which will turn into a portal, which will turn into a point of light if it is cared for and nurtured. That point of light is then reflected and carried in the hearts of all of those who cared for and nurtured that point of light. We have challenged the Keeper and the Keeper's Keeper to do exactly this, as in their travels with this work, they can effectively ignite 144 points of light on the globe. Then after they leave that portal can be nurtured by local lightworkers who will then become reflectors of the light. This work is not restricted to the challenge we have offered the Keeper. We also challenge each of you to do the same and ignite Points of Light in your own circles. You may accept the same challenge, and take it upon yourself to ignite one of the points wherever you go. A new point may be in a new country or a new city or a new group of people, for the actual location makes little difference. In all instances, the point of light must be tended and grown by local people after it is first ignited. Each of those people who tend the light will actually ignite 144 Points of Light within their own being and radiate it out through their very being from that point on. This global challenge is also an individual challenge, as it must be carried from one heart to another. Although this work has great global and cosmic effects, this is also a very personal and intimate mission that Lightworkers may choose to undertake. To be a conscious transmitter of light is your next step in evolution as Lightworkers. It is not something that will be done in one sitting. It is not a task that will be done in a very short time or even over a year or two. We also tell you, it will also have inter-dimensional ramifications. Not only will it affect all the other dimensions of time and space that share your planet, but it will also reach beyond the metaphysical community into religions, corporations, governments and organizations of all sorts. The 144 points of light will reach into all dimensions of all reality.

## The Microcosm and Macrocosm of Lightwork

Igniting these points can be accomplished in many ways. There are both microcosms and macrocosms of the new Lightwork. We have offered you one vision of traveling to various places on the Earth and gathering hearts in a unified purpose. Yet, there are also things each of you can do on a smaller scale,, on personal levels that lend to the same purpose. It is important to remember that, without the individuals who tend the fires, the Light will not remain lit.

An example may be the time you are asked to be a listener for a good friend who is having difficulties. She may be having trouble in her marriage and she sits and talks to you as you counsel her. You make a difference when you empower this person. At this point, she may choose to pass it on to all she comes in contact with. That is a point of light that now takes your energy and goes forward: 144 of those situations will ignite your own matrix. Take responsibility on an individual basis to step into your passion, to do those things you have come to do and that bring you the greatest joy, for those are the things that will ignite the 144 Points of Light. Go forward from this day to be a conscious purveyor of light and watch the magic happen in your life.

## The Atlantean Power Crystals

It has been no secret that the energy of Atlantis has been held within the crystals that have been buried deep within the area you call the Bermuda Triangle. Currently it will still be another 20-25 years before you uncover the actual crystals. It is not really important that you find the crystals. What is important is that you utilize the energy from the Crystals. It is the unused energy from these crystals that has caused so many turbulent discharges in the form of hurricanes in that area. Your use of this energy will reduce the need for these discharges and, in the days, ahead these occurrences will return to their normal rate.

The Crystal energy is returning to planet Earth. Ready or not, you have reached a high enough vibration to reveal the secrets of Crystal energy once again. This is the same energy used for daily life in the days of Lemuria and Atlantis. The crystals are now activating all by themselves for, when they were hidden, they were set with an automatic trigger point where they would activate when humanity reached a high enough level of vibration. Now all that is left is to use that energy and that is the reason for activating the 144 Points of Light

When one point of light begins, others are activated. If they are nurtured, they remain lit and allow the Crystal energy a path to travel. One after another, and pretty soon you will have exponential numbers of that happening all over the planet. At that point, life gets very exciting. That is what is directly ahead for you. You are returning to the days of Lemuria and Atlantis. You will walk in a constant connection to the Web of Love with a constant knowing.

## Evolution Becomes Commonplace

It was not that long ago that many of you were discovering the word 'ESP' (extrasensory perception). It was an anomaly and very strange at first. It was something different. It was a new word that became the buzzword among those leading the vibrational movement. Is it not interesting that the word no longer exists in your language? Even when you start talking about ESP, it takes you back to the days of the 70s. It is an old word. What happened to that gift called extrasensory perception? It became part of you. It became integrated, and everyone was aware that it was commonplace. You began making space in your life to use it on a daily basis. Therefore, you no longer need the words to describe it as something separate from you. It is now integrated. That is happening with the concept of the Web of Love. That was Tyberonn's dream in the beginning as he sought to blend the heart energy on to the crystal power grids of Atlantis. That was part of bringing the heart energy back to planet Earth.

Many of you do not believe you are healers or teachers. You may think you are here by mistake, or feel that you know what it is you came to do but are not doing it. We tell you that is about 92.3% of you on the planet. Get over it. You have work to do and we need you now more than ever before. It is time to stop thinking and start feeling. Step in the direction of your heart and activate your own life now.

## Critical Mass and a Flash of Light

There is a message and you are hearing it loud and clear. Now you listen in a new way, for the connection to your own higher selves is strengthening every day. Each one of you has a beautiful gift to give. Find ways of giving it and that will start to ignite the 144 Points of Light. Then, as you ignite a point of light, it will remain an energetic structure. And if it is supported and fed even, it will grow. If it is not fed and if it is not supported, the light will grow dim and fade away. Choose to ignite the light. If you ignite the light and if fades, do not let that discourage you, for that is part of the normal process. It is nothing to be feared and nothing you did wrong. Your job is to simply ignite the point of light and, if it is to be fed, it will be fed by others. Ignite it and let it go in love. Do not take responsibility for what happens after that point. You are the precursors of the light. You are the igniters and you will set those 144 Points of Light.

If you follow the call to nurture the light in a particular space, your job is just beginning. Many of you have been in training for this as guardians of the vortexes and the portals. When you feel a pull to an area of the Earth that has special meaning, you have the opportunity to tend the fires of Light. Follow these directions, for they are an important part of the process. Those of you holding the energy in areas of Earth are more important now than ever before. Small groups of lightworkers gathering to hold and strengthen the energy are at the heart of this process.

Certainly it is understood that there are many more than 144 Points of Light on Earth. As one is lit, it may stay lit and grow stronger, or it may fade. The truth is, at this time on Earth, most will fade, yet that is not important. The intent here is to get 144 Points of Light glowing brightly at the same instant. The moment that happens, a magical, critical mass is reached. Much like what you call the Hundredth Monkey Theory, all points of Light everywhere ignite and a great flash of Light not seen since the beginning will permanently change the direction of all that is. That is the Web of Love incarnate.

Currently the Web of Love is nothing more than a thought of God. You are God. You are the creators and all is in motion through your own thinking, through your own thoughts and ideas. When God has a thought, it is like a blueprint that is sent out for the universal energy to create. Such is the Web of Love. You have created it through your thoughts and your use of it, only this is a collective thought, so there is an exponential power behind it. As you use that as a tool for yourselves, it grows stronger. Now, what would it be like not to have the tool outside, but to have it inside? That is what is ahead. As you ignite these 144 Points of Light, you become permanently connected to the Web of Love and it takes a form in your reality.

We tell you that the Web of Love first began as a communication grid. It started in the early days when a messenger was sent to another village to carry messages back and forth. The path they created to go from one village to another started a matrix upon Earth. Later, over periods of time, that grew into spreading the messages by horseback, and the path they traveled created a larger grid of communication. It was not long before wires were strung and these same paths became telegraph lines. Here the grid took its first physical form. Of course, that grew to be the grid of what you call telephone wires strung all over the planet. They are not evenly distributed, mostly in areas of dense population. Then the Internet evolved from those telephone lines and began connecting hearts globally. The next step is to turn that grid into a light grid of communication. Then, after you become accustomed to light grid, it will become integrated into each of you, and there will no longer be a need for a physical grid to be outside of yourselves. The next incarnations of this grid will be more evenly distributed throughout the planet and not only aid communication between you, but will draw in connection with Gaia Herself, and connect you all together as one. That has already begun. There will come a time when you no longer need the light grid itself because it is a part of who you are.

## Gifts of the Light Grid

We began to prepare you for this movement with the Web of Love experiment where you began to conceptualize, and therefore create, the next incarnations of this grid. The 144 Points of Light are the next step in activating this heart grid. Soon, you will begin to experience the gifts of the 144 Points of Light. Imagine having a thought automatically spread to everyone on Earth. Imagine feeling an emotion that is automatically available to everyone else on Earth. You have a collective conscious awareness that has never before been a part of the Human experience. This is an awareness of the collective heart of God. Please understand, you will not lose identity when these gifts are added to you. Rather, you will learn the unique beauty of who you are is more appreciated and honored unconditionally. As awareness of the collective increases, the need for ego and separation diminishes. This is your path this very day, for your choices for integration rather than separation will determine how fast these points of light will activate.

To draw strength or to give strength is automatically attainable by everyone on that grid. Those are your connections and possibilities. We say possibilities here because you still retain free choice in your human experience. Nothing is imposed upon you; it is simply available as instant, accessible communication. The Internet has begun to prepare you for that kind of information accessibility, yet at this point, the Internet is still unable to convey emotions. The access to human hearts and minds of the one heart will change the human experience over a relatively short period of time. This unity is the same connection you experience when you return Home in what you call Heaven. You are simply evolving to use it on Earth. This is your birthright and you are simply returning to it. Your dedication to creating Heaven on Earth is opening this door now. It has been with you all along, yet to play the Game and put the veil on, it was necessary for you to forget that connection. It was necessary for you to bump into the walls, not re-membering who you were, looking for your imaginary path. Oh, you know you have one, you just don't know where it is. Even when you are on it, you doubt it.

## If It Were Easy, Everyone Would Be Human!

Being human is such a wonderful game of spirit. We love the human experience and, although we have not been human, we watch you with the greatest of love. We tell you it is not easy being human for if it was, everyone would be human. The reality is that it takes the highest of vibration to come into the most difficult Game board on all planets. Then you agreed to play this Game, not only with total free choice, but with the veil so effective that you can play with total free choice. That veil is lifting by your own accord. That veil is lifting because you no longer need it to be so complete. As it lifts, there will be people who will say, "Follow me, for I see the future." In the second wave of empowerment, you all have the same gifts. Are you ready for such a paradigm shift? Are you ready to release the game of follow the leader to begin playing the game of follow yourself? You are the One Heart of Earth, and all eyes in the cosmos are upon you as you boldly take this next step.

## The Hearts of Atlantis

Today you set the energy of Atlantis into motion. When you left Atlantis, you hid the crystal energies from yourselves. Not only was it important to bury the crystals and to keep them from surfacing accidentally, but you, as spirits, had a meeting where you decided that you would hide this energy from yourselves for the duration of the Game. Yet now you have passed the time originally set for the end of the Game, and that agreement no longer holds. We tell you further, your collective vibration now has even passed the levels you reached in the days of Lemuria and Atlantis. Now you start pulling away the veil to take your true power while you are still in physical bubbles of biology. This has never been done before anywhere in any universe. All of the cosmos are watching planet Earth because of the choices you are making today. We cannot wait to see where you take it from here.

Dear ones, step forward. Know that you are honored beyond your imagination. Know that you are honored and supported and loved more than you will ever know. You are the greatest hope of Heaven pretending to be human, and we are so very proud of you. Even in the times when you feel lost, we hold the magnificence of who you really are. As you take that feeling deep within you and let it grow, it ignites warmth within your own chest. It ignites a warmth within your soul. That is the beginning of a Point of Light you will ignite, for you will be one of the 144. You will be those who take the challenge and make a difference on this planet. Those 144 Points of Light will ignite and every being everywhere will watch this transformation.

You are the Masters of the Game board. Cheer yourselves on, dear ones. You have no idea how you are seen throughout the rest of the cosmos. Know that you will be greeted at Home as the greatest of heroes. Take the challenge. Find a way to ignite one point of light and focus your energy on that. Take the challenge to ignite and nurture 144 Points of Light throughout your existence.

We leave you with only three simple reminders. Treat each other with the greatest of respect for you are heroes. Nurture one another at every opportunity as you are looking in the eyes of God. Re-member that it is a wonderful Game ... and play well together.

Espavo.

the Group

## About the Author

Steve Rother was comfortably settled into life as a general building contractor in the San Diego area when, through a synchronistic series of events, he was placed firmly in the middle of his contract. Steve and his wife, Barbara, began shifting their focus on life and living on New Year's morning, 1995, when they found themselves unexpectedly expressing their intent for the coming year during a ceremony that took place as the sun rose over a California beach. From that day forward, their lives were never to be the same.

**Barbara & Steve**

Soon after, Steve began receiving divinely inspired messages from 'the Group,' which he published monthly as the 'Beacons of Light.' These monthly writings from 'the Group' are about re-membering and accepting our own power, and living comfortably in the higher vibrations now on planet Earth. The Group calls Steve the 'Keeper of the Flame' or just 'Keeper' for short.

Steve never returned to his contracting business. Today, he and Barbara, his wife of 30+ years present empowerment seminars to Lightworkers throughout the globe. They have presented these in many countries, and are five time presenters at the United Nations on two continents. In April of 2000 at the UN in Vienna, Austria, Steve and Barbara presented a class on channeling, believed to be the first such class ever presented at a U.N. facility.

Steve and Barbara make their base in Las Vegas, Nevada, where they work together in Love and Lightwork. They have formed the nonprofit corporation of Lightworker and, together with the volunteers and staff, plant seeds of Light through personal empowerment on a global basis. More information about Steve, Barbara and the Group, including their seminar schedule, can be found at the web site: http://www.lightworker. com.

## Connect with spiritual family:

http:// www.Lightworker.com

'The Beacons of Light Re-minders from Home'
monthly messages from the Group, are available online or
as a free e-mail service by request.

http://www.Lightworker.com/Schedule

Connect with original spiritual family on the message boards
and in the chat rooms. Set your creations into motion in the 8
Sacred Rooms. Lightworker is a large site where the Groups information is translated into 20 languages. Come spend time creating
Home.

Re-member... You are not alone... Welcome Home

# Paths to Empowerment Seminars
## from Lightworker

Paths to Empowerment Seminars provide practical applications of the information for living in the higher vibrations of the new planet Earth, based on information from the Group. All gatherings include practical techniques for evolving as empowered humans, together with a Live channel from the Group through Steve Rother.

## One day informational seminars

Designed to connect family and introduce a new way of thinking ad living as empowered humans.

## Two day Interactive seminars

Experiential seminars over two days that apply practical applications of the material being covered. Each workshop is desdribed in greater detail on the web site.

## Three day OverLight Trainings

Three days of working with one of the OverLight modalities for healers shows the applications of the specific modality. Certified trainings. Several OverLight modalities have been adapted for a three day intensive. More on the OverLight modalities including a detailed description of each can be found at http://Lightworker.com/OverLight

## Six day OverLight Facilitator Trainings

Spiritual Psychology, Transition Team Training, Spiritual Communication, Human Angel Harmonics and Inverse Wave Therapy are th first of these with more added each year. The six day trainings are for those wishing to have a complete understanding of this material and its uses in daily life or for facilitators who wish to offer these modalities in their own work as facilitators. These are Lightworker certified courses.

Check the schedule on the web site at:
http://Lightworker.com/Schedule

You will receive notification of events in your area by adding your name to our mailing list at:
http://Lightworker.com/Signup

# Re-member:

## A Handbook for Human Evolution

This book will re-mind you how to:

- Discover and step into your 'Plan B' Contract.
- Purposefully craft your own reality and create your own version of Home on Earth.
- Adjust to the new levels of vibration affecting your biology.
- Master the arts of Time Warping and moving between Alternate Realities.
- Re-discover your gifts and tap into your own guidance and Re-member your power.
- Play "the Game" to the Highest Outcome and enjoy the journey.
- Prepare for the next phase of our evolution and the Crystal Children who are coming.

It's an exciting time on Planet Earth. In this enlightening book, Steve Rother and the Group offer a look at Higher Truths that will change the paradigms and the way we perceive ourselves. We Humans have just won the Grand Game of Hide-and-Seek and are now moving the Game to a new level!

"Mankind is evolving. We are moving from a motivation of survival to a motivation of unity. We are reaching for 'Higher Truths' in all areas as a quiet revolution is taking place. This transition does not have to be difficult. This book documents not only profound information for the planet, but also the LOVE journey of two enlightened and high-vibrational people."

— LEE CARROLL, author of The Kryon Writings

"This book will remind you of why you are here on the planet at this time. Peace is real now, and Steve's work will help you find that magic place within yourself."

— JAMES TWYMAN, author of Emissary of Light, The Secret of the

# Spiritual Psychology
## The Twelve Primary Life Lessons

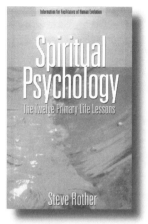

Have you ever wondered why it is that one person can grow up with every conceivable advantage, and yet seem incapable of mastering even the simplest things in life?

Have you ever known someone who, despite being highly intelligent, keeps on repeating the same mistakes over and over again?

It is only when we begin to view the human experience as the evolutionary process of a soul that we can begin to understand all these strange forces at work in our lives.

We see ourselves as human beings searching for a spiritual awakening when, in fact, we are spiritual beings trying to cope with a human awakening. But what causes us to seek these experiences in the first place? What is it, precisely, that sets certain life patterns into motion? Why do these patterns emerge in our own behaviors repeatedly? More importantly, what would happen if we could find ways of identifying this higher purpose and in so doing transform seemingly destructive patterns into positive attributes?

Spiritual Psychology offers a radically different view of life and the human experience. This book offers a view of humanity from the higher perspective of our own spirit.

"This book gives us help for our bodies, sanity for our minds and food for our Souls."

— CHARLES L. WHITFIELD, MD, author of Healing Your Inner Child and The Truth about Mental Illness

— BARBARA HARRIS WHITFIELD, RT, author of Spiritual Awakenings

"The word 'psychology' originally meant 'study of the soul' (psyche). After exploring far afield, we are returning full circle to encompass an understanding of ourselves as spiritual beings into our understanding of human health and behavior. Steve Rother's remarkable pioneering work is a cornerstone in challenging us to expand our knowledge and skills as empowered and empowering healers."

— PAULINE DeLOZIER, Ph.D., Clinical Psychologist

Welcome Home
The New Planet Earth

# Welcome Home

## The New Planet Earth

Welcome to the 5<sup>th</sup> dimension. Did you feel the ascension? The world we knew is rapidly evolving. Life on planet Earth is becoming increasingly unpredictable. The old rules no longer function. According to 'the Group,' these changes have greater implications than we imagine. As unexpected as recent events have been, they merely mark the beginning. The evolution of mankind has begun.

The Group's purpose is to prepare us for what lies ahead. In Welcome Home, they otter us keys to unlocking the secrets of developing our full power as creators, and using them in our lives now.

Welcome Home is divided into four sections:

1. Current Events: A cosmic view of where we are, how we got here and where we are heading.

2. The New Planet Earth: The new attributes of life in the 5<sup>th</sup> dimension and how we can apply them right now.

3. Questions and Answers on a wide range of topics taken from live presentations.

4. Where do we go from here? Prepare to be surprised!

"Steve Rother has tapped into the root of a new consciousness blossoming in the hearts of Humanity. Re-Member offered practical step-by-step instructions on how to awaken to the Pathway of the Soul. Welcome Home is the next step … useful, loving, wise, and beautifully engaging – another tremendous book for the 'enlightened seeker.'"

    – ISHA LERNER, author of Inner Child and Power of Flower cards

"Steve and the Group present an exciting new way to look at our world. This book provides a deeper understanding of the power and miracles that are now available to us."

    – Ronna Herman,  author and messenger for Archangel Michael

"Did anyone notice that life has changed? Perhaps you also feel that time has sped up and the spiritual rules are getting overhauled. Are you asking the question, 'What's next?' If so, you have the right book in your hands! Join Steve, Barbara and the Group for more loving insights into one of the greatest energy shifts our planet has ever seen."

    – LEE CARROLL, author of The Kryon Writings

Each month the Spiritual Family gathers for
the **Virtual Light Broadcast.**

Lightworker presents a 3-hour international broadcast free of
charge on the Internet to connect spiritual family on the new
planet Earth.

---

*Each month see:*

Special Guests each month, leaders in Lightwork.

2-minute readings from Steve & the Group

Lightworker events and attractions.

The "Beacons of Light" message from the Group presented
live.

---

Watch it live on the Internet at http://Lightworker.com

or

Attend in person in Las Vegas, Nevada

or

Watch the shows at your convenience in their entirety:

http://VirtualLightProject.com